OSS and the
Yugoslav Resistance,
1943–1945

Kirk Ford, Jr.

OSS and the Yugoslav Resistance, 1943–1945

Texas A&M
University Press
COLLEGE STATION

The paper used in this book meets the minimum requirements
of the American National Standard
for Permanence of Paper
for Printed Library Materials, Z39.48-1984.
Binding materials have been chosen for durability.
∞

Library of Congress Cataloging-in-Publication Data

Ford, Kirk, 1944–
    OSS and the Yugoslav resistance, 1943–1945 / Kirk Ford, Jr.
        p.   cm. – (Texas A&M University military history series ;
28)
    Includes bibliographical references and index.
    ISBN 0-89096-517-X
    1. World War, 1939–1945 – Underground movements – Yugoslavia.
2. World War, 1939–1945 – Secret service – United States.   3. United
States. Office of Strategic Services – History.   4. Yugoslavia –
History – Axis occupation, 1941–1945.   I. Title.   II. Series.
D802.Y8F67   1992
940.53′497 – dc20   92-11220
                                              CIP

Contents

Illustrations

Preface

In the summer of 1942, Capt. John Milodragovich was in training at Camp Davis, North Carolina, with a cadre of officers scheduled to become part of a newly authorized battalion at Fort Bliss, Texas. While waiting for his transfer to come through, Milodragovich received orders to report to the camp commandant's office where he was asked a series of questions concerning his military status and willingness to accept an overseas combat assignment. Milodragovich knew this would be no ordinary assignment when the interviewer emphasized that his chances of returning would be less than fifty-fifty. Confessing that he "chewed on that for a while," Milodragovich nevertheless replied that he would accept the assignment. After a few more routine questions, the interview came to an end.

There was no immediate follow-up to the meeting, and Milodragovich subsequently received the expected orders transferring him to Fort Bliss. While there he received some orders that he had not expected, directing him to report to Q Building in Washington, D. C. Reporting as ordered, Milodragovich soon found himself being shuffled from one office to another in what was the "damndest runaround" he had ever seen. Angry and confused, he was making his way down a hallway to yet another office when he overheard some men conversing in Serbian. He walked over to the group and introduced himself. One of the officers, Capt. Nick Dragash, turned and greeted Milodragovich with a broad smile and warm handshake. Dragash asked, "Where have you been? We have been trying to get you for a long time." Milodragovich soon learned that the "we" to which Dragash referred was the Office of Strategic Services (OSS). At the time, he knew nothing about the organization but sensed that that was about to change.

Literally hundreds of men shared an experience similar to Milodragovich's. Eager to serve their country in a unique way, they volunteered to fill the ranks of Maj. Gen. William J. Donovan's OSS. Trained to gather and report intelligence and conduct sabotage operations behind enemy lines, these men formed an important element of America's first venture into the murky waters of clandestine warfare. By war's end oss had established bases all over the world and had liaison officers operating in virtually every major theater of the war.

This study focuses primarily on the operational aspects of oss's work in one of those theaters, and more specifically in one country—Yugoslavia. Relying upon field intelligence reports taken from the operational files of oss, correspondence and interviews with numerous participants, and relevant published sources, I have attempted to show the kind of work American liaison officers did in Yugoslavia and to assess the extent to which their efforts either advanced or influenced the goals of Allied policy there.

oss directed its Balkan operations, which included Yugoslavia, first from Cairo and later from bases in Italy—Caserta and Bari. Ideally, the agency sent its liaison officers into the country to establish contact with the resistance, provide means whereby these forces could be supplied, and, insofar as possible, to integrate their activities into the overall scheme of Allied military strategy. The first American officers who parachuted into Yugoslavia in August, 1943, and those who followed, quickly discovered that idealism would have to yield to the realities of the environment in which they were to operate. Forces they did not always understand and over which they exercised little or no control often defined the limits of their actions.

In the first place, the Middle East was a British military theater in which oss functioned as a junior partner vis-à-vis its British counterpart, Special Operations Executive (soe). This relationship, reluctantly accepted by oss, worked harmoniously enough as long as military considerations dominated Allied thinking. However, when political issues began to come to the fore during the latter months of the war, dissonant chords could be heard with greater frequency between the two services and within the ranks of each.

Second, the civil war between Tito's Partisans and Mihailovich's Chetniks or Nationalists was a pervasive problem that limited the effectiveness of oss and absorbed resources and energy that would otherwise have been expended against the Germans and Italians. The political and military objectives of these resistance groups and the tactics employed to achieve them were not always compatible with Allied interests. With some justification, Nationalist and Partisan leaders suspected that the Allies were willing to expend Yugoslav blood in pursuit of general military objectives that had little bearing on their own aspirations. On the other hand, Allied planners were understandably reluctant to see what limited supplies they could send to the resistance squandered in a civil war that profited no one but the enemy.

The internal struggle in Yugoslavia gave rise to serious discussions within oss concerning the extent to which the organization might attempt to disassociate itself from British policy and pursue a more independent course of action. The civil war also set off acrimonious debate inside oss, exacerbating ideological differences in the agency between those who supported the Partisans and those who supported Mihailovich's Nationalists.

Lastly, OSS had to contend with the growing influence of the Soviet Union in eastern Europe and by the fall of 1944 with the physical presence of Soviet forces in that region. In Yugoslavia this prompted the Partisans to adopt a more independent, and at times hostile, policy toward their western benefactors – Britain and the United States – circumscribing the freedom of action and influence of their liaison officers even more.

OSS operations in Yugoslavia offer many examples of individual acts of courage and heroism. Facing the certainty of torture and death if captured, OSS field personnel risked their lives to provide useful intelligence on enemy troop movements and order of battle, to sabotage enemy communications and transportation centers, and to locate and assist in the evacuation of Allied airmen. On the other hand, there were examples of pettiness, bureaucratic jealousy, chicanery, and disloyalty.

Those who have previously written exclusively about the Yugoslav resistance or about aspects of Allied policy toward Yugoslavia without access to the operational records of OSS will find that some of their conclusions are challenged while others are confirmed. Tito's military contribution to the Allied war effort and the decision of Churchill and Roosevelt to support him on that basis can hardly be questioned. On the other hand, to justify that support by suggesting that Mihailovich and his forces were at best totally inactive or at worst collaborationist is to perpetuate a myth. The totality of evidence I have examined for this study rejects the portrayal of Tito as liberator or Mihailovich as collaborator. Hopefully, the time has come to consider this aspect of Yugoslavia's wartime history in terms other than those of victor and vanquished.

For the convenience of the reader, I would like to note a couple of conventions I have followed in this book. Generally, Serbo-Croat spellings for proper names have been used in the text with two notable exceptions: Mihailovich and Chetnik. In these two instances I have used the anglicized spellings that appear in the vast majority of OSS reports. Proper names occurring within quotations are given as they appear in the original source. Two other names, those of Constantine Fotitch (Fotić) and Boris Todorovich (Todorović), are given in the anglicized form under which their books were published in this country. A guide to the pronunciation of Yugoslav's names is given in appendix A.

The second matter to which I would like to draw the reader's attention, concerns the maps. Individual maps showing OSS coverage for the years 1943–45 are intended to show the general zone of operation for teams in Yugoslavia for a given year. Placement markers reflect only the province in which the teams operated and are not intended to show the exact location of specific teams.

Briefly acknowledging here those who assisted me in the preparation of this book seems a most inadequate expression of my appreciation. Many of those whom I first approached as sources of information have through the years become friends. Whatever measure of personal satisfaction I feel in bringing this work to completion, I wish to share with those who made it possible.

The contributions of some were so numerous as to require specific mention in the endnotes of various chapters. This is certainly true of many of the former OSS and air force personnel – officers and men – who made their personal papers available to me, granted my requests for interviews, or patiently responded to innumerable letters of inquiry. To whatever extent this study has brought to life the personalities and events of almost fifty years past, the credit is theirs.

My debts to John Taylor in the Modern Military Branch of the National Archives are legion. His encyclopedic knowledge of the OSS collection, his familiarity with many personal contacts, and his wry sense of humor made my trips to Washington both informative and pleasurable. I must also thank Terri Hammet, Larry MacDonald, and Sim Smiley, who assisted me in many ways and greatly facilitated my work at the Archives. I also wish to express sincere appreciation to the staff of the Interlibrary Loan Division of the Robert Manning Strozier Library at Florida State University for making the Ultra documents available to me on microfilm.

Dr. Arthur L. Funk, Professor Emeritus of the University of Florida, Mr. Franklin A. Lindsay, a former OSS officer who served in Yugoslavia, and Dr. Kenneth G. McCarty of the University of Southern Mississippi, graciously consented to read the initial draft of my manuscript. I found many of their comments encouraging but profited most from their suggestions and criticisms. Each will see evidence of his handiwork in this final version.

The contributions rendered by M. Mike Sujdovic, George and Mirjana Vujnovich, and David Martin, too numerous and varied to list here, are noted throughout the book. To Mrs. Mary Lea Nations, who transcribed many of the more recent personal and telephone interviews cited in this study, and Mrs. Wanda Mikhail, who wrought order from chaos by transforming my rough draft into finished copy, I express my heartfelt thanks. Natasha Pantić freely gave of her time to check the spelling and accent marks for the Serbo-Croat names and to provide a pronunciation guide. Errors of omission or commission in this or any other area of this book are solely my responsibility. Prints of the photographs used in the book were prepared by Just Black & White of Jackson, Mississippi.

I am also grateful to those colleagues of Mississippi College who have been so supportive of this effort: Drs. Edward McMillan and Ron Howard, my former and current departmental chairmen; Pat Turner and Alice Smith of secretarial services; J. B. Howell, former head librarian; Professor Steve Cook, who took time from a very busy schedule to prepare the maps and charts; and members of the faculty development committee who made funds available to defray travel and other related expenses.

Throughout the years I have been engaged in this work, my wife, Gayle, has been a constant source of strength and encouragement to me. Proofreader, critic, and sounding board, she has assumed many roles with patience and understanding. I dedicate this book to her and to our son, Kyle, to whom I shall now be able to give an unqualified yes to the question: "Daddy, will you play with me?"

OSS and the
Yugoslav Resistance,
1943–1945

I. Greetings First American

During the early evening hours of August 18, 1943, a single Halifax bomber lifted slowly from the airfield at Derna, North Africa, turned to a northerly course over the Mediterranean, and gradually vanished into the darkness. On board the plane was Marine lieutenant Walter R. Mansfield, who in February, 1943, had transferred into Gen. William J. Donovan's Office of Strategic Services (OSS).[1] Since joining OSS, Mansfield had undergone extensive training in the United States, England, and the Middle East in methods of gathering intelligence and conducting sabotage operations behind enemy lines. All that he had been taught over the past months would soon become quite real, for in only five hours he would be parachuting into the rugged mountainous region around Ivanjica, Serbia, in enemy-occupied Yugoslavia. OSS was about to establish its first direct liaison with the Nationalist resistance forces of Gen. Draza Mihailovich, and Mansfield had been chosen to make this initial contact.[2]

As Mansfield settled in for what proved to be an uneventful flight, except for a brief encounter with German antiaircraft fire over southern Yugoslavia, a three-man detachment from Mihailovich's headquarters prepared the drop site where they hoped to receive the OSS officer that evening. The area had to be secured and the proper pattern established for the signal fires that would be lit as the time for the plane's arrival approached. With these tasks done, there was little to do but wait and listen.[3] Inside the plane Mansfield knew that his wait was almost over. Mansfield recalled that as his plane neared the prearranged drop site:

We spotted the signal fire almost immediately, and made a pass at the field, during which I could see the fires from the hole through which I jumped. As soon as we checked our flash signal with the one on the ground, we did a circle of about 10 miles and came back. Then I shook hands with the RAF dispatcher, gave our 'thumbs up' signal, and when the light went green shoved off. When the chute blossomed, I immediately saw the fires, realized I was away off to one side, and landed in a pile of

3

rocks hurting my hip slightly. I found myself on a cove mountainside and in a few minutes found myself surrounded by a group of big bearded Chetniks who tried to smother me with kisses yelling 'Zdravo purvi Amerikanc!' (Greetings First American.)[4]

In addition to the Chetniks, his greeting party consisted of Col. William Bailey, head of the British mission to Mihailovich's headquarters, and Maj. Kenneth Greenlees, Bailey's chief of staff. Mansfield quickly gathered his gear and, with the other members of the team, set out for the British camp about an hour's journey away. Upon reaching the British mission, which consisted of a crude peasant hut and two parachute tents, Mansfield met Lt. Col. William Hudson, who had been in Yugoslavia since September, 1941, and was the first Allied officer to have established contact with the resistance. Shortly thereafter, Mansfield was escorted to Mihailovich's headquarters for his first meeting with the general.[5]

Only four days after Mansfield dropped to Mihailovich, Capt. Melvin O. Benson parachuted to Josip Broz Tito, leader of the Partisan resistance forces, whose headquarters were located in an area of Bosnia known as Metropolje. Benson had been assigned to the Secret Operations Branch of oss-Cairo in February, 1943, after having been associated with soe (Special Operations Executive) for little more than a year, during which time he received much of the specialized training required for service in Yugoslavia. Like Mansfield, Benson parachuted alone to Partisan headquarters where he was greeted by Capt. F. W. D. Deakin, Maj. Basil Davidson (who, until his arrival in Yugoslavia only a few days earlier, had served as head of the Yugoslav Section in Cairo), and Gen. Vladimir Velebit of Tito's staff. Benson reached Partisan headquarters around 2:30 A.M. on August 22, and on the evening of the same day had a very cordial dinner with Tito himself.[6] At last oss had eyes and ears of its own at the headquarters of both Mihailovich and Tito.

The arrival of Mansfield and Benson marked the beginning of oss's direct involvement in Yugoslavia. Still, it should be remembered that by the time these officers set foot on Yugoslav soil, the country had been under Axis occupation for almost two and one-half years. Not all of the events during that period can be recounted here, but some of them must be since they directly affected the political and military environment within which oss and its representatives had to function inside Yugoslavia.

On March 25, 1942, the Royal Yugoslav Government ended weeks of tortuous diplomatic maneuvering by signing the Tripartite Pact. Hitler's decision to move against the Soviet Union dictated the need for friendly or at least neutral countries on his southern flank. Britain and the United States, on the other hand, were determined that no other countries should be drawn into the Axis orbit. Both sides in this diplomatic tug of war subjected the Yugoslavs to intense pressure, but in the end the proximity of German power and Hitler's demonstrated willingness to use it won the day. Prince Paul, Yugoslavia's first regent, summed up his country's dilemma quite well when, during the height of the crisis, he lost his temper and shouted at the American ambassador, Arthur Bliss Lane, "You big nations are hard, but you are far away."[7]

Yugoslavia's adherence to the Tripartite Pact seemed to give Hitler yet another easy victory. Even as news of the signing began to circulate within the country, German officials in Belgrade informed Berlin that the government was "entirely master of the situation."[8]

Events were afoot which would soon change all of that. In the early morning hours of March 26–27, a group of nationalist air force officers led by generals Bora Mirković and Dušan Simović and army major Živan Knežević effected a bloodless coup d'etat. The conspirators swept away the regency, installed Simović as prime minister, and elevated Peter Karadjordjević, King Alexander's son, to the throne as King Peter II.[9] Louis Fortier, who had been kept informed about the planned takeover by then colonel Draza Mihailovich, was in the streets of Belgrade with Lane when news of the coup was announced and noted that "complete calm prevailed."[10] This too would soon change.

In Berlin, Hitler, who first thought the reported coup was "a joke," responded by ordering his staff to prepare for the military destruction of Yugoslavia in a "lightning like undertaking" which should be "carried out with unmerciful harshness."[11] Hermann Goering's Luftwaffe inaugurated the campaign on Sunday, April 6, with a devastating air attack on the "open city" of Belgrade. Axis forces smashed across Yugoslavia's poorly defended borders and in only eleven days of fighting completely overwhelmed the Yugoslav Army, which surrendered unconditionally on April 17.[12]

After crushing her army and forcing the flight of her government to Athens and later London, the victorious Axis forces dismembered Yugoslavia. Germany occupied Serbia proper and recognized Ante Pavelić, leader of the Ustasha terrorists, as head of the Independent State of Croatia – the western portion of which was occupied by Italy. The Italians also occupied Montenegro and annexed territory along the Dalmatian coast and in Slovenia. Hungary, Bulgaria, and Albania also acquired territory from the defeated Yugoslavs.[13] Greece, which had also been invaded by Axis forces on April 6, surrendered only eight days after the capitulation of Yugoslavia. In little more than two weeks and with minor losses in men and material, Hitler had made himself master of the Balkans; or had he?

Germany and her allies had defeated the Yugoslav Army with relative ease. Conquering the Yugoslav people would prove to be another matter altogether. The latter, long accustomed to the hardships of military occupation, prepared to do once more what they had done for centuries – resist.

The first group to raise the standard of revolt in Yugoslavia consisted of a small number of regular army officers and noncommissioned soldiers led by Draza Mihailovich. Although a regular army officer, Mihailovich refused to obey the order for unconditional surrender, choosing instead to retreat into the mountains and continue the struggle in the Chetnik tradition.[14]

Rooted in Serbia's historical resistance to Turkish domination, the Chetnik movement existed largely as independent guerrilla bands organized on a territorial basis under the leadership of a commander or *vojvoda*, whose authority over his men was virtually exclusive.[15] Not surprisingly, Chetnik leaders who had been unable to agree on how to resolve Yugoslavia's problems in the interwar period also found themselves divided on how to respond to their country's military collapse. Recognized leaders like Kosta Pećanac and Dimitrije Ljotić openly collaborated with the Axis. Other Chetnik groups placed themselves in the service of Gen. Milan Nedić, former minister of defense in the Royal Yugoslav Government, who subsequently became head of the puppet regime in German-occupied Serbia. There were also a number of independent Chetnik commanders who owed no allegiance to Pećanać, Ljotić, or any other Chetnik leader for that matter and who openly resisted the Axis occupiers. Lastly, there were the followers of Col. Draza Mihailovich, most of whom came from the regular army and who might be considered Chetniks only because they took to the hills to fight as guerrillas.[16]

Mihailovich came to be regarded as leader of the resistance by the Yugoslav government-in-exile and was frequently depicted as head of the wartime Chetnik movement by the Allied and Axis intelligence services. The latter was an association that was neither accurate in the spring of 1941 nor particularly advantageous in the months ahead. In the first place, Mihailovich preferred that his troops be called "The Yugoslav Army in the Fatherland" rather than Chetniks.[17] Second, although Mihailovich would in time assert his authority over larger guerrilla bands operating in the country, the handful of officers and men who followed him to Ravna Gora in western Serbia in May, 1941, hardly constituted a movement. More by circumstance than by any personal desire on his part, Mihailovich inherited the responsibility of consolidating an ideologically fractionalized movement, dispersed in isolated pockets throughout an occupied country and led by individual commanders long accustomed to the freedom of independent action. Over such a movement, his control was more nominal than real in the early stages of the resistance.[18]

Mihailovich hoped to lay the foundations for an army that could be mobilized quickly to deal with Axis forces at the decisive moment when help from the Allies would be close at hand. He therefore worked to strengthen his position within the country while avoiding any premature action that might lead to the destruction of his army.[19] Furthermore, as a Serb, he saw little to be gained from sabotage operations that would only discomfit the Germans temporarily but would result in the death of hundreds or thousands of Serbs whom he could not protect and from whom he drew most of his support.[20] The execution of between two and three thousand civilians in the towns of Kraljevo and Kragujevac in mid-October, 1941, convinced him that he should initiate actions against the Germans only when the results could justify the inevitable reprisals that would follow.[21]

Political considerations also influenced Mihailovich's policies. Though not a politician, he was committed to preserving the status quo in Yugoslavia insofar as that implied defense of the monarchy and of Serbia's dominant position within the country. Both of these would be threatened if, during the war, Serbia's population were decimated and the internal political balance shifted in favor of the Croats.[22] The wholesale slaughter of Serbs in Croatia by Pavelić and his Ustasha henchmen provided ample proof that such fears were well-founded.

Mihailovich faced a new, and in time more formidable, challenge when in the wake of the German attack on the Soviet Union in June, 1941, the Communist-dominated Partisan movement led by Josip Broz Tito initiated active resistance against Axis forces in their country. Tito, a Croat and dedicated Communist, had worked in the outlawed Yugoslav Communist party in the 1930's, survived the great Stalinist purges, and in 1937 became chairman of the Yugoslav Communist party. Between 1937 and 1939, he and hs followers conducted a vigorous anti-Fascist campaign inside the country. However, when the Russo-German Non-Aggression Pact became public, the Communists began emphasizing the need to keep Yugoslavia out of imperialistic wars. Germany's invasion of the Soviet Union in June, 1941, cast the war in a new light by which the Yugoslav Communists could see the wisdom of opposing Nazi aggression in their own country.[23]

From the outset it was clear that the Partisans would embrace a resistance strategy quite different from that of the Chetniks. Not inclined to husband their resources and wait for the right moment to rise against the invaders, Tito's Partisans favored immediate all-out resistance. Since the Partisans depended less on the peasantry for support, they were not as likely to feel the pressure of mass reprisals against the civilian population. In fact, severe retaliation by the Axis forces served in many instances to radicalize the peasants, drive them from their land and homes, and virtually force them into the ranks of the Partisans. Thus, at a very early point in the development of the resistance, Tito's highly mobile force of dispossessed workers and uprooted farmers drawn from virtually every part of Yugoslavia stood in stark contrast to Mihailovich's land-based Serbian peasantry that was the foundation of his movement.[24]

Obviously, not all of those who joined the Partisans did so out of political conviction. Most of the rank and file simply wanted to rid their country of the Axis invaders and were not imbued with the revolutionary zeal of the

Partisan leadership. Emphasizing nationalism rather than communism and pursuing an aggressive resistance policy, the Partisans presented themselves as a viable alternative to the more conservative Chetnik formations under Mihailovich.[25]

Tito and Mihailovich undoubtedly recognized the desirability of a common front against the Axis, but neither was willing to sacrifice his political beliefs to achieve that end. Two face-to-face meetings between the rival leaders, at Struganik on September 19 and at Brajići on October 27, failed to reconcile the political and military differences that separated them.[26]

On the night of September 20–21, one day after the collapse of the Struganik talks, a joint Anglo-Yugoslav mission slipped over the side of a British submarine and made its way in two rubber dinghies to a desolate stretch of beach on the Montenegrin coast. It was a modest beginning, but as Deakin points out, "The story of the competition between Communist and Nationalist groups within Yugoslavia for Allied aid and recognition begins with this journey of the first mission to the centre of events."[27]

Initially the mission was to have been exclusively a Yugoslav operation, but SOE-Cairo insisted on sending in its own observers. Created officially in July, 1940, following the collapse of France, SOE was to be the means by which Britain would strike back at Hitler within occupied Europe. Equipped with capabilities in the areas of intelligence gathering, sabotage operations, and propaganda, SOE was to be the instrument by which Churchill hoped to "set Europe ablaze."[28]

This colorful charge, typically Churchillian in its defiant tone, envisioned a role that, for the present at least, was inconsistent with SOE's policy and well beyond its means. Lacking the resources to provide adequate supply for the various resistance movements in Europe, SOE instructed its agents to patiently tend the embers of revolt while waiting for the decisive moment to fan them into the consuming blaze called for by the prime minister.[29] Clearly, at the time SOE dispatched its first mission to Yugoslavia, British strategic thinking vis-à-vis the resistance was far more in accord with the ideas of Mihailovich than with those of Tito.

Capt. Duane Hudson, selected by SOE to head the mission, had been a consultant mining engineer in Serbia before the war, knew the country quite well, and was fluent in the Serbian language. Accompanying Hudson were majors Mirko Lalatović and Zaharije Ostojić, and sergeant Veljko Dragičević, the mission's radio operator.[30] Two days after Hudson's team reached Mihailovich's headquarters on October 25, circumstances affecting the resistance began to change rapidly. Talks between Tito and Mihailovich at Brajići on October 27, proved unsuccessful. By November 2, Partisan and Chetnik forces were fighting each other in the town of Užice in what proved to be the opening round of a civil war. And, in late November, as if all of this were not enough, the

Axis launched their first major offensive aimed at crushing all guerrilla bands in the Užice region.[31]

In the chaos that followed, Hudson, who had returned to Partisan-held territory to report on conditions there, became separated from Mihailovich's headquarters and was forced to retreat with Tito's forces. He subsequently reached Mihailovich's new headquarters in Montenegro in April, 1942, and reestablished contact with Cairo in late May.[32] At that time Hudson reported having proof of the collaboration of local Chetnik leaders in Montenegro with the Italians and of Mihailovich's continued inactivity against the Axis forces. Although Hudson thought Mihailovich was "perfectly capable of coming to any secret understanding with either Italians or Germans," to prevent the communization of Yugoslavia, he remained convinced that the general would "undertake a grand finale against the Axis" once victory seemed assured.[33]

Hudson's reports convinced some in Cairo that Mihailovich was neither the only source of resistance in Yugoslavia nor perhaps the most effective. Accordingly, SOE decided to send in a more senior officer to Mihailovich's headquarters both to relieve Hudson and to report fully on the Chetnik organization. On December 25, Col. S. W. Bailey, an officer whose background and qualifications were quite similar to Hudson's, parachuted to Mihailovich's headquarters then located about ten miles north of Kolašin in Montenegro. Bailey soon confirmed Hudson's earlier reports concerning agreements between the Montenegrin Chetniks and the Italians, but found "no evidence of direct collaboration between Mihailović himself and the Germans and Italians."[34]

Accepting Hudson's and Bailey's evaluations of Mihailovich's ultimate intentions, SOE was not unduly concerned about arms deals between the Italians and the Chetniks. Besides, the Partisans were engaging in the same kind of activity. According to one German secret service officer, "the longer the guerrilla warfare lasted, the more frequent became deals in arms and munitions between Italian units and the partisans. Things reached such a pitch that there was a fixed and recognized price for all weapons."[35]

Partisan-Italian relations notwithstanding, Bailey informed Cairo that "the time has come to treat Mihailović firmly. He must be made to realise that we can make him or break him. . . . If our work is to prosper . . . he must now be . . . made to realise that we will no longer tolerate deceit."[36] Just how the British were to convince Mihailovich that they could "make him or break him" is not clear. As one SOE official pointed out quite correctly, the paucity of supplies sent by the British to Mihailovich left Bailey with "no cards in his hand at all."[37]

Though Hudson and Bailey never questioned Mihailovich's ultimate loyalty, their reports did reveal the limitations imposed on British military planners by continued exclusive support of the Chetnik leader. It was not that the Chetniks were doing any less than before; it was simply that the changing military situation in the Mediterranean dictated that they do more. Gen. Bernard Law Montgomery had thrown Erwin Rommel's vaunted Afrika Korps into retreat after El Alamein in October, 1942. Less than a month later, Allied forces landed in North Africa. These developments transformed the Mediterranean into a major theater of operations, which in turn substantially altered British thinking about the role of the resistance. Supply lines running through Yugoslavia and Greece needed to be cut in order to weaken Axis resistance in North Africa. Active resistance would also be required to pin down Axis forces and preclude their timely response to future Allied initiatives in the region.[38]

It seemed unlikely that Mihailovich either would or could fulfill the new role expected of him by the British. His conception of resistance had been shaped by forces and circumstances peculiar to his own country—historical traditions coupled with the complex political and social issues developing in the wake of the Axis invasion. These were internal matters largely unaffected by the changing tide of military events in the Mediterranean. To imagine that Mihailovich would radically alter his strategy as a result of events in North Africa was to misunderstand the raison d'être of his movement altogether. Obviously, the bond of mutual self-interest which had for slightly more that two years held Mihailovich and the British together was beginning to unravel. As it did, the British had to choose between short-term military policy, which suggested the extension of military support to the Partisans, and long-term political interests, which implied continued support of Mihailovich.

Brigadier C. M. Keble, chief of staff to Lord Glenconner (SOE-Cairo), took the initiative in resolving the dilemma on military grounds.[39] Assisted by Maj. Basil Davidson, chief of the Yugoslav Section, and Capt. F. W. Deakin, intelligence officer of the Yugoslav Section, Keble prepared a convincing brief advocating the extension of military support to the Partisans. Churchill received the document in late January, 1943, and approved it shortly thereafter, prompting Basil Davidson to exclaim that "the Cairo 'partisans' had won."[40]

The Foreign Office did not share Davidson's enthusiasm. A Foreign Office memorandum dated March 6, 1943, claimed that "Mihailovich is still the best man to back" and "represents the best instrument for conversion to our use. . . ."[41] Such views coincided with those of the British Chiefs of Staff, but SOE-Cairo, buttressed by Churchill's support, prevailed, and in late March the British decided to send missions to Partisan forces in Slovenia and Croatia.[42]

Perhaps the most important of the missions sent into Yugoslavia at this time was a joint SOE–Military Intelligence mission (TYPICAL) which reached Partisan forces near Mount Durmitor in Montenegro on May 28. The mission, which included Captain Deakin, arrived just two weeks after the Axis forces had launched their fifth offensive and found the Partisans locked in a desperate struggle for their very existence.[43] Deakin, who had served as Churchill's literary secretary prior to the war, found himself witness to an epic battle as the Partisans tenaciously fought to extricate themselves from the Axis trap. His messages describing the fighting stood in stark contrast to the majority of reports coming out of Mihailovich's area and may well have served to focus Churchill's attention on Tito's plight.[44]

At the same time the British initiated contact with the Partisans, they also sent additional missions to Mihailovich's forces in Serbia.[45] According to Bailey, who was at the time senior British officer with the Chetniks, these missions generally confirmed "that a policy of procrastination and downright inactivity was common to all Mihailović's forces."[46] Deakin added to this gloomy appraisal, charging that the Chetniks were collaborating with both the Italians and Germans – characterizing relations with the latter as "close, constant and increasing" over the past two years. This first instance of a British officer accusing the Chetniks of collaborating with the Germans came at a time when the German High Command was opposed to making agreements with the Chetniks. Furthermore, intelligence then being gleaned from the Ultra intercepts did not support such a sweeping indictment, nor did it directly implicate Mihailovich in any collaborationist activity.[47]

By the early summer of 1943, however, it was not necessarily Mihailovich's loyalty that was in question, but his value as an ally.[48] Still, conflicting intelligence coming out of Yugoslavia and divided councils in Britain's policy-making machinery left the British reluctant to make an irrevocable decision in favor of either Tito or Mihailovich. As a result, London moved toward a policy of equal support for both elements of the resistance, while at the same time attempting to ensure that the meager supplies which could be provided were not squandered in a debilitating civil war. To this end, the Middle East Defense Committee submitted a plan to the Chiefs of Staff in London on June 8, calling for assistance to Chetnik forces east of the Ibar River and to Tito's forces west of the river. Obviously the British hoped by this measure to secure immediate military results from the resistance without jeopardizing their own political interests or tipping the internal balance in favor of either faction.[49]

This policy may have been consistent with the principles of high Allied strategy, but it lacked an element of reality when applied to Yugoslavia. Mihailovich and Tito each had programs of his own, and neither was inclined to accept any limitation on military operations that implied or might later result in a corresponding limitation of political authority. With no consensus in mid-1943 either to abandon Mihailovich or embrace Tito, the British tried to resolve their dilemma by supporting both. Given these circumstances, the British undoubtedly viewed with some apprehension the prospect of direct American involvement in Yugoslav affairs through the Office of Strategic Services.

2.   A British Show

The British had invited OSS participation in Yugoslav operations at the time they notified Washington of plans to infiltrate missions to the Partisans.[1] At that time the State Department was quite reluctant to plunge headlong into the turbulent waters of Yugoslav politics without testing the strength of the currents or knowing where they might lead. The department raised legitimate concerns that the United States might be drawn into the quarrel between Mihailovich and Britain or might become associated with British policies with which the Americans disagreed.[2] The United States would at the outset, for example, have to abandon its policy of exclusive support for Mihailovich and the Royal Yugoslav Government and accept the British policy of equal support just to get observers into the country.

OSS did not share this reluctance. In Donovan's mind Yugoslavia offered yet another opportunity for his organization to demonstrate that it could fulfill the mission for which it had been created. Consequently, he vigorously defended the prerogatives of OSS, particularly in the field of secret intelligence, and insisted upon its right to operate in every major theater of the war, including those on the periphery of American military and political interest.

Two agreements negotiated with SOE officials in June, 1942, and July, 1943, provided the basis for OSS participation in the Balkans generally and Yugoslavia specifically. The first of these made the two organizations coequal partners in the field of intelligence but identified certain regions where each country would have control over special operations. Since the Balkans lay within a British theater of operations, SOE was given control of special operations activities in that region.[3]

On paper the agreement appeared workable, but in practice some problems surfaced from time to time that required Donovan's personal intervention to resolve them.[4] With some justification the British regarded themselves as the senior partner in this joint intelligence undertaking and were less than enthusiastic about sharing the field on a "coequal" basis with the Americans.

Maj. Gen. William J. Donovan, director of the Office of Strategic Services, 1942–45.
U.S. Army photograph, courtesy Geoffrey Jones, president, Veterans of OSS.

OSS Coverage, 1943

Missions with Partisan forces

1. Benson
2. Farish
3. Wuchinich
4. Selvig

_____

Missions with Chetnik forces

A. Mansfield
B. Seitz
C. Musulin

One British SOE officer undoubtedly summed up the sentiments of many of his colleagues when he suggested that "liaison with Americans was like having an affair with an elephant; it is extremely difficult, you are apt to get badly trampled on, and you get no results for eight years."[5]

British resentment was not always confined to witty analogies and at times manifested itself in actions toward OSS that clearly constituted obstructionism. Intelligence would sometimes be circulated on a very restricted basis or perhaps not passed through channels as quickly as it should have been. In operational matters where SOE had greater control, mission departures would at times be delayed, supplies would not be dropped on time if at all, and virtually all communications went through British channels.[6]

Admittedly, OSS reciprocated when it could but frequently had to be satisfied with lodging official complaints that tended to have little effect. An attempt was made to resolve some of these problems in the summer of 1943, by which time it was apparent that the Balkans would soon become a theater for joint OSS-SOE activities. In addition to placing OSS operations in Yugoslavia under control of SOE-Cairo, the July agreement provided for OSS officers to be attached to British main missions at Partisan and Chetnik headquarters and for the creation of joint OSS-SOE or wholly OSS submissions in the country.[7]

Washington had earlier decided to proceed with plans to establish an OSS mission in Cairo from which liaison officers could be infiltrated to Tito and Mihailovich. In March, Col. Ellery C. Huntington, a high-ranking OSS official from Washington who would later head the Independent American Military Mission to Tito, along with Col. Gustav Guenther and Maj. Louis Huot, flew from London to Cairo by way of Algiers to establish the mission. Guenther remained in command, with Huot and Lt. Comdr. Turner H. McBaine heading the special operations and secret intelligence sections. Their British counterparts at the time were Lord Glenconner, head of SOE-Cairo; Brigadier C. M. Keble, his chief of staff; and Basil Davidson, head of the Yugoslav Section.[8]

The first two OSS officers sent to Cairo for infiltration into Yugoslavia were George Musulin and George Wuchinich, both Americans of Yugoslav ancestry. They arrived in Cairo on May 23, 1943, but were not able to enter the country immediately because the British would not consent to OSS having its own communications network as Donovan insisted. At one point in early July, Musulin, accompanied by Capt. George Selvig, flew from Cairo to Derna preparatory to joining Bailey at Mihailovich's headquarters in Serbia.[9] Capt. Melvin O. Benson was to be the third member of this team. Of course, this mission never became operational because of the differences with the British alluded to earlier, and all three were forced to return to Cairo.[10]

The OSS-SOE agreement concluded in July settled, at least temporarily, the troublesome communications issue and paved the way for Mansfield and Benson to enter the country the following month. Prior to their departure, SOE-Cairo briefed both men, though neither was favorably impressed with the information provided by his British comrades. Benson described his briefing as very sketchy since "reliable information about the Partisans at that time was very meager."[11] Mansfield said much the same in his report when he described Colonel Bailey as a "capable, broad minded, intelligent and patient officer who was far more familiar with the problems faced in dealing with Mihailovich than officers with whom I had talked in Cairo."[12] This is perhaps a good example of the British not being as forthcoming with their American colleagues as they might have been. Seven months earlier SOE-Cairo had persuaded Chur-

Capt. Melvin O. Benson, first American liaison officer sent to Partisan forces, pictured here in Dalmatia. National Archives

chill to dispatch British missions to Tito's Partisans. It is difficult to believe that the same information which proved so convincing to the prime minister would have been so lightly regarded by Benson and Mansfield.

In any case, shortly after the two OSS officers reached Yugoslavia, events occurred that would have rendered any briefing somewhat obsolete. On September 8, news of the Italian surrender reached the British missions at Tito's and Mihailovich's headquarters, setting off a three-way scramble for Italian arms among the Partisans, Chetniks, and Germans. Both resistance leaders accused the British of giving the other side advance warning about the capitulation, but there is no direct evidence to substantiate these charges.[13]

Benson, who was with the British mission at Partisan headquarters at Jajce when news of the surrender arrived, recalled that Tito immediately requested that he and Deakin proceed to Split to assist in disarming the Italians there. In less than an hour the two officers, accompanied by their wireless operator, were on their way by car to Bugojno where they were to join the First Proletarian Division under the command of Gen. Koča Popović.[14] This division, numbering about six thousand men, set out the next day and, by a series of forced marches, reached Split on September 16. On the following day Popović and members of his staff met with Italians to discuss the terms by which the latter would surrender their arms and supplies. Benson represented OSS during these negotiations but, like Deakin, more in the capacity of an observer than a participant.[15]

Besides Benson and Deakin, Maj. John Burke, head of the British mission in Dalmatia, attended the negotiations, as did Ivo Lola Ribar, who served as Tito's representative. There was in fact little to negotiate. The Italian representative, Gen. Emilio Becuzzi, commander of the "Bergamo" Division, was mainly concerned with using Deakin's radio to get a message to his wife that he was safe. Obviously, the Italians were not prepared to resist the Partisans, who had already relieved them of most of their arms and equipment and were moving them up into the mountains. With negotiations concluded, Deakin returned to Bosnia to meet Brigadier Fitzroy Maclean, who was to assume command of all Anglo-American missions attached to Partisan forces. Benson and Burke remained in Split until September 24, when they evacuated the town and rejoined Popović's division, which was preparing to attack the town of Livno.[16]

Ustasha troops occupying Livno had no more appetite for a battle with Popović's forces than had the Italians in Split. They hastily evacuated the city at the beginning of the attack, leaving behind so much food, guns, and ammunition that the Partisans suspected a trick. Popović occupied the town and moved on to Kupres, which also fell with very light resistance. The engagements at Livno and Kupres were not impressive actions from a military standpoint, but when the BBC announced that the Partisans had taken the two towns, no one seemed overly concerned with details as to how they had done it.[17]

At Mihailovich's headquarters, news of the Italian surrender found the Chetniks as unprepared as the Partisans. Mansfield was surprised that Cairo had not provided some advance notice of the surrender so that Mihailovich's forces could have moved to disarm nearby Italian garrisons in advance of the Germans. On September 9, Cairo did instruct Bailey to do everything possible to obtain the surrender of all Italian units in his area.[18] In the company of Maj. Voja Lukačević and his command, Bailey immediately set out for Berane, hoping to obtain the surrender of the Italian "Venetzia" Division. Mansfield repeatedly wired Cairo for permission to accompany Bailey, but received no reply for over a week. Rather than sit idly by waiting for instructions from Cairo, he and Hudson left headquarters on September 11 for Priboj with intentions of negotiating the capitulation of the two thousand Italians garrisoned there. At the time Mansfield and Hudson arrived, the Priboj garrison, which was under the command of headquarters at Berane, had not received orders to surrender. The orders arrived two days later, at which time the Italian commander surrendered his forces to Mansfield and Hudson while Chetnik forces occupied the town.[19]

In the meantime, Bailey secured the capitulation of the "Venetzia" Division, whose commander entered into an agreement for joint action against the Germans. Bailey followed earlier instructions from Cairo which stipulated that where such agreements could be reached, the Italians need not be disarmed. This agreement also applied to the garrison at Priboj where, as in Berane, only a small Chetnik force was left behind. Lukačević's men later disarmed the Priboj garrison when the area was threatened by Germans, but all of the Italian arms at Berane ultimately fell into Partisan hands. Tito's forces occupied the city and disarmed all of the Italians there despite the latter's agreement with Bailey to join the Chetniks in actions against the Germans.[20]

While negotiations were being conducted with the Italians, Mihailovich issued a general order to his troops throughout Yugoslavia to attack German supply lines, communications installations, and troop concentrations. Mansfield saw these orders, had them translated, and forwarded them to Cairo. Mansfield also confirmed that for several days after these orders were issued, reports came in from various corps commanders detailing extensive sabotage activity in Serbia, Hercegovina, Bosnia, and Dalmatia. Chetnik commanders in Bosnia and Dalmatia also reported that the Partisan forces had attacked their units while they were engaged in combat with the Germans. Another report claimed that Chetnik forces took the town of Gacko and drove the Germans out, only to have the Partisans walk in and claim that they had liberated the town from the Germans. Even while en route to Berane, Lukačević's men engaged German troops in an all-day battle in the town of Prijepolje, which they captured—killing about one hundred of the enemy in the process. This action was far more significant than the Partisan engagements in Livno, Kupres, and

Gacko, but BBC made no mention of it, reporting exclusively on the Partisans.[21]

Without question the Partisans benefited much more from the Italian capitulation than did the Chetniks. Tito later claimed that his forces succeeded in disarming ten Italian divisions and secured enough arms to equip eighty thousand additional men.[22] This was, however, only the first in a series of events that would strengthen Tito's hand, militarily and politically.

The second, which occurred while the race to gather Italian arms was taking place, was the arrival of Brigadier Fitzroy Maclean at Tito's headquarters. The increased military importance of southeastern Europe, including Yugoslavia, was in part responsible for the British decision to upgrade their missions in the region.[23] But Fitzroy Maclean was no ordinary brigadier randomly chosen from the ranks to represent British interests in Yugoslavia. He was a man with extensive Foreign Office experience, a Conservative Member of Parliament, and a personal acquaintance of Churchill. Clearly, his arrival in Yugoslavia on September 17 "marked the opening of a new chapter, political as well as military, in Britain's relations with the Partisans."[24]

By comparison, Brigadier Charles Douglas Armstrong, selected to go to Mihailovich's headquarters, was a professional soldier with a distinguished record of service in India who, by virtue of being known by Field Marshal Montgomery, was asked to go to Yugoslavia. Armstrong believed that he was being sent to Mihailovich's headquarters to "counterbalance the Brigadier Maclean mission which was being sent to Tito."[25] To a degree that was true, but the balance was one of rank, not of influence.

OSS had also decided to upgrade its representation at the headquarters of Mihailovich and Tito. Maj. Linn Farish joined Maclean's mission, which dropped to Tito on September 17, while Lt. Col. Albert B. Seitz parachuted with Armstrong to Chetnik headquarters one week later.[26]

Seitz, a West Point graduate with prior service in the Royal Canadian Mounted Police, arrived in Cairo on July 1, 1943, anxious to get some combat experience, and had been recruited by OSS through Colonel Guenther. Linn Farish also brought a varied and colorful career to OSS. He had been chosen for the Olympic team while attending Stanford University and after graduation pursued a career as an oil engineer in California. Before the United States entered the war, he joined the Canadian Army, then transfered to the Royal Engineers and was sent to Persia. Farish later requested and received a transfer to a British commando unit and was sent to Cairo. There he met Seitz, with whom he traveled to Haifa where both men underwent parachute training.[27]

The trip from Cairo to Haifa took about twenty-four hours by rail, and according to Seitz "one trip on what passes for a train will cure you of ever wanting to take another." After reaching Haifa, Seitz and Farish were "rattled and bumped" for six more miles by truck to a tent camp called Ramat David where their actual training would take place. Having been forewarned about the arduous regimen that lay before them, the two men retired early that evening and, with lights out, spent quite some time talking. Farish told Seitz, "You know, Al, here we are, grown up men, forty-three and forty-four years old, supposed to have horse sense, here to learn parachuting. I never even ride in a plane if I can help it, too many trips over the Andes." Seitz now understood why Farish had insisted on traveling by train rather than by air. The irony of the situation, given their reason for being in Ramat David, invited some good-natured retaliation by Seitz, who professed great indignation at having been subjected to the intolerable conditions of the train ride for such a poor reason. Farish took the banter in stride, replying with some degree of resignation, "Well, we're here in time, anyway, but aren't we a couple of dam [sic] fools?"[28]

Seitz and Farish became the best of friends and, with the completion of their training, returned to Cairo together – this time by air. Upon arriving, Farish learned that his transfer to the United States Army had been effected and that he had been assigned to operations with Partisan forces in Yugoslavia. Pledging to meet for Thanksgiving dinner, the two officers went their separate ways, Farish to the Partisans and Seitz to the Chetniks.[29]

Almost immediately after Armstrong and Seitz arrived at Mihailovich's headquarters, tensions began to develop between American and British personnel, and relations with Mihailovich noticeably deteriorated. Armstrong had inherited Bailey's thankless, if not impossible, task of prodding Mihailovich to greater activity without the inducement of adequate supply. Frustrated by the circumstances, he notified Cairo in early November that "it is 'Perfide Albion' attempting to purchase strategic benefits with Serb blood without any intention of giving an adequate quid pro quo."[30]

Relations with the Americans were complicated by the fact that Armstrong and Seitz disliked one another personally and never developed a working relationship comparable to that enjoyed by Mansfield and Bailey.[31] Furthermore, Armstrong was probably overzealous in his efforts to minimize the influence of Mansfield and Seitz, fearing that Mihailovich might attempt to play one side against the other and thus create an embarrassing schism in Anglo-American resistance policy. Armstrong barred the two oss officers from his first meeting with Mihailovich, which, according to Seitz, turned into a "bickering match with the Brigadier definitely outclassed." After the meeting Armstrong told Seitz that "the mission was British and the whole show would remain a British show." The Americans were there only "to give an Allied illusion to the Yugoslavs." Accordingly, Seitz could see Mihailovich only at Armstrong's discretion and then in the company of Colonel Bailey. Mansfield was denied direct access altogether.[32]

Seitz immediately complained to Cairo, only to be told that Armstrong was acting within his authority on all points. SOE did inform the brigadier, however, that he was to send all OSS messages verbatim after reading them.[33] Armstrong later claimed that "Colonel Seitz sent his reports off without my ever seeing them," and insisted further that "I certainly didn't censor them, and I certainly didn't stop him from sending any reports."[34] Nevertheless, in Seitz's view, the Americans had been relegated to a "supernumerary news gathering capacity and at that, sending items gathered by the Stab (headquarters) from various Korpus (corps) commanders by radio and courier."[35]

Mansfield, who witnessed the personal conflict between Seitz and Armstrong as well as the growing disillusionment with which Mihailovich and the British viewed one another, observed that "from the very outset relations between Mihailovich and the British were tenuous. Although General Mihailovich enjoyed a warm personal relationship with Colonel Bailey, it was readily apparent that he reflected a general distrust toward the British. The attitude toward American officers on the other hand, was one of warmth in which Mihailovich made no bones about his dislike for the British."[36]

Subsequent events proved, to Mihailovich in any case, that his suspicions of the British were well founded. Less than a week after arriving in the country, Armstrong accompanied Hudson on a successful mission to destroy a bridge near Vardiste on the narrow gauge Belgrade-Sarajevo railroad, which served as an important line of supply between Belgrade and Dubrovnik. Mihailovich sanctioned the operation with the understanding that his men would receive additional supplies if the bridge was destroyed, but none were sent. Mansfield later reported that "despite clear wires from the British mission on pin points for landing grounds on Zlatibor, signals received from Cairo indicated either a complete misunderstanding or ignorance of our signals."[37]

A larger operation was carried out on October 2, in the presence of Hudson, Seitz, and Armstrong, in which about 350 Germans and Ustasha were killed and a significant quantity of arms and ammunition captured. After the attack, the Chetniks, with help from some British sappers, demolished the bridge at Višegrad, closing traffic between Sarajevo and Belgrade by way of Kragujevac. Armstrong "personally reported the success of these operations to headquarters in Cairo, asking for assurance that the BBC would put it out on their news and give credit to General Mihailovich's forces."[38] Incredibly, BBC attributed these actions to the Partisans despite the fact that they had been witnessed by three ranking Allied officers and personally reported to SOE-Cairo by the chief of the British mission.[39]

Mihailovich had reluctantly consented to the Višegrad operation with the understanding that the British would respond by sending additional supplies, which he desperately needed. In the end, he received no supplies and the Partisans got credit for what had been a very successful Chetnik attack. Also, following the action at Višegrad, the Chetniks had taken the town of Rogatica, which they still held at the time BBC announced that the Partisans had captured it from the Germans.[40]

Indignant that his reports from the field were being ignored and outraged that BBC was undermining his work with Mihailovich, Armstrong angrily advised Cairo, "If you persist refuse listen us here don't blame if you get poor results." He continued, "Sorry but most [sic] keep on at you about political aspect and suggested remedies. One is for Heavens sake tell BBC to 'put a sock in it.'"[41]

Writing of the period between August and November, 1943, David Martin claims that "man for man and gun for gun, the permanent Chetnik units fought as hard . . . killed as many Germans, and took as many German prisoners as did the Partisan units."[42] After Višegrad, however, it all seemed in vain, and Mihailovich once again lapsed into a policy of passive resistance. George Musulin, who entered Yugoslavia on October 19, 1943, and remained with Chetnik forces in Serbia until May 28, 1944, reported that "Mihailovich is not fighting the Germans at the moment. He has his own reasons for not fighting the Germans, but the fact remains that during my stay in Serbia I did not see a German-Chetnik clash."[43] Armstrong reluctantly advised Cairo that he had reached "tacit deadlock" with Mihailovich and his efforts were largely "restricted to badgering him operation by operation into doing the absolute minimum with which he thinks he can regain our nominal support."[44]

Circumstances were markedly different at Partisan headquarters, where Brigadier Maclean had quickly established a very amicable relationship with Tito. On the other hand, Farish had been as effectively, if more diplomatically, removed from the center of events as had Seitz. Maclean had sent him to the town of Glamoč where, according to Benson, he remained for several days "with a radio which didn't work and a wireless operator who couldn't fix it."[45] The treatment accorded Seitz and Farish clearly suggests that the British, while inviting OSS participation in Yugoslavia, wished to keep a very short rein on Donovan's men. OSS personnel outside the country, however, had other ideas.

Soon after the invasion of Italy, OSS established an advanced base on the Italian coast at Bari. The site had been selected by Turner McBaine, who, with a jeep, a driver, and a map had undertaken a reconnaissance of the coast for that specific purpose. McBaine, a Naval Reserve officer called to active duty in mid-1941, had been recruited by the Coordinator of Information (COI), the forerunner of OSS, shortly before Pearl Harbor. He worked directly under Donovan in Washington before transferring to the Middle East, where he was instrumental in setting up OSS operations in Cairo.[46] Bari, or Special Bari Section (SBS), remained under the control of OSS-Cairo but became the center for operations in the Balkans and later for operations aimed at the penetration of central Europe. McBaine initially assumed command of the base and was

Lt. Comdr. Turner McBaine, second from left, and Capt. Hans Tofte, fourth from left, discuss progress on Operation AUDREY in Bari, Italy. National Archives

succeeded by Maj. Robert Koch in late December, 1943.[47] From Bari a group of enterprising oss officers planned and executed one of the organization's largest and most successful supply efforts – Operation AUDREY.

Logistically the stage had been set for this operation by the Allied invasion of Italy and Partisan successes in western Yugoslavia that had left Tito's forces in control of the Dalmatian coast and several offshore islands. If the Partisans could hold these areas, it would be possible to ship supplies to them in far greater quantities than either they or Mihailovich had been receiving by air. This, in essence, was the plan that Capt. Hans V. Tofte and Lt. Robert S. Thompson submitted to Major Huot on September 12. Within six days Huot pushed the plan through oss channels and, with Donovan's backing, obtained General Wilson's approval.[48]

By October 9, oss had secured the use of berth two at Bari for its shipping operation. Two days later Huot undertook his first of three reconnaissance missions to the Yugoslav coast to determine the location and capacities of receiving points under Partisan control. He returned on the fourteenth to find a representative from General Wilson's headquarters conducting his own investigation, which concluded with the issuance of an order transferring fourteen vessels from the Royal Yugoslav Government to the control of the commander-in-chief of MEDTO (Mediterranean Theater of Operations), thus placing them at Huot's disposal.[49]

Two days later, Huot, accompanied by Lieutenant Thompson and Comdr. Sergei Makiedo, a representative of the Partisan Eighth Corps, set out from Bari aboard an RAF crash boat en route to the island of Vis. After being received by Partisan officials there, Huot's party proceeded first to Hvar and then to Podgora. There the group met Col. Pavle Ilić, commander of the Eighth Corps, with whom Huot had extensive discussions concerning the means by which the Partisans would receive and distribute supplies coming from Bari.[50] Ilić also mentioned the possibility of a meeting with Tito if the major could return within a few days. Huot knew that such a meeting would constitute a violation of standing orders. Still, he returned to Vis on the evening of October 20 and met with Makiedo and Ilić prior to traveling inland to meet with Tito at his headquarters at Jajce.[51]

Huot gained the impression from Ilić that the British mission under Maclean "had all but worn out its welcome among the Partisans" because of its inability to provide adequate supplies. When a conference with British officers on the following day failed to convince Ilić that SOE could increase the flow of supplies, he repeated his suggestion to Huot concerning a personal meeting with Tito. Rather than going to Korčula to inform Maclean of his intentions as he should have done, Huot decided that he would set out for the mainland without further delay. Accompanied by Makiedo and Ilić, he boarded a small launch, which the Partisans had derisively dubbed "The Chetnik," and under the cover

Maj. Louis Huot, center, was a key figure in the planning Operation AUDREY. Lt. Robert Thompson, left, worked with Huot in the Trans-Adriatic shipping operation. The officer on the right is Maj. Carleton Coon. National Archives

of darkness made his way to the coast, arriving there in the early morning hours of the twenty-second. Traveling overland in a small Italian staff car and armed with a Schmeiser submachine gun, Huot's party reached Jajce in the early evening of the twenty-third and found Tito on hand to greet them.[52]

On the preceding day, news had reached Partisan headquarters that tons of stores had been delivered to the Island of Vis by the Americans. Members of the British mission dismissed the story as misinformation, claiming that any such shipment must have been the work of SOE and, more specifically, Brigadier Maclean. When Huot arrived the following day, however, no one remained in doubt for long as to who was in charge of the shipping operation. That night he and Benson enjoyed a very cordial dinner with Tito and members of the Partisan staff—a function from which the British were conspicuously absent.[53]

Benson gave Huot a verbal report covering his experiences over the past month and photostatic copies of fifty-five captured documents purporting to show collaboration between the Chetniks and the Germans. In a subsequent meeting with Tito, Huot discussed the issue of Chetnik collaboration as well as matters relating to the shipping operation. He also secured an agreement to place an American intelligence officer at each Partisan corps headquarters.[54] Huot was obviously impressed with Tito, whom he described as "a force to reckon with, a leader men would follow through the very gates of hell."[55]

After concluding his discussion with Tito, Huot sent a message to Livno requesting that Farish stand by to meet him as he passed through on his way to the coast. Based on the verbal report received from Farish on the twenty-sixth, Huot recommended that he return to Italy and submit a formal written report concerning his observations of the Partisan movement. Having spent the last few days in "complete idleness," Farish readily agreed. Aware that his actions "would inevitably require lengthy and painful explanations with Brigadier Maclean," Huot proceeded with his plan, convinced that it would be possible to "square the situation" with Maclean. It obviously was not.[56]

Maclean lodged a vigorous protest with OSS headquarters over Huot's unauthorized trip to Tito's headquarters, which resulted in Huot's being relieved from his duties in Bari. Captain Tofte assumed command of the shipping operation, and Huot received orders to report personally to Col. John E. Toulmin, who had succeeded Guenther as acting director of OSS Middle East (OSS-ME). After meeting with Huot, Toulmin wrote to Donovan on November 3, describing the success of AUDREY to that point and conceding that "this is to Huot's credit." But, the colonel continued, "He is almost impossible to control and one of these bright days I may have to send him back to Washington."[57] Huot was later transfered out of the theater and ultimately dismissed from OSS altogether, but the operation he had begun continued to funnel supplies to the Partisans in ever-increasing amounts.[58]

Tito, left, pictured with members of his staff in the mountains of Yugo-slavia. National Archives

Soon after Tofte replaced Huot, oss concluded an agreement with the British by which overall control of the operation would fall to soe-Bari (Force 133) while the actual shipment of supplies from Italy to Tito's headquarters would remain the responsibility of Special Operations Special Bari Section (so-sbs). When these arrangements were made in early November, Tofte had about twenty-five ships in his fleet. By December the number had grown to forty, and the number of Partisan workers engaged in loading the ships had increased from one hundred to six hundred.[59] Additional oss personnel also joined the operation during this period. Lt. (jg) Ward E. Ellen took charge of ships maintenance while Lt. John Hamilton, better known perhaps as Sterling Hayden, opened a new shipping base at Monopoli in mid-December.[60] Melvin Benson served as liaison on the islands of Hvar and Vis, receiving the supplies and supervising their transport to the mainland, until December 22, when he was relieved by Hamilton.[61]

Figures vary on the total tonnage of supplies sent to the Partisans between October 15 and December 31. One report claims 11,637 tons, but Tofte gives a figure of 6,500 tons. In addition to the supplies, oss also transferred to Yugoslavia approximately two thousand Partisan troops recruited from internment camps in Italy and evacuated seven hundred Partisan wounded along with thousands of refugees. AUDREY was quite successful but hardly a secret operation. According to Tofte, war correspondents visited the base regularly, and in early November alone, more than thirty enemy agents with wireless sets were arrested in the town. oss also avoided many "subtle" attempts by the British to gain control of the shipping operation, which, if successful, would have diminished the importance of the American contribution significantly.[62]

Even as AUDREY was coming to a close, controversy continued to swirl around those involved in the operation. On December 22, McBaine assembled a five-man rescue party, including Tofte, under the command of Maj. Richard Weil, to enter Yugoslavia and assist in the evacuation of some twenty-five nurses whose plane had been forced down. That same evening Tofte approached McBaine to suggest that Hamilton should go on the mission in place of one of the other officers. McBaine, who was to leave Bari in a few days, recommended that Tofte take the matter up with Weil, which he did. When Weil refused the request, Tofte pursued the matter outside oss channels with the commanding officer whose personnel were the object of the proposed mission. Keenly aware of Huot's previous exploits, McBaine had no appetite for more of the same from the major's former subordinates. He therefore recommended to Toulmin that Tofte be recalled from Bari and given another assignment, that letters of censure be written to each of the officers concerned, and that any promotions should be cancelled.[63]

Huot also continued to be a considerable thorn in the side of oss even after he had expelled from the organization. The cause célèbre in this instance was the scheduled publication in early 1945 of his book, which oss had apparently decided not to contest despite scathing protest from those who had read the manuscript and were personally familiar with Huot's record. Conyers Read, head of the oss history project, objected to the publication on the grounds of security, distortions and inaccuracies in the work itself, and the effect it might have on morale. Claiming that the book would constitute an "insult" to many in oss whose contributions exceeded those of Huot, Read argued that "they knew Major Huot and they knew how to appraise him. They will shudder to think that his performance is put forward as the one public record of their gallant adventures."[64] Maj. Carleton Coon, who had initially been sent to Bari to replace Huot[65] and was later assigned to edit the history of Yugoslav operations, shared Read's opinion. He described Huot's account as "highly inaccurate, highly romantic in a nauseating manner," and one that "takes all the credit for Huot which should be given to others." Despite strong opposition within the agency, Huot's manuscript was published in 1945, leaving Coon to speculate that "either the oss has seen fit to release this . . . or Huot has pulled a fast one, as usual, and put it through the War Department without reference to oss."[66]

Those responsible for the planning and execution of Operation AUDREY may have demonstrated more initiative and resourcefulness than prudence, but that should not detract unduly from their accomplishment. One measure of their success may be found in a report that Donovan submitted to the Joint Chiefs of Staff in late November, indicating that between October 12 and November 5 over 1,000 tons of supplies had been sent to the Partisans. By way of comparison, only 190 tons of supplies had been dropped to the resistance between July and September – 107 tons to Mihailovich and 82½ to Tito.[67]

Shortly after Huot and his men began ferrying supplies to the Partisans, oss dispatched Lt. George Musulin to Mihailovich's forces. Musulin, who had been an outstanding tackle at the University of Pittsburgh in the mid-1930s, may well have been the heaviest American soldier to make a successful parachute jump during the war.[68] He had joined the army in May, 1941, and was assigned to the Twenty-ninth Infantry Division at Fort Meade, Maryland. His ethnic background, knowledge of the Serbo-Croatian language, and willingness to undertake hazardous duty behind enemy lines made him a prime candidate for oss, which recruited him in July, 1942.[69] Trained in the United States, Musulin arrived in Cairo in late May, 1943, for further briefings before entering Yugoslavia in mid-October.

Musulin was supposed to join Seitz and Mansfield in the First Corps area but for reasons that are not altogether clear was dropped into territory held by the Second Corps. When he later informed Cairo of the error, he was advised to remain with the soe mission then under the command of Capt. Peter Maynard. Musulin had hardly settled in before the Germans sent out a recon-

Capt. George Musulin, left, shown with full beard and Chetnik headgear during his first mission to Mihailovich's forces. Musulin subsequently re-entered the country as commanding officer of the HALYARD mission. Courtesy George Vujnovich

naissance in force from the nearby town of Čačak. Over the next two weeks the mission remained constantly on the move, giving Musulin an opportunity to witness firsthand the destruction and personal tragedy the people of Serbia had experienced during two and one-half years of German occupation.[70] On November 17, Musulin left Second Corps headquarters and traveled to the First Corps area, which was under the command of Capt. Zvonko Vučković.

To understand the significance of Musulin's observations and subsequent report, it must be remembered that at the time he entered the country Britain and the United States were committed to a policy of equal support for Tito and Mihailovich. In fact, no such equality existed. While tons of supplies were pouring across the Adriatic to Tito's forces, Musulin claimed that "the only thing the British sent in there in the areas where I was . . . were some Italian carbines and some Italian black shirts with lice. And they tried to give that to Mihailovich, and he was insulted and refused."[71] Musulin finally became so disgusted with the paucity of supplies being sent to Mihailovich that he angrily reminded Cairo, "We can't fight Jerry with bare feet, brave hearts, and Radio London."[72]

The result of all of this was that in the span of four months – September to December, 1943 – the military balance of power in Yugoslavia had shifted dramatically and irrevocably in favor of the Partisans. Vucković, whose troops fought the Partisans before and after this period, discovered that "while fighting against them in the spring of 1944 during their attempt at reentering Serbia, I was amazed at the quality and quantity of fire power they could deploy against us."[73]

The rapid increase in Partisan strength beginning in September paralleled an equally rapid deterioration in relations between the British and Mihailovich. Rather than simply observe and report on these events, Mansfield and Seitz proposed to make a general reconnaissance of Mihailovich's forces in Serbia to determine his numerical strength and military needs. Armstrong approved the plan, as did Cairo, and on November 7, the two OSS officers began their tour. Mihailovich assigned Capt. Boris J. Todorovich (Todorović) to serve as liaison with the mission, while Armstrong sent Hudson along as interpreter.[74]

While Seitz and Mansfield proceeded with their inspection, Armstrong and Bailey set forth a detailed proposal that they hoped would end the civil conflict and offer some hope of achieving a united resistance in Yugoslavia. Briefly, the plan called for the British to reiterate their stand on the restoration of pre-1941 Yugoslavia as a war aim, guarantee free elections to determine the form of government after liberation, and provide equal support to all resistance elements. For their part, Tito and Mihailovich would agree to subordinate their activities to the policy of the Allies, place themselves under the command of the Allied theater commander in chief, confine their activities to defined operational zones, and refrain from fighting one another. Supplies would be cut off from either group that failed to abide by these agreements.[75]

Had the recommendations submitted by Armstrong and Bailey been presented six months earlier, their chance for success would have been much greater. At that point the Partisans would have gained from any arrangement by which they would have been accorded equality of treatment by the Allies in terms of recognition, material support, and propaganda. By early November, however, they had all of those things. The chief of the British mission to Tito's headquarters was Churchill's personal representative. OSS was shipping tons of supplies daily to the Partisans on Vis. And the BBC had conveniently forgotten about Mihailovich. Armstrong based his proposals on the assumption that the British were still the arbiters in the Yugoslav situation. They were not. Virtually everything the British might threaten to withhold from Mihailovich was already being withheld, and almost everything they could promise Tito, he already had.

Tito believed that his best opportunity lay in avoiding any agreement that would limit his authority while continuing to establish a position of dominance in Yugoslavia that would command recognition by the Allies at the conclusion of the war. In this belief he had reason to be encouraged by the actions of the western Allies and by public statements of the Royal Yugoslav Government that implied a favorable shift of opinion toward his movement.[76] Partisan stock had also risen considerably in some segments of the American press since the first of the year. The political implications of Tito's movement were soft-pedaled, and when they were raised, the Partisans were often described as a "coalition of all democratic and progressive parties . . . and a small minority of communists."[77]

Such assessments were not confined solely to the press. In a memorandum to the president in late October, Donovan reported that the Partisans were engaged in hostilities throughout the country "in favorable contrast to Mihailovich's relative lack of activity and narrow field." He further noted that their political program, calling for a federated Yugoslavia with a government selected by democratic elections, was "extremely popular." Lastly, Donovan wrote that "there is no factual foundation for the allegation of communism made against the Partisans. Such inclinations are found only among a small part of the rank and file of the leaders."[78] Similar characterizations were also applied to Mao and his "agrarian reformers" in China.[79]

In time, Donovan's views about the Partisans would change. In the fall of 1943, however, he appears to have been poorly informed, as was the president through him, about the character of the movement. Measuring Communist influence among the Partisans largely in quantifiable terms would be comparable to counting Napoleon Bonaparte as one more French soldier on the field of battle. A more accurate assessment of the degree of control exercised by the Communists over the Partisan movement is provided by M. R. D. Foot. He shows that the command structure of the Partisan army "from Tito at its head down through brigade and battalion to company commanders, was in the hands of communists; non-communists, however talented, however brilliant, could command nothing stronger than a platoon."[80]

On one hand it seemed to make little sense for the Allies to be overly concerned about the politics of the Partisans while providing every possible assistance to the Soviet Union.[81] On the other, Allied leaders had some responsibility for considering the extent to which pursuit of their own short-term military interests might lead to the imposition of a Communist regime on the people of Yugoslavia. These points and others were given forceful expression in Brigadier Maclean's now famous report of November 6, which called for the abandonment of Mihailovich and the transfer of all support to Tito.[82]

Maclean credited the Partisans with dominating "the greater part of Yugoslavia" with an army of some twenty-six divisions that enjoyed the "whole-hearted support of the civil population." He admitted that the Partisan movement was "essentially revolutionary . . . and there can be no question of a return to the old order." As for Mihailovich, Maclean suggested that while he might deny any personal collaboration with the Axis, he could not "deny the open and active collaboration of many of his principal commanders, of which there is irrefutable evidence." The brigadier therefore recommended that aid to Mihailovich cease since "by it, we are in return for no corresponding advantage, prejudicing our position with the Partisans and driving them more and more to the conclusion that the Soviet Union is their only friend." Maclean conceded that the Partisans intended to assert their control over the country after liberation and warned that only military intervention on a large scale could prevent them from doing so. Consequently, exclusive support of Tito would substantially increase Yugoslavia's contribution to the war effort and "should establish Anglo-Yugoslav relations on a firm basis, which would do much to consolidate our position in the Balkans after the war."[83]

It is difficult to read the Maclean report and remain convinced that the British were still motivated primarily by military concerns. Donovan certainly did not think so. He viewed Maclean's appointment as evidence that the Foreign Office had superseded s o e as the principal agency responsible for implementing British policy in Yugoslavia. Vane Ivanović, who served with the Political Warfare Executive in London between 1943 and 1945, may have been closer to the mark when he observed that Maclean's appointment had reduced "the Foreign Office, s o e and all other British factors . . . to the role of spectators."[84] In any case, Donovan advised the Joint Chiefs in late November that "the policy of dealing with the situation has been dictated by the considered long-range political necessity of the British in the Balkans rather than the immediate and vital military problem here or its relation to over-all Allied

operations."[85] Donovan stopped short of criticizing the military recommendations in Maclean's report, and well he might. A week earlier Maj. Linn Farish
had filed a report, the substance of which was very similar to that of the
brigadier's.[86]

Just as Maclean's report found its way to Churchill, Roosevelt obtained a
copy of the Farish report sometime before the Teheran Conference. The timing of the report and the fact that it was the first direct analysis from an American officer in the field gave the document greater impact than it might otherwise have had. At Teheran, Roosevelt shared with Stalin a copy of Farish's
findings, which the president described as "a most interesting report from an
American officer who had spent six months in Yugoslavia in close contact with
Tito."[87] Actually, Farish had been in the country only six weeks and during
most of that time had not been in close contact with Tito.

Farish believed that the Partisan movement was of "far greater military and
political importance than is commonly realized in the outside world" and described their struggle against Axis forces as being "at times almost beyond the
imagination." He agreed with Maclean that the Allies were in a position to
cultivate favorable relations with the Partisans if adequate supplies could be
sent to them at this critical point. As Farish put it, "Cold, hungry, and inade-
quately armed men will surely remember from whence aid came when they
were fighting for their very existence."[88]

Farish did not claim with the same degree of certainty as Maclean that the
Partisans would dominate Yugoslavia in the postwar period. He did concede,
however, that "if ever a movement had the background of indomitable will
and courage with which to build great things, it is to be found in Yugoslavia."
He regarded the Communist party as only one of several elements within Tito's
forces, though it was definitely the most aggressive in pursuit of its social,
political, and economic goals.[89]

As for the Chetniks, Farish maintained that they had initially opposed the
enemy forces and had cooperated with the Partisans in so doing. Unfortunately,
as time went by and Partisan strength increased, Mihailovich committed a "fatal
mistake" in allowing his policies to be governed by political rather than military considerations. In short, Mihailovich "feared Communism more than he
feared the common enemy." This decision split his forces. Some units defected
to Tito while others began "fighting with the Germans and Italians against
the Partisans."[90]

Farish's conclusions and recommendations paralleled many of those in
Maclean's report, particularly regarding Chetnik collaboration, support for the
Partisans, and the suggestion that through such support the Allies might secure
some political advantage in the postwar period. As noted earlier, however, the
significance of this report does not lie exclusively in its findings. The timing
of its submission, both in terms of the Teheran Conference and Maclean's own

report, is important. Also, Farish was the first OSS officer to come out of the country to deliver a personal report, something no observer – British or American – with Mihailovich's forces would do for almost four months.

Other factors, if they had been known at the time, might have resulted in the report being evaluated more critically. In the first place, Farish did not speak the Serbo-Croatian language, nor was he accompanied by an American or British interpreter during the major portion of his stay in the country. Furthermore, Maclean sent him to Glamoč to build a landing zone, which left little time for inspection tours and the gathering of firsthand information.[91] These restrictions alone would suggest that six weeks was a relatively short period in which to assess accurately a military-political organization of the magnitude attributed by Farish to the Partisan movement. But Farish labored under even greater handicaps. As noted earlier, when Benson arrived at Glamoč, he found Farish there with a radio which was not working and an inexperienced British radio operator who could not repair it. At this time there were no fewer than five newer, working sets at Maclean's headquarters. Farish sent Benson on to Jajce, but "remained in Glamoc, freezing with a starving detachment from October 11th to the 25th waiting for an aircraft that never came."[92] Such were the conditions under which Farish gathered the information for his initial report. No evidence has been found, however, which suggests that Roosevelt or any ranking officials in OSS were aware of these facts.

Farish's report coupled with some of the information Roosevelt had been receiving directly from Donovan gave the president little reason to challenge Churchill's recommendation at Teheran that Allied aid should be shifted exclusively to Tito. Roosevelt agreed with his top military advisers, most of whom believed that the alternative to stimulating resistance activity in the Balkans was an invasion of the area – something they adamantly opposed.[93] The Farish report, therefore, had little, if any, impact on the course of Allied policy. Its true significance lay in the fact that it supported a strategy to which the Allies, particularly the United States, were already committed.

In due course, the Big Three agreed at Teheran that Tito's forces represented the most effective resistance element in Yugoslavia and determined that his movement would be exclusively supported by the Allied powers. The Yugoslav government, led at the time by Božhidar Purić, openly criticized the decision, which it described as "fatal." King Peter obviously believed that Roosevelt had "let him down," and found no consolation in Churchill's assurances that Tito would be "his man."[94]

The Teheran decisions affecting Yugoslavia represented the culmination of Allied policy, not a turning point. In the words of Carl Norden, a State Department official on Robert Murphy's staff, "Teheran gave us sanction."[95] This was certainly true insofar as continued support of Tito was concerned, but what about the basis of that support? Was it still military, the grounds on which the British had justified all decisions related to the Partisans since they first sent liaison officers into the country in April? Or, was it, as Donovan suspected, primarily political?

By late 1943, British policymakers had concluded that the monarchy was incapable of commanding the degree of popular support required to sustain political unity in the postwar period. They also believed that the Partisans intended to dominate Yugoslavia politically at the end of the war and that they were capable of doing so with or without Allied support.[96] Maclean had virtually said as much in his report. Acting on these assumptions, Churchill supported Tito, in part for military reasons but also because the Partisans were seen as the only means by which British influence might be maintained in Yugoslavia after the war.

Of course, OSS was not totally oblivious to the connection between wartime military support and possible political influence in the postwar period. A report originating in OSS headquarters in Cairo argued that the United States should not support "to the bitter end groups hostile to the Partisans and regarded by them as reactionary, anti-democratic or downright Fascist." Suggesting that the Partisan movement could represent the "wave of the future in southeastern Europe," the report concluded that the United States should "consider whether our Allies should ride the crest and relegate us to the trough or whether we by our own absence of alertness should find ourselves there."[97]

There is little in this statement or in those attributed to Maclean and other British leaders to suggest that the Allies were motivated exclusively by military concern in late 1943. I raised this specific question with Robert Murphy, who served as American political adviser to the Supreme Allied Commander, Mediterranean Theater. Murphy replied that "while, of course, the military consideration was involved, certainly Mr. Churchill's regard for Tito was inspired by political considerations." As for Roosevelt, Murphy wrote: "The demands made on his time and energy were such that he was willing to permit the British to play the major role in the Mediterranean Theater. After all, they were more directly concerned in that area and able and eager to do so."[98]

In the final analysis the Allies might make whatever distinctions they wished to justify sending supplies to Tito. Once the supplies reached his hands, however, all such distinctions were meaningless. The military and political aspects of the Partisan movement were so inextricably bound together that it was impossible to support one without the other. Tito knew that. London and Washington probably knew it too, though one could never prove it from their policy statements.[99]

3.   A Hostile Brief

Following the Teheran Conference, Churchill and other members of the British delegation stopped in Cairo, where the prime minister talked with a number of British liaison officers about their respective theaters of operations. Among them was Deakin, who briefed Churchill on captured German and Chetnik documents that revealed ties between Mihailovich and some of his subordinate commanders who were suspected of collaborating with the Italians and the Germans. The meeting was very formal and Deakin realized as it progressed that he was "compiling the elements of a hostile brief which would play a decisive part in any future break between the British government and Mihailović."[1]

Later, during the course of a dinner party, Churchill called a number of officers aside and informed them that while no final decisions had been made he was "minded to support the King in Greece and Tito in Yugoslavia." The prime minister acknowledged the apparent inconsistency of his position but reminded his audience rather pointedly, "It is my policy and I still have some influence here."[2]

Inconsistent or not, Churchill decided in early December that the British would sever all ties with Mihailovich and recall all military missions operating in his territory. The Special Operations Committee in Cairo proceeded with plans to implement the withdrawal order, brushing aside suggestions that the decision be postponed until Colonel Bailey could come out of the country to report.[3] To strengthen its case against Mihailovich, the committee also recommended that he should be called upon to "carry out by a given date some specific operation known to be within his powers in the certain knowledge that he would fail to do so."[4]

The major reason for devising such a test for Mihailovich stemmed from the fact that the most convincing evidence the British had of his inactivity and the collaboration of some of his subordinates with the Germans came from the Ultra intercepts, which, of course, could not be divulged.[5] Accordingly, Middle East Command sent what amounted to an ultimatum to Mihailovich that he agree by December 29 to destroy two railway bridges—one over the Ibar River and one over the Morava.[6]

Mihailovich agreed to carry out the operations provided he could obtain adequate supplies. Cairo informed Armstrong, however, that no further shipments would be made until the bridges had been destroyed. The British had failed to keep similar promises in October, and Mihailovich had little reason to believe that circumstances would be different now. He thus declined to carry out the operations and gave the British the justification they needed for breaking relations with him.[7]

In reality there was little, if anything, Mihailovich could have done to change the course of events at this point. On December 15, almost two weeks before the deadline for agreeing to destroy the bridges, the British advised Armstrong to prepare to withdraw from Chetnik headquarters.[8] Michael Lees, a British officer with Mihailovich's forces in southern Serbia, received a message on December 10 advising him of the break with Mihailovich and ordering him to cease all operations. The message continued: "British Liaison Officers should plan to evacuate if possible, or make their way to Partisans. Mihailovic has not yet been informed. We will instruct you of date to move."[9] At the time these messages were sent, Seitz and Mansfield were away from Mihailovich's headquarters still engaged in their inspection of Chetnik forces. In fact, Mansfield was in the village of Krljani in Maj. Radomir Cvetić's area when he received a penciled note from Capt. Bob Wade, a British liaison officer who had been ordered by Cairo to cross over to the Partisans in preparation for leaving the country.[10] Musulin, who had joined Seitz and Mansfield in late November, had returned to Captain Maynard's mission at Second Corps headquarters on Christmas Day when he learned of the British decision. He had previously informed Cairo of plans to destroy the antimony mines at Lisa, but was subsequently ordered not to take part in that operation.[11]

Given these facts, it seems unlikely that the British would have altered their plans to break with Mihailovich even if he had carried out the operations requested by Cairo. In a note to the Foreign Office dated December 28, the British ambassador to the Royal Government implied as much when he pointedly asked, "If he carries this out do you propose to ignore the fact [and break with him in any case]?"[12] The fact that such a question was seriously raised suggests that Mihailovich's suspicions about the value of British promises were justified.[13]

Britain's decision to withdraw its missions from Mihailovich's territory again confronted OSS with some difficult choices. Robert Joyce, a foreign service officer on loan to OSS and chief of the SI Branch in Bari, advised Donovan, "If we follow too closely the lead being taken at the present time by our British cousins we are letting go by default a force very well disposed to the United States and whose strategic potential and diplomatic value in time to come is considerable."[14] Aware that his proposals inevitably touched upon political matters, Joyce nevertheless insisted that the United States should develop its own policy in Yugoslavia and "go ahead independently of the British." He noted that Britain had interests in the Balkans which did not coincide with those of the United States, and he speculated that London and Moscow might have reached a secret agreement about southeastern Europe without informing Washington—a prophetic supposition that anticipated the Churchill-Stalin "percentages" deal by almost a year.[15]

Joyce's call for greater freedom of action was not without support from officers in the field. Seitz had earlier complained that the absence of a clearly defined policy placed OSS in a "position of blindly following our fellow allies in their manipulation of these guerrilla forces."[16]

Donovan agreed with these arguments, and, in late February when the British formally requested that the United States withdraw its officers from Mihailovich's area, he pursued the matter with Roosevelt.[17] On March 2, he informed the president of the British request concerning the withdrawal of American personnel, but he challenged the British assertion that no "useful military purpose" could be served by remaining in Mihailovich's area. To buttress his position he attached a copy of Mansfield's report, an evaluation of which had prompted OSS-Cairo to recommend that the Allies avoid a break with Mihailovich and maintain "observers" with his forces. Having advised the president that Cairo had prepared at least two intelligence teams for dispatch to Mihailovich's territory, Donovan pressed for permission to send an officer to Chetnik headquarters "immediately" for the dual purpose of gathering intelligence and continuing plans for the infiltration of teams into central and southeastern Europe.[18]

In late March, Roosevelt replied to Donovan's request in a letter approved by the State Department, agreeing in principle with the OSS proposal. The president concurred with Donovan that withdrawal of all Allied missions from Mihailovich left "no sources of intelligence whatever in a part of the Balkans which may become an important area at some stage of war."[19] Roosevelt emphasized, however, that any mission that might be dispatched to Mihailovich would have to refrain from making any commitments to the Chetniks and avoid at all costs becoming involved in political issues.[20]

At this point Donovan had every reason to believe that he had secured for OSS the right to maintain an intelligence-gathering capability at Mihailovich's headquarters free of British control. His victory proved to be a very short-lived one. SOE-Cairo, having attempted without success to persuade Donovan not to proceed with the proposed missions to Mihailovich, appealed directly to Churchill.[21] Accordingly, on April 6, the same day he met with Hudson and Bailey following their evacuation from Yugoslavia, Churchill complained to Roosevelt that if OSS were now to send a mission to the latter's headquarters,

OSS Coverage, 1944

Missions with Partisan forces

1. RAKEOFF	16. HACIENDA/ACRU
2. FLOTSAM	17. ASH
3. CALIFORNIA	18. WILLOW
4. CUCKOLD	19. TOLEDO
5. DURAND	20. WALNUT
6. MULBERRY	21. ALUM
7. RELATOR	22. COLUMBIA/ACRU
8. REDWOOD	
9. GEISHA	
10. ABBEVILLE	_____
11. SPIKE	
12. ALTMARK	Missions with Chetnik forces
13. DUNKLIN	
14. ARROW/ACRU	A. HALYARD
15. IAMM	B. RANGER

Source: RG-226, E. 154, B. 21, F. Bari SI-PRO-6, "Teams in Yugoslavia."

it would "show throughout the Balkans a complete contrariety of action between Britain and the United States."[22] Roosevelt pointed out that the OSS team was being sent for intelligence purposes only and would have "no political functions whatsoever," but he agreed nonetheless to abide by Churchill's wishes and cancel it.[23] As one OSS report put it, "The hatchet men had done their job at the highest level."[24]

Donovan, not willing at this point to admit defeat, tried a new tack. Rather than sending in two or three teams as originally planned, he proposed sending only one team under Capt. Gil Flues. Roosevelt, however, would not budge, and on April 13 this plan was also cancelled.[25]

OSS-Washington had no choice but to notify Col. Edward Glavin in Algiers that "by order of highest authority, the plans to send representatives to Mihailovich have been held up." At the same time, perhaps in response to demands for clarification of American policy aims in Yugoslavia, Washington outlined the principles that were to govern OSS actions in the country. The United States favored strengthening the military capability of the resistance without becoming involved in the "internal political affairs of Yugoslavia." Acknowledging that the British and the Russians might have interests in the Balkans that the United States might not wish to support, Washington emphasized the need to disassociate itself from policy initiatives that went beyond the prescribed limits of "non-intervention." The United States desired to see a united Yugoslavia in the postwar period and to that end would have no reluctance to "continuing political and diplomatic relations with a reconstituted Government, even though it may represent quite new 'elements.'"[26]

Donovan realized, even if Washington did not, the inherent contradictions implied between stated American policy aims toward Yugoslavia and continued acceptance of British initiatives. From the very beginning, London had emphasized the strategic location and hence great military value of Serbia. Even when the decision was made to contact the Partisans, relations were maintained with Mihailovich in part because he controlled sizable forces in this important region. At Teheran, the British continued to insist that their support for Tito was based on military considerations, though Donovan and others in OSS thought otherwise. Their skepticism seemed justified when in early 1944 the British decided to strip Serbia of all Allied missions including those solely concerned with the collection of intelligence. This action served no military purpose, nor was it intended to do so. It was a political action fashioned to serve political ends.

There is evidence that Churchill agreed to withdraw all liaison officers from Mihailovich, in part, because Tito would not otherwise consent to the dispatch of British missions to his forces in Serbia.[27] If true – and certainly there is little in subsequent British dealings with the Partisans to suggest otherwise – the recall of all SOE missions from Serbia was the first in a series of actions undertaken by Churchill wherein he exhibited an uncharacteristic deference toward Tito and his movement. As will be seen, Churchill came to treat Tito less as a resistance leader and more as an equal on matters both military and political. When Tito began to act as an equal, however, the prime minister's attitude underwent a rather remarkable change, though too late to alter the course of events in the country.

It should be remembered that the British proceeded with plans to break with Mihailovich even after they became aware of the political decisions of the Anti-Fascist Council of National Liberation of Yugoslavia (AVNOJ) in mid-December. This was the second session of AVNOJ. The first had been held in November, 1942, in the Bosnian town of Bihać where the Partisans had established their headquarters at the conclusion of the Third Axis Offensive. At that time the Partisans contented themselves with adopting a six-point program described by one OSS analyst as "an unexceptionable document embodying democratic and almost mildly conservative ideas."[28]

A year later, when the Partisans held the second session of AVNOJ in Jajce, their internal political and military situation had improved tremendously, and recognition from the major Allies seemed almost certain. Disregarding Stalin's advice,[29] they transformed the AVNOJ into a provisional government, deposed the Royal Government, and forbade the king's return until the people could decide the issue after the war.[30] In the aftermath of these decisions the British had to realize, as Deakin points out, that "any hopes of sending military aid, which was now being actively organised, to the Partisan movement could not now be divorced from the political issues involved."[31]

Ironically, at the very time the United States was moving to follow Britain's lead in severing all ties with Mihailovich, OSS provided the first direct intelligence from American — indeed, the first from Allied — officers attached to Chetnik forces. Mansfield emerged from Yugoslavia in mid-February, followed a month later by Seitz. The extent to which their reports were at variance with British evaluations of Mihailovich's movement supported Donovan's argument for maintaining American intelligence teams in Serbia. The president, however, was not about to risk another confrontation with Churchill.

Between November 7 and December 23, 1943, Seitz and Mansfield had traveled together through central Serbia and contacted a number of Mihailovich's subordinate commanders on whose strength — real and potential — Mansfield made very detailed notes. When these officers came in contact with Captain Wade's mission as it was making its way out of the country, Mansfield gave his notes to Seitz, who joined the British party in an attempt to get the information to Bari as quickly as possible.[32]

Mansfield remained in Cvetić's area until early January when he moved into territory controlled by the forces of Voja Lukačević, who was to escort the Allied party to the coast. Despite several close brushes with Partisan and German forces, Mansfield continued to wear his GI pants and leather jacket with insignia. At the town of Goražde, however, where his party crossed the Drina River, he disguised himself in peasant clothing, put his equipment in a sack, and "walked right in front of the German guards"; he was not stopped.[33]

Pushing on to the town of Priboj, Mansfield met Lt. Col. Zaharije Ostojić, who gave him letters from Mihailovich to Donovan, Roosevelt, and Eisenhower. These Mansfield sewed in his jacket lining and continued on, ultimately join-

Maj. Boris Todorovich, left, Mihailovich's liaison officer with the Anglo-American mission, pictured here with Lt. Walter Mansfield, first American officer attached to Chetnik forces. Courtesy Mrs. Boris Todorovich

ing Lukačević and Colonel Bailey—the latter also en route to the coast. By this time the escorting party had grown to almost 180 men, making detection by either Germans or Partisans more likely. At one point the column did encounter a German patrol, and only some quick thinking by Lukačević averted a disaster. The Chetnik commander and some of his men came forward and demanded to see the German commandant on the pretext that they had information about an impending Partisan attack against his forces. After some time, Lukačević convinced the Germans that he and his men were interested only in fighting the Partisans, and they were allowed to pass.[34]

On the following Day, Mansfield and his group reached Lt. Col. Peter Bačević's headquarters not far from the coastal city of Dubrovnik. Anticipating their arrival, Bačević had selected a spot on the coast from which the Allied personnel could evacuate. After overcoming some problems with his batteries, Bailey succeeded in contacting Cairo, which advised the party to stand by at its pin point for three nights. The group made its way to the coast on the first night, dodging Ustasha patrols along the way, only to have their hopes dashed by a storm that made it impossible for them to embark. Mansfield's party, now numbering ten, returned to the home of their guide, which was located in one of the villages held by the Ustasha. There they remained through the night and following day, nervously watching the Ustasha through a crack in a window. When no vessel arrived at the pin point on the next two nights, the mission moved further inland and found shelter in the home of a friendly peasant family. Their troubles, however, were far from over.[35]

Having eluded the Ustasha, they now discovered through one of Bačević's spies who worked in the local Gestapo headquarters that the Gestapo knew of their presence in the general area and was trying to locate them. To compound the problem, Bailey's batteries were dead and needed to be recharged. A peasant carried them into the village to be charged by a local establishment that was also servicing batteries for the Germans. Unfortunately, Bailey's batteries, which were of a different type than those of the Germans, could have attracted more unwanted attention and had to be retrieved before they could be charged. Mansfield and some others resolved the battery problem by stealing one from a railroad car that provided sufficient power for them to reestablish contact with Cairo.

Having been advised to return to the embarkation point on the night of February 14, the party did so, and after a twenty-minute wait, a British vessel arrived to effect their evacuation. Mansfield arrived in Bari at 9:00 A.M. the following morning, undoubtedly convinced that it was a great deal easier to enter Yugoslavia than to leave.[36]

While Mansfield and Bailey had been dodging German and Ustasha patrols along with the Gestapo, Seitz and Hudson were having their share of problems with the Partisans, whom they had joined in late December. Upon discovering that Seitz's party had come from Chetnik territory, Tito's men began questioning members of the team about the Chetniks. The officers made it clear that they would answer no questions nor would they divulge any information of a political or military nature. This exchange put an end not only to inquiries about the Chetniks but also to Partisan efforts in behalf of the mission's evacuation. When Seitz later learned from a young Partisan radio operator that he and his group were in fact being held up for information and for their radio, he told the Partisan commander to either furnish guides or they would "go on alone and to hell with him."[37]

The commander yielded and furnished Seitz and Hudson the guides they requested. After a few days of travel the Partisan force to which the Allied team was attached became involved in a skirmish with German and collaborationist Chetnik units near the village of Jablanica. While Partisan troops clambered up the adjacent hillsides to clear them of enemy forces, Seitz and his party continued moving along the road, and soon came under fire themselves. Seitz realized that their attackers were not Germans or Chetniks, however, but Partisans. That evening as the column halted its march, Seitz confronted the Partisan commander about the shooting incident. Showing him a bullet hole in the left pocket of his battle dress, Seitz said, "The loss of one of our party considering the fact that Chetniks were attacking us would have been wonderful propaganda, wouldn't it?" He then asked if he could see the Chetnik prisoners but was told that they were not available. Seitz responded tersely, "I thought not," and turned and walked away.[38]

Seitz, Hudson, and the rest of their party reached Berane in early February, but a heavy snowfall on the fifth rendered the airfield totally inoperative and further delayed their evacuation. Nightly entertainment provided by the Partisans made the time pass a little more quickly, but the two-hour propaganda session that preceded each program soon became too great a price to pay for the amusement, especially for Seitz.[39]

Relations between the Anglo-American mission and the Partisans reached a new low when, on the second Sunday morning of their stay in Berane, Seitz and Hudson found that their guard would not allow the waitress to enter their room with breakfast without written permission from the commandant. The two officers, who were by this time "righteously angry" and "damnable hungry," threw the guard down a half-flight of stairs and told him at gunpoint to go to his headquarters and get his orders straight.[40] The guard returned in a few minutes but still would allow no one to enter the room without written permission. This proved to be the last straw for Hudson and Seitz. They disarmed their antagonist, kicked him down the stairs, and Seitz promised to "kick his teeth in" if "he showed his filthy face" around them again.[41]

Finally on March 15 planes arrived to evacuate the mission and a number of wounded Partisans to Italy. Seitz noted that a fight almost broke out be-

tween the Partisans and Italians as to which of the wounded should be evacuated, and after everything had settled down, his plane had on board "ten remarkable healthy specimens," one of whom was the mistress of a Partisan in
Italy. Less than two hours after Seitz's plane left Yugoslavia, it touched down
in Lecce, Italy. Almost six months after he had entered the country, his mission to Mihailovich was completed. And, though no one could have foreseen
it at the time, the experiences of Seitz and Hudson were a portent of things
to come insofar as relations with the Partisans were concerned.

Viewed in their totality, the Seitz and Mansfield reports were generally favorable to Mihailovich and his movement, though some significant weaknesses
were noted. For example, there was little question that Mihailovich was allo-
cating most of his resources to the war against the Partisans—roughly 65 percent according to Mansfield—with the result that the Chetnik army in Serbia
was reduced "to a static condition where everybody is waiting for 'D-Day.'"[42]

Mansfield characterized the Chetnik general staff as "very second rate" but
found the area and corps commanders to be "on the whole fairly capable leaders." In evaluating Mihailovich himself, Mansfield reported that the general
lacked the ability to delegate authority and frequently overestimated his talents
as a diplomat and politician, particularly in his dealings with the British. His
stature among the Serbian people, however, was another matter. "They talk
of him," Mansfield wrote, "as one would of the Messiah."[43]

As for the size of his army, Mihailovich told Mansfield that he had 57,440
men mobilized and could mobilize over 450,000. Mansfield's own estimate of
men actually under arms was 35,000, and they were "in an extremely ragged
condition." Furthermore, the ratio of unarmed to armed men was fairly high
in virtually all of the areas visited by Mansfield and Seitz. In Vuckovič's area,
for example, there were over 600 unarmed men at one inspection. At Račić's
headquarters an inspection was held for 4,000 armed men while "some 13,000
unarmed, but trained men were scattered through his Korpus, praying for
something besides a flail or knife to fight with." The rifle was the most common weapon among the Chetniks, but according to Mansfield, "the average
rifle often looks more like a museum piece, than an instrument ready for use
on the battlefield." Lack of ammunition was also a serious problem. As a rule
an individual soldier had between ten and one hundred rounds for his weapon
and at best might have enough for one day's fighting.[44]

As far as the issue of collaboration was concerned, neither Mansfield nor
Seitz found direct evidence in north-central Serbia to support the charges that
had been leveled against Mihailovich and his commanders by Partisan and
British sources. Nikola Kalabić, the Chetnik commander in the Čačak region,
admitted that he maintained liaison with two garrisons of Nedić troops, but
insisted that most of the men in these units were loyal to Mihailovich. In fact,
both OSS officers had the opportunity to talk to the commanding officer of

one of the Nedić formations who admitted that he was loyal to the Chetniks and would help them in any way that he could. Kalabić also stated that he could disarm the Nedić troops anytime he wished, but chose not to do so because they served as a valuable source of information for him as far as German plans and operations were concerned.[45]

Mansfield concluded that there was "very little" collaboration in Serbia, where Germany was still regarded as the primary enemy. In Hercegovina, however, some of Mihailovich's leaders saw collaboration as one means by which they could defeat the Partisans in the civil war. Chetnik leaders justified these tactics by pointing out that they were in fact "fighting former Croat Ustachi, many of whom are presently fighting with Pavelic; and that the British are feeding arms to the Partisans which are being used by the Partisans against the Chetniks."[46]

oss officers attached to Partisan units confirmed Mansfield's reference to the Ustasha-Partisan relationship. Among the more prominent figures in the Ustasha movement who later joined the Partisans were Antun Augustinčić, a famous Croat sculptor who before joining the Partisans created a bust of Ante Pavelić; Vladimir Nazor, a well-known Croat poet who had been closely associated with the *Spremost,* the official Ustasha organ; and Gen. Franya Pirtz, who had been highly decorated for his actions against the Russians on the Eastern Front.[47] This defection of former Ustasha into the ranks of the Partisans and the natural Chetnik reaction to it served to transform the civil war into an ethnic as well as political conflict and gave certain evidence that the age-old Serbo-Croat feud was still very much alive.

Seitz described the Ustasha-Partisan-Chetnik relationship as one in which "either of these groups do and would perpetrate any atrocity on either of the others with a clear conscience." He saw absolutely no basis for collaboration among the three groups but did not doubt that "either of them would collaborate with any outside group in order to harm or preferably destroy the other two."[48]

Seitz also wrote that "as far as collaboration of Mihailovich with Nedic goes, it is true by my own knowledge."[49] As oss report prepared in Bari and forwarded to William Langer, head of the Research and Analysis Branch of oss, stated that Mihailovich could not have returned to Serbia without Nedić "and therefore German consent."[50] This report identified certain of Mihailovich's commanders who also had ties with Nedić, among them Račić, Predrag Raković, and Dragutin Keserović. Claiming that Mihailovich was "imposed" on the Serbian population by Allied propaganda, this document suggested that the general should be viewed in the same light as Nedić, Ljotić, and the Bulgarian occupation forces. Lastly, the report charged that Mihailovich's movement was "cooperating with the enemy" and had "accepted for its political program an Axis-devised plan for the partition of Yugoslavia."[51]

It would be difficult to imagine that the Partisans themselves could have devised a more damning critique of Mihailovich's movement or one more at odds with the findings of Seitz and Mansfield. Lt. Col. Robert H. McDowell put a far different construction on the Nedić-Mihailovich connection. In a report prepared for the Joint Intelligence Collection Agency, he pointed out that it was "erroneous to conclude that all those who oppose Axis are patriots and workers for democracy, while all those in the service of the Axis are unpatriotic and anti-democratic." McDowell claimed that Nedić was using his position to secure German arms for "Serb bands which will work in conjunction with Mihailovich to stop Partisan effort aimed at Serbia."[52]

Tito and those sympathetic to his cause used Chetnik ties with Nedić to depict Mihailovich and his entire movement as collaborationist. Chetnik propagandists, on the other hand, never succeeded in exploiting the Partisan-Ustasha relationship to their advantage. Indeed, throughout most of the war the Chetnik leadership failed to adopt or pursue a vigorous political or propaganda campaign. Mihailovich may have believed that as the representative of the legitimate and recognized government of Yugoslavia, he should not have to engage in such activities. However, after the formation of the National Liberation Committee of Yugoslavia in November, 1943, and the absence of any Allied opposition to it, Mihailovich and his political advisers moved to establish a political program of their own. The result was the Saint Sava Congress held in the village of Ba near Valjevo from January 25 to January 28, 1944.

Delegates from virtually all major political parties in the country, except the Communist party and those groups aligned with the Fascists, attended the meeting.[53] Mihailovich delivered a personal address to the assembly but did not become openly involved in the subsequent political deliberations. The election of Dr. Živko Topalović, respected journalist and chairman of the Yugoslav Social Democratic party, as president of the Congress was a victory for the moderates in the Chetnik camp and a defeat for the extreme Pan-Serb element represented by Dr. Stevan Moljević and Dragiša Vašić. Also the political program adopted by the Congress reflected the shift of influence away from the Pan-Serb forces.[54]

At the outset the delegates resolved that Yugoslavia should be constituted within the territorial boundaries submitted by her delegates to the Paris Peace Conference in 1919. Politically, the state would be a constitutional and parliamentary hereditary monarchy with the Karadjordjević dynasty in the person of King Peter II at its head. Furthermore, in all of the federal units of the state the people would have the opportunity to satisfy their "individual provincial, economic, cultural, social, and other interests and needs through a broad, popular autonomy." The Congress denounced as illegal and unconstitutional the formation of the Independent State of Croatia under Pavelić and the National Liberation Committee of Yugoslavia under Tito, asserting that King

Peter was the legally constituted head of the Yugoslav state and as such could only be removed from power by the people of Yugoslavia through legally adopted means.[55]

In many respects the Saint Sava Congress held in Ba was a significant and important conference. The more than three hundred delegates came from all parts of Yugoslavia and represented a broad spectrum of political opinion within the country. Also, by accepting the recommendations of the Congress to organize Yugoslavia as a federal state, the Chetnik leadership did much to undermine Partisan charges that Mihailovich was irrevocably committed to the restoration of a Greater Serbia.[56]

In reality the Congress had very little effect either inside Yugoslavia or on external relations with the Allies. Vane Ivanović described the Congress as "too little and too late,"[57] and Dr. Topalović later admitted that the Congress was not as "imposing nor as grand as its own propaganda and the publicity given to it by its friends abroad made it appear to be."[58]

The only Allied representative to attend the conference was Musulin, and he did so largely on his own initiative. The British had no firsthand intelligence at all on the Congress, and not until April did SOE-Cairo contact Musulin to request a report on the meeting.[59] The Allies, particularly the British, were reluctant to accept the Nationalist program at face value. They believed that Mihailovich's position in the country was gradually becoming more desperate, and they were not enthusiastic about underwriting what they viewed as a last-minute attempt to salvage a lost cause.[60]

While the conference was in session, Mihailovich passed on a bit of information to Musulin which the latter thought might be used to justify the continued presence of an OSS mission in Serbia. Mihailovich indicated that ten American airmen had crashed south of the town of Niš, but that all of them had been picked up and were being cared for by his men. When this crew and others that had been forced down ultimately made their way to Musulin's location, he radioed Cairo that he could, with Chetnik assistance, get the airmen to the coast if arrangements could be made for their evacuation to Italy. Noting that Musulin had made no reference to his own evacuation, Cairo replied on March 6 that the airmen would accompany him to Mihailovich's headquarters where he and they would prepare to leave the country.[61]

Musulin delayed his departure in part because of personal illness, but also because he wanted very much to remain in the country as an observer attached to Mihailovich's forces. As late as May 20, he requested that Cairo grant him permission to continue his efforts at gathering intelligence and assisting in the evacuation of Allied airmen. Cairo refused, and on the night of May 28 Musulin reluctantly returned to Italy. It should be noted that at a time when the United States and Britain were claiming that their resistance policies were based exclusively on military considerations, OSS had unsuccessfully asserted

An unidentified American airman, left, with Maj. Richard Weil of the CALIFORNIA mission. National Archives

its right to maintain observers in Serbia for the legitimate purposes of gathering intelligence and assisting the return of downed Allied airmen to their bases.

Musulin arrived in Bari a very bitter and disillusioned man. He felt that he had been abandoned while he was in the country, had been forced out for political reasons, and now that he was back, no one was interested in what he had to say. In a fit of rage he stormed into oss headquarters and shouted, "Listen you bastards, you think I went in and risked my life for almost a year for nothing?" The outburst was certainly understandable. Musulin had for some time been without direct contact with American sources, and the British had contacted him only for the purpose of ordering his evacuation. When he arrived in Bari, the chief point of concern was not his report about current conditions in Yugoslavia but the fact that five members of Mihailovich's political staff arrived with him—a matter to which the British strongly objected. Musulin told Robert Joyce that Mihailovich had requested that the men be allowed to leave the country with the mission, and since there was available space, he granted the request. He also told Joyce that if the British insisted on making an issue of the matter, he wanted to be court-martialed for the act so that all of the facts could be presented to the public.[62]

Musulin was so discouraged at the treatment he received in Bari that he decided there would be no point in his writing a report at all. He recalls: "I came to Bari and saw Partisans all over the damn town. I saw them in our headquarters. They were packing supplies on our planes in Brindisi. They had Partisan dispatchers. There were more Partisans outside in Italy propagandizing than there were inside fighting, it seemed to me at the time. And I really was sick and didn't want to write a report because I felt that it would have no significance. These people forgot that I was even alive."[63]

Nelson Deranian, head of oss-so (Special Operations) in Bari, and Robert Murphy encouraged Musulin to write a complete report of his activities, assuring him that it would be seen by the proper officials. Reluctantly, Musulin prepared a nineteen-page report outlining his experiences and observations in Yugoslavia between October 19, 1943, and May 28, 1944.[64]

In many respects Musulin's report substantiated the conclusions of Seitz and Mansfield. In fact, when the latter two officers made their inspection tour of the First Corps area between November 26 and December 4, they were accompanied by Musulin, who joined them on Thanksgiving Day at Seitz's invitation. Musulin's report focused primarily on his experiences with First Corps, the strength of which he estimated at 1,230 armed men with a potential mobilization strength of 12,000, if adequately supplied. He estimated Mihailovich's total strength at between 60,000 and 90,000, but pointed out that these figures reflected information supplied by various corps commanders and that strength reports "have a tendency to be highly magnified in Yugoslavia."[65]

Lt. B. Nelson Deranian, chief of Special Operations, oss-Bari. Courtesy
B. Nelson Deranian

In terms of arms and supplies the First Corps fared better than most Chetnik units in Yugoslavia, but even so the men were poorly equipped with outdated weapons of various manufacture, had virtually no heavy weapons, and had only between ten and one hundred rounds of ammunition per rifle. About one in fifty First Corps soldiers had been issued British battle dress; only 25 percent of the men had shoes of some kind; few, if any, had a change of clothing; and medical supplies were nonexistent.[66]

Musulin confirmed that a policy of live and let live governed Chetnik-German relations for the present, confirming the findings of Seitz and Mansfield. As part of his report Musulin included a radio message he had intercepted on May 10 from Mihailovich's headquarters to the various Corps commanders which he said "clearly defines Mvichs present policy." The cable, dated May 7 and coded "most confidential," stated:

The attempt of the Communists to penetrate into Serbia has been repulsed by us and now we are to further our operations until their extermination, which can be accomplished if our units are not in conflict with outer forces. German forces have not interfered with us in this last operation even though we do not have any contact or agreement with them. So that we will not make difficult or jeopardize the arranged operations against the Communistic group, it is necessary to stop all operations against the Germans, but the propaganda must continue. This is necessary because whoever attacks Germans would directly aid the Communists and make the situation grave for our forces. Therefore, until further orders all armed operations against the occupying forces will cease. Let it be known that we have large numbers of enemies. We cannot fight against all simultaneously. Now, the most important enemies are the Communists. Let it also be known the Communists attack only us and evade contact with Germans and Bulgars.[67]

Musulin confirmed that Chetnik forces were not able to fight the Germans and Partisans at the same time and that most of the Nationalist effort was being aimed at the Communists who "contrary to many opinions . . . attack Mvich in strong force." The oss officer also charged that if German forces were pushed into northern Yugoslavia, the Partisan forces would "then have their hands free to mass their forces against Mvich in an effort to liquidate him."[68]

Regarding the question of German-Chetnik collaboration, Musulin reported that he never personally witnessed anything or found any evidence to support the charges that Mihailovich and his forces were collaborating with the Germans. There were reports that some Chetnik commanders in Hercegovina, Montenegro, and southern Serbia were receiving weapons and supplies from the Germans, but these reports were unconfirmed. Some of the information Musulin obtained about these commanders came from peasants who reported that the Germans would pull their trucks loaded with ammunition and guns off the side of the road and lose themselves while the Chetniks unloaded the

vehicles. In other cases the Germans would simply unload the trucks themselves and leave the supplies beside the road for the Chetniks. Mihailovich
may have suspected that such activities were going on, but Musulin never obtained conclusive proof that the Chetnik leader either knew of or approved
such relations with the Germans.[69]

Musulin had been in Yugoslavia for approximately seven months when he
came out to prepare his report. Seitz and Mansfield had been in the country
for roughly six months before submitting their reports. All three officers had
traveled extensively in the areas controlled by Mihailovich's troops and had
been allowed complete freedom of movement. Most of what they reported about
Mihailovich's forces came from firsthand observation and experience, and not
all of it was flattering to the Chetnik movement. This was in stark contrast
to the circumstances surrounding the gathering of intelligence for the Maclean
and Farish reports, which reached Churchill and Roosevelt just prior to the
Teheran Conference.

There were also very important substantive differences between the Seitz-
Mansfield-Musulin reports on one hand and the Maclean-Farish reports on
the other. The former placed active Chetnik forces in the field considerably
below the figures provided by General Mihailovich and described these units
as poorly armed and supplied. There was also little doubt that Mihailovich
was directing most of his meager resources against the Partisans and was for
the most part not actively engaging the Germans. There was evidence that
some of Mihailovich's subordinates had reached accommodations with the Germans in order to fight the Partisans, although there was no conclusive proof
that Mihailovich was personally involved in these negotiations. On the other
hand, there was no doubt that Mihailovich and his forces remained favorably
disposed to the western Allies and constituted a potential threat to the Germans if adequately supplied.

Once again the candor with which these reports discussed the strengths
and weaknesses of the Nationalist movement was markedly different from the
Maclean and Farish reports, which gave unqualified acceptance to the most
optimistic appraisal the Partisans could present on their own movement. Indeed, Lawrence Modisett has said of the Maclean report that "it is doubtful
that Tito himself would have changed a word."[70]

Unfortunately the written reports of Seitz, Mansfield, and Musulin played
no role whatsoever in Allied decision making about the resistance. The British
proposed and the United States agreed to abandon Mihailovich without con-
sulting a single liaison officer – British or American – who had been attached
to his forces. Seitz had informed Cairo in December that his report "might
cause our government to change its view" and had requested that Washington
not commit itself irrevocably to any policy until the report could be evaluated.
His pleas fell on deaf ears.[71]

Insofar as field intelligence influenced the decision to break with Mihailovich, all such information came from liaison officers attached to and obviously impressed with Tito's movement. The Ultra intercepts also provided a great deal of information about resistance activities in Yugoslavia, although the picture that emerges from this source is not as clear as one might imagine.

It is interesting to note that the British seemed to have been convinced of Mihailovich's alleged collaborationist activities to a much greater degree than were the Germans with whom he was supposedly collaborating. In fact, the Germans remained committed to Mihailovich's destruction throughout the period of May to September, 1943, and ordered that "no Cetnik formations whose leaders were proved to be in touch with Mihailovic are to be spared."[72] While the word "Cetnik" appears many times in the intercepts, the Germans frequently made distinctions between those Chetnik bands that were loyal to Mihailovich and other units that were not associated with his movement.[73] For example, a signal dated December 9, 1943, refers to "pro-German Cetniks" who were apparently operating with German forces in a joint operation against Partisan units,[74] while a later transmission notes the "increasingly anti-German attitude of Mihailovich formations in area Zagaza, 70 KM north east of Nisch."[75]

The intercepts do reveal that the Germans were receiving intelligence on a routine basis from some Chetnik units regarding the location and movement of Partisan forces, but there is no indication that these units were affiliated with Mihailovich. On the other hand, some signals identify particular Chetnik commanders as participants in joint operations with the Germans against the Partisans. On December 29, 1943, for example, the Second Panzer Army reported on an action against Tito's forces in which a number of subordinate groups participated—one of which was "Gruppe Lukacevic."[76] In May, 1944, another report from the Second Panzer Army stated that the "battle strength and spirit of Cetnik formations, Djurisic and Lasic" were insufficient for liberating Montenegro from the Partisans. This same report also suggested the possibility of "utilising Gruppe Djurisic" and forces from the Moslem Legion to check a Partisan thrust into the Sandžak area.[77]

Of course, by the spring of 1944, the Allies had broken with Mihailovich and the Germans had begun to reexamine their policy toward him, perhaps with the idea in mind of reaching some agreement similar to the one they had with Nedić.[78] Nevertheless, a signal dated April 3, 1944, refers to a German operation against Mihailovich's headquarters in Homolje in which an English officer was taken prisoner.[79] Obviously the Germans remained committed to Mihailovich's destruction at the very time his movement was being abandoned by the Allies. Perhaps the best explanation of this complex and seemingly contradictory set of circumstances is offered by John Ehrman, who suggests that Mihailovich's "aims remained honourable; his practice, thanks to their irrelevance, was tortuous and uncertain. Neither a consistent opponent nor a consistent supporter of the Germans, he was now regarded by them with a wary tolerance punctuated by armed reprisals, and by the Allies with growing irritation and suspicion."[80]

Collaboration was not the only issue by which the Allies sought to justify their decision to break with Mihailovich. There was also the charge that his forces were not conducting any operations against the Germans and were instead concentrating all of their efforts against the Partisans. Timing has a great deal to do with the validity of this allegation – particularly insofar as the matter of inactivity toward the Germans is concerned. In the months immediately following the Teheran Conference, Mihailovich's forces were admittedly far less active against the Germans than before. Seitz, Mansfield, and Musulin all agree on this point. It is important to focus on the months immediately preceding the Teheran Conference, however, since the case against Mihailovich concerns his activity, or lack of it, during that period.

In 1978, David Martin published a work that included information from an operational log found in the files of SOE in the Public Record Office. This document covers the period from August to December, 1943, and contains specific and substantiated references to military actions and sabotage operations carried out by Mihailovich's forces against Axis occupation units. Some of these reports also make reference to Partisan attacks on Chetnik units while the latter were fighting Axis forces – charges later confirmed in Mansfield's written report.[81]

Two years after Martin's book appeared, Basil Davidson published a memoir in which he dismissed Martin's work as one that "adduces no new evidence, makes many baseless and indeed libelous assumptions about the British officers concerned and can be accepted as no serious contribution to the subject."[82] Davidson's own conclusions regarding the issue of Chetnik inactivity are best summed up in a statement he makes describing the status of the Chetnik movement in late 1941. At that time, Davidson charges, "For their part, the chetnik officers and their bands retired to mountain tops, folded their arms, and sat down to await the end of the war. That would be their time to fight: against, of course, the Partisans."[83] A more blatant distortion of, or flagrant disregard for, the facts could hardly be imagined.

Wilhelm Hoettl, in a very different assessment, characterized "the power of Mihailović in the first years of German occupation" as "unbelievably great," and described the Chetnik leader as being the "true master of Serbia."[84] Michael Lees, a British liaison officer in Serbia, cites numerous instances of Chetnik forces supporting various sabotage operations against the Germans. Many of these, it is true, were conducted at the initiative of individual Chetnik commanders like Bora Manić and were contrary to the standing orders of Mihailovich.[85] According to Lees, however, Mihailovich later revised his policy to allow for the approval of specific sabotage operations.[86]

Despite this alteration in Mihailovich's strategy, the Chetniks never matched the level of resistance activity sustained by the Partisans during the latter half of 1943. The Ultra intercepts reflect this disparity, and although the Germans frequently used the term guerrilla rather than Partisan or Chetnik, it is clear that the vast majority of such references were to Tito's forces.[87] The Partisans effectively carried out sabotage actions against German-held transportation and communication lines and harassed smaller German garrisons. However, they were never able to withstand German movements in force and often found themselves compelled to yield some of their "liberated" territory in the hope that circumstances would allow them to reclaim it in the future. Thus, while Tito's claim to be the leader of an army found a receptive audience in some Allied circles, the Ultra decrypts and most of the field intelligence reports coming from officers attached to Tito's units revealed that his movement was, in terms of its tactics and capabilities, essentially a guerrilla force.[88]

One other aspect of the Allied—primarily British—case against Mihailovich should be considered in light of the Ultra intercepts. Throughout the course of their dealings with Mihailovich, the Allies appear to have placed a disproportionate share of the responsibility for the civil war on his shoulders. Being named minister of war increased his responsibilities but not his authority. Certainly it did not strengthen his hand in dealing with the Partisans. The British earlier had tried without success to achieve some satisfactory resolution of the internal conflict, appealing to the Soviets to use their influence with Tito to achieve a united front in Yugoslavia. How was Mihailovich supposed to succeed where they had failed?

Ultra decrypts clearly show that the civil war in Yugoslavia was not a unilateral undertaking initiated and sustained by Mihailovich and his forces. Chetnik units attacked Partisan forces when it was to their advantage to do so, and Tito's troops retaliated in kind when circumstances were in their favor.[89] Seitz and Mansfield confirmed this in their written reports, and other OSS officers sent to Mihailovich's headquarters in the late summer of 1944 reported on the increasing scale of Partisan aggression against the Chetniks. Still, the Allies never stopped the flow of supplies to the Partisans even in the face of incontrovertible evidence that the latter were continuing their efforts to destroy the Chetniks. London and Washington well knew that the civil war in Yugoslavia was the result of two competing resistance elements with irreconcilable political aims, each struggling to gain ascendancy during the war in order to impose its system on the country in the postwar period. Saddling Mihailovich with the blame for this unfortunate turn of events was not so much a cause for the Allied decision to abandon him as it was a justification. Robert Lee Wolff, who was very familiar with Yugoslav affairs through his work in the Research and Analysis Branch of oss-Washington, probably expressed the views of many when he wrote: "I thought that Mihailovich was trapped into something like a pro-Axis position, that Tito was somewhat independent of Stalin and was killing Germans and that on the whole Churchill was right. I still think so which is not to say that Mihailovich was not to be pitied or Tito to be loved."[90]

4. Uninformed and Misinformed

Wolff's assessment of Mihailovich would have been more accurate had he substituted "anti-Partisan" for "pro-Axis," although his analysis as written closely approximated the information given to Churchill by his two most trusted advisers, Maclean and Deakin. On the other hand, there was little question about the military contribution made by the Partisans to the overall Allied effort between November, 1941, and November, 1943. By the time of the Teheran Conference, Tito's forces had weathered five Axis offensives and, in the process, had tied down a number of troops that might well have been used elsewhere. The Axis coalition of German, Italian, Ustasha, and collaborationist Chetnik units, while usually enjoying superiority in numbers and armament against the Partisans, never succeeded in destroying them as a fighting force. An oss report prepared by the si Branch in Bari concluded that the Axis Sixth Offensive, launched in September, 1943, "has shown concretely and indisputably that the Partisans are not only the most formidable resistance group in Yugoslavia, but also that they are the only anti-Axis force in that country."[1]

The Partisans responded to the various Axis offensives hurled against them in a fairly predictable manner: "by resolute opposition to start with, and then by a controlled disappearance, as soon as it was clear that the main attack could not be mastered."[2] To their credit, however, the Partisans had managed to survive Axis efforts to destroy them for almost two years, during which time they had received almost no material aid from the Allies. The Italian surrender and the success of Operation AUDREY alleviated many of their supply problems, and, of course, after the break with Mihailovich, Tito was the sole recipient of all supplies earmarked for Yugoslavia.[3]

oss had played and would continue to play a major role in the effort to supply the Partisans. Also, in the months after Teheran there was a significant increase in the number of personnel assigned to operations in Yugoslavia. In late November, 1943, when Donovan wrote to the Joint Chiefs of Staff about American intelligence operations in Yugoslavia, oss had only six men with the Partisans. Three of them were assigned to Tito's headquarters, while the others were attached to subordinate units in the country. By October, 1944, there were approximately forty OSS personnel attached to fifteen military missions in various corps areas throughout Yugoslavia.[4]

On November 27, 1943, one day after Donovan's memorandum to the Joint Chiefs, Cairo began building up the number of OSS personnel in Yugoslavia by dispatching 2d Lt. George Wuchinich to Slovenia as head of the ALUM mission. Described in one OSS report as a man who was "under the impression that he is destined to go over there to sell American democracy to those people," Wuchinich had been slated to go into Yugoslavia several months earlier, but his departure, like George Musulin's, had been delayed when the British declined to allow independent means of communications for the American missions. One accomplishment Wuchinich apparently was very proud of concerned his introducing the word *bazooka* into the Serbo-Croat language. Unfortunately, this led to a rather embarrassing situation for Bari when Partisan demands for bazookas far exceeded the number that could be supplied, and there was some fear that Wuchinich might have inadvertently damaged OSS's credibility with the Partisans.[5] Wuchinich proved to be a "prodigious" source of information, but his strong affinity for the Partisan movement led some of his fellow officers to depict him as an advocate of Tito's cause rather than an impartial observer.[6]

One week after Wuchinich reached Slovenia, Capt. George Selvig, in the company of a number of British officers, infiltrated into Bosnia where he joined the British mission at Tito's headquarters then located at Jajce. As a member of the Special Operations Branch of OSS, Selvig was under the command of Brigadier Maclean, although Farish was his immediate American superior. In early January, when the Partisans abandoned Jajce during the course of the German Sixth Offensive, Selvig moved into western Bosnia to the town of Potoci. He later traveled to Bosanski Petrovac on January 17 to greet Maclean, Farish, Eli Popovich, and Randolph Churchill, who arrived three days later.[7] Shortly after entering the country, Maclean ordered Selvig to Partisan Eighth Corps headquartered at Tičevo, where he relieved British liaison officer Maj. John Henniker-Major as head of the RELATOR mission on January 25.[8]

Roughly three weeks after Selvig entered the country, Captain Benson was recalled to Cairo, not to report on his experiences while in the country but as a diplomatic gesture designed to assuage the feelings of the British—mainly Maclean—over an incident that had occurred during Operation AUDREY. While based on the island of Vis, Benson sent a signal to Cairo that read in part, "The British are meeting the German threat to these islands with more liaison officers and batmen."[9]

Unfortunately for Benson, this signal received general distribution and ultimately came to the attention of Brigadier Maclean, who lodged a complaint with Lt. Col. Paul West, chief of Special Operations, oss-Cairo. West ordered Benson to come to Cairo to explain the matter, after which it was agreed that the issue would not be pursued if Benson would send a formal letter of apology to Maclean. On January 7, 1944, Benson sent the letter; Maclean accepted it and later told West that he would be pleased to have Benson serve under his command in the future.[10]

This might be viewed as a rather trivial incident if it were not indicative of a more fundamental problem which had affected and would continue to affect the nature of relations between oss and soe in Yugoslavia. Benson explained that at the time he sent the signal he was the only American officer attached to Partisan units on the islands of Vis, Hvar, Brać and Korčula. Maclean, on the other hand, was in command of fourteen officers and forty-five additional personnel. It was not the numerical imbalance to which Benson objected but the fact that the British were using their control of communications between Bari and Vis to intercept messages sent to Benson about the shipment of supplies. This information was then relayed to British missions on the mainland in order that they might take credit for the supplies when they arrived.[11] Selvig, who encountered similar difficulties in working with the British, reported that "there was always a tendency for them to take credit for everything that was done for the Partisans without regard for the person doing the work."[12]

With the Huot episode still fresh on his mind, Maclean was not inclined to let Benson's ill-advised remark pass unchallenged. However, there was more at stake here than Maclean's personal feelings. Having decided even before Teheran that Tito would be his man in Yugoslavia, Churchill regarded the control of supplies to the Partisans as the means by which the British could stimulate the resistance, cultivate better relations in the country, and diminish the influence of the Soviet Union. Maclean was Churchill's man on the spot, and it was primarily his responsibility to see to it that the Americans did not jeopardize British plans by seizing the initiative in the area of supply.

The importance Churchill attached to this issue was emphasized by the fact that he undertook a direct correspondence with Tito in early January, 1944, wherein he gave Tito his personal assurance that the British government would send no more supplies to Mihailovich and would urge the Royal Yugoslav Government to dismiss him as minister of war.[13]

Anthony Eden, who believed that Churchill was relying too much on Tito's good faith, argued in vain that, if for no other reason, the British should maintain relations with Mihailovich to strengthen their bargaining position with Tito.[14] Carl Norden of the Division of European Affairs shared Eden's view and warned the State Department in mid-January that failure to subordinate Tito to some authority in Yugoslavia would greatly jeopardize chances for "securing a free choice of government after liberation."[15]

Donovan, who for some time had been convinced that the British were playing a political game in Yugoslavia, had seen little in the weeks following Teheran to persuade him otherwise. The State Department obviously agreed. Accordingly, when the British extended an invitation for American officers to join the Maclean mission on its return to Yugoslavia in January, Assistant Secretary of State Adolf Berle advised against it on the grounds that the mission was essentially political in nature. In a refreshingly candid memorandum, Berle argued that the United States had no interest in being part of a British mission wherein they "would share the responsibility with no power to act." He continued, "If we plan to have any part in the Yugoslav picture to the extent that Tito (Marshal Broz) dominates it, we should have to have independent representation."[16]

Donovan had in fact secured the right of SI personnel to operate in Yugoslavia independently of the British in late November, 1943, and in early 1944 plans were underway to infiltrate a mission to Tito's headquarters when the German offensive closed all sea routes to the mainland. Turner McBaine considered going in himself, but command responsibilities precluded that possibility. Instead he sent Maj. Richard Weil, who was breveted lieutenant colonel for the mission.[17] Since his student days at Yale, Weil had been identified as an outspoken admirer of Tito. That fact, coupled with his well-known family ties to the Macy fortune in New York, did not endear him to many of his OSS colleagues with whom he served in Yugoslavia. A number of them saw Weil as the very epitome of the "Oh So Social" tag which some pundits tried to pin on Donovan's organization.[18]

Weil's CALIFORNIA mission parachuted into Yugoslavia on the morning of February 27, landing near the village of Preka, which was the location of the Anglo-American mission attached to Gen. Koča Popović's Fifth Army Corps. Popović greeted Weil most cordially and proceeded rather quickly to inquire if he had brought any bazookas with him. Wuchinich's efforts had apparently not been in vain. Weil had lunch at General Popović's headquarters and was joined by Maclean, who had walked over from Drvar to meet him.[19]

On the following day, Weil traveled to Drvar, arriving in time to dine with Maclean and the members of his staff, which included Major Farish and Maj. Randolph Churchill. After dinner Maclean questioned Weil concerning the exact status of his mission and told him in no uncertain terms that he was not pleased with his arrival at Partisan headquarters. Weil told Maclean that all appropriate headquarters had been advised of and had approved OSS's decision to send an independent mission to Tito and that he had been selected to command the mission. Making no effort to conceal his displeasure, Maclean argued that since he was General Wilson's representative in Yugoslavia all Allied personnel were supposed to be responsible to him. Weil was not, and Maclean deeply resented it.[20]

Some of the American and British officers responsible for the evacuation of Allied airmen from Partisan-held territory, pictured here at the Glina airstrip in Croatia, May, 1944: standing, left to right, Major McKuen (SOE), Capt. George Selvig, Lt. Col. Linn Farish, Capt. John Hamilton [Sterling Hayden], and Capt. John Blatnik, all of OSS; kneeling, left to right, an unidentified British officer and Lt. Eli Popovich. Courtesy Eli Popovich and M. Mike Sujdovic

Maclean suggested to Farish that Farish switch his communications to Weil's radio, advised the American officers that he, Maclean, would no longer be responsible for the safety of the members of the American mission, and warned Weil against lending himself "to any Partisan efforts to create a competitive spirit between the two missions." Farish seemed no more enthusiastic about Weil's arrival than Maclean. He told Weil that he had advised Colonel West against sending an independent mission to Tito because the Anglo-American mission had been operating so effectively. Moreover, Farish did not relish the idea that Weil was now the senior American officer in Yugoslavia while he remained only senior American officer on Maclean's staff.[21]

Farish left the next morning to survey some airfields, but Weil met with Maclean and found him to be in a more agreeable mood. The brigadier recounted his unfortunate experiences with Huot and Benson, suggesting by inference that he may have overreacted to Weil's arrival because of these previous incidents. Later in the day Weil met with Tito for about an hour, presenting a letter of introduction from General Donovan and explaining the nature of his mission. In what Weil described as a routine but satisfactory meeting, Tito promised his cooperation and later arranged for a member of his staff to brief the American on the disposition of Axis and Partisan forces in the country.[22]

Weil also had the opportunity to meet with other American personnel who were serving under Maclean's command and found them to be rather dissatisfied with the contribution they were making to the war effort. Captain Selvig, who had been at Sixth Army Corps since mid-January, complained of having little to do and told Weil that he did not think the United States could accomplish very much under present circumstances. Lt. James M. Goodwin, an American officer who had entered the country with Maclean in January, had been ordered to go to Slovenia to work with Maj. William B. Jones, a British officer who had arrived in the country in May, 1943. Maclean himself had told Weil that Jones was "uncontrollable and insane and had been for some months." Indeed, Maclean subsequently relieved Jones and temporarily turned the mission over to Goodwin.[23]

Shortly after arriving in Slovenia, Goodwin sent a message to Farish requesting reassignment because of the very minor role American personnel were playing in that area. He told Farish that he considered this a matter of national prestige and insisted that his "loyal instincts for the U.S. does [sic] not permit me to play a willing part in it."[24]

The under-utilization of American officers could not be blamed exclusively on Maclean, who told Weil that he had attempted to represent American interests in the country to the best of his ability despite the lack of instructions from American military or political authorities. Furthermore, Maclean indicated that he had told Farish he could meet with Tito whenever he liked, but that Farish had done so only twice for fifteen minutes during the entire time he had been in the country. As a result, Maclean had decided to use Farish's engineering skills to survey prospective airdromes and dropping zones, which meant that he was away from Tito's headquarters most of the time.[25]

Weil's findings confirmed the need for independent representation by OSS at Tito's headquarters, and Maclean agreed but with the important condition that he continue to control the flow of supplies to the Partisans. According to Weil, "This last crack was not very subtle, since everybody knows that whoever controls the supply line has the greatest leverage and influence at headquarters." Weil even suggested that the quest for influence might well extend beyond the war years. He reported on a conversation with a British officer from Croatian headquarters, Major Rogers, who told him that he thought Maclean was "negotiating some post-war economic concessions in Yugoslavia for Great Britain, more or less as quid pro quo for the help now being given."[26] Weil never confirmed this allegation, but such speculation did little to allay the growing suspicions of some in OSS about the motives of British policy in Yugoslavia.

Having determined the need for OSS representation at Tito's headquarters, Weil decided that it was more important for him to report his findings directly to the president than to remain in Yugoslavia. Therefore, acting on his own authority, he left the country on the evening of March 19 and returned to Bari. He subsequently flew to Algiers, where he sought and got permission from Colonel Glavin to take his report to Washington.[27] Although Weil did not see Roosevelt, he did have tea with Mrs. Roosevelt, who gave him a personal note from the president to be delivered to Tito.[28]

Whatever advantages may have accrued from Weil's impromptu travels were largely offset by the fact that during the critical weeks when the Allies were shifting their support to Tito and attempting to extricate their personnel from Mihailovich's territory, OSS had no independent representation at Partisan headquarters. Although Weil succeeded in establishing the principle of independence for SI operations in Yugoslavia, six months passed before OSS dispatched the Huntington mission to take advantage of that fact.

The Partisans were, of course, eager to have an American mission at Tito's headquarters since it would suggest a further degree of commitment and recognition on the part of the United States and might provide the leverage necessary to gain acceptance of a Partisan mission to Washington. The Partisan High Command was so insistent on this matter that by the summer of 1944 it actually prohibited the expansion of SI operations along the Dalmatian coast until an American military mission had been sent to Tito's headquarters.[29]

Clearly, American interests in Yugoslavia would have best been served had Weil chosen to remain at Tito's headquarters or at least taken care to provide for continued representation after his departure. His report of March 20, despite the drama of a personal visit to the White House, did not have a major impact on Allied policy in Yugoslavia, the course of which had been determined even before he had entered the country. His findings did, however, challenge many of the assumptions upon which that policy had been based and should have given pause for thoughtful reflection upon earlier assessments of Tito's movement.

In the first place, Weil questioned the accuracy of Partisan claims of damage to the enemy. He charged that the Partisans were prone to exaggerate the scope of their activities, kept few records, and maintained incomplete and irregular communications among their units. Weil was certain that "the Partisans' announced claim . . . that they, by their sole efforts, are 'containing' 17 German divisions and well over one-half million enemy troops in their country, is unquestionably false."[30]

In terms of numbers of men under arms, Weil's findings, taken from Partisan sources, coincided with previous reports that put Partisan strength between 290,000 and 310,000 men. He also noted that the Partisans claimed that they could enroll 200,000 more men. Unlike Maclean, Deakin, and some American officers who had recently reported on the Partisans, Weil considered that Tito's forces, regardless of how numerous they might be, could not "be anything but guerrillas." Their conception of intelligence was poor, their medical facilities were appallingly bad, and their equipment, though vastly superior to that of the Chetniks, was greatly inferior to that which the Germans could bring to bear against them in a pitched battle. In fact, Weil subsequently told Cavendish Cannon, assistant chief of the Division of Southern European Affairs, that if Tito established a fixed line the Germans would "knock hell out of him."[31] Other American officers confirmed Weil's conclusion on this point. Dan Desich, who served with the ALUM mission in Slovenia, stated that "all the time I spent in Yugoslavia with the Partisans which was ten months, I never saw where, as far as the Partisans were concerned, they could stand head-to-head with the Germans and have a battle front."[32]

Given these facts, Weil maintained that "there is no territory anywhere in the country which cannot be entered by enemy troops at will, and with a minimum of resistance." Indeed, without outside assistance, he considered it unlikely that the Partisans could either drive the enemy from their country, prevent the enemy from withdrawing, or annihilate the enemy in their country.[33] Subsequent events would prove Weil's assessment of Partisan capabilities quite accurate.

Goodwin, who also served in Slovenia, reported that the Germans eventually abandoned the strategy of trying to crush the Partisans through a series of offensive operations because the latter would not fight. Instead, the Germans "permitted the Partisans to occupy a rather large unimportant area considerable distance from their communications with two strong German garrisons almost in the center of the 'Free Territory.'"[34]

Partisan Corps Areas, May,1944

Source: RG-226, E. 154, B. 21, F. Bari-SI-PRO-6

Weil was also openly critical of Allied, particularly American, intelligence-gathering capabilities in Yugoslavia. He charged that the information coming out of the country was

substantially defective in the only four ways information can be defective. We are substantially uninformed and misinformed. The analysis we have received is incorrect and incomplete. We are uninformed in that we do not know whether Partisan reports about action against the enemy are accurate, exaggerated, or utterly untrue. This is because, for the most part, we have taken the Partisans' word for what went on in enemy actions since we have seldom had our own observers with them to make independent observations and reports.[35]

Despite the shortcomings enumerated in his report about the Partisans, Weil believed that they would dominate Yugoslavia in the postwar period "even if it involves internal strife and bloodshed to assert and maintain this control." He recommended that support for Tito continue, arguing that the United States had the capability to influence the political situation in Yugoslavia as much if not more than either Britain or the Soviet Union by so doing.[36]

A State Department analysis prepared for Cavendish Cannon found the Weil report to be lacking in new information and contradictory in some of the more general conclusions—the most notable being Weil's statement that the Partisans would be the future masters of Yugoslavia regardless of the many weaknesses found to exist in the movement. The most biting criticism, however, questioned Weil's recommendation for continued exclusive support of the Partisans when "Mihailovich controls or is contiguous to territory strategically important, according to military observers to Allied big-scale operations."[37]

The question was a simple one, yet from a purely military standpoint there appeared to be no satisfactory reply. Intelligence reports from OSS sources throughout late 1943 and early 1944 had consistently placed Partisan forces in western Yugoslavia where they posed only a minor threat to German strategic interests and lines of communications. Granted, the Partisans may have been more active during this period than their Chetnik counterparts, but as one OSS report noted, "it must be recognized that for many months the Partisans had the advantage of operating in territory not formally under German rule."[38]

For this reason Partisan claims about liberated and controlled territory came more and more under question, particularly since intelligence on this subject was so contradictory. For example, a Joint Intelligence Committee report dated May 18, 1944, put Partisan strength at 300,000 and claimed that these forces were in control of two-thirds of the country. Yet, only one month later when the Political Intelligence Committee, Middle East released its very favorable report on Tito's forces, the statement was made that the Partisans "never attempt to hold any given liberated area, still less a town, against a serious enemy attack." While in Cairo, Lt. Col. Robert H. McDowell conducted a study of intelligence reports emanating from Partisan sources and concluded that there were "so many serious contradictions in Partisan claims as to require rejection of the communiques as serious military documents."[39]

McDowell challenged the claims of Weil, Farish, and Maclean, all of whom had placed Partisan strength between 250,000 and 300,000. Citing a report on Partisan strength by Gen. N. V. Korneyev, head of the Russian mission to Tito's headquarters, that estimated Partisan forces to be about 18,000 and an MID (Military Intelligence Division) report dated June 26, 1944, that placed Partisan strength at 15,000, McDowell contended that much of what had passed as intelligence on the Partisan movement had in fact been the unsubstantiated claims of the Partisans themselves.[40] When McDowell discussed with Robert Joyce some of the findings of American and British officers concerning the Partisan movement, Joyce admitted that some Allied officers were "starry-eyed" when they came out of the country to file their reports and had allowed themselves to become emotionally involved to such an extent as to preclude objective analysis.[41]

While debate continued about the strength of the Partisan movement, Reuben

Markham of the Office of War Information (o w i) submitted a report that challenged Partisan claims about the extent of territory under their control. This document, presented to Lincoln Macveagh, American ambassador to the Yugoslav government-in-exile, included a map showing territory that Tito claimed was controlled by his forces. Markham described the areas in questions as "wild, barren, or wooded mountain regions in which but few people live and at that in a primitive manner." He suggested by way of comparison that "if Elizabeth Dilling and her ardent supporters should dominate Upper Maine, East Tennessee, Nevada, Montana, the Dakotas, and West Texas, except the cities and main railroad lines, she could hardly be said to have freed half of America from Mr. Roosevelt – though she might make such a claim."[42]

Critics of the Partisan movement have charged that Tito took advantage of his relatively isolated position to prepare for an ultimate showdown with Mihailovich instead of continuing to harass the Germans to the fullest extent. In fact, there is evidence to suggest that as early as March, 1943, Tito had adopted such a strategy. M. J. Milazzo offers the following assessment of Tito's position in the spring of 1943: "With practically all of his forces outside of the German operation zone and the Italians obviously unenthusiastic about fighting anybody, Tito saw his chance and seized it. The Partisan leaders, with as much reason as Mihailovich to expect a rapid Italian and ultimate German defeat, began to discriminate among their opponents in essentially the same way the Chetniks had been doing all along."[43]

Likewise, Jozo Tomasevich, in his very critical treatment of the Chetnik movement, cites a message from the provincial committee for Bosnia and Hercegovina, dated March 29, calling for the destruction of Mihailovich's forces because "they represent the greatest danger for the further course of the national liberation struggle." In this same period the "chief goal" of the German Brandenburg Regiment was the capture of Mihailovich and the destruction of his staff.[44]

Deakin also concedes that "during the next critical six weeks, Tito's forces concentrated with impunity, on carrying out the same task as the Germans themselves had outlined in Operation 'Schwarz' – the liquidation of the Mihailović movement, and for the same reasons – to control the hinterland of Hercegovina and Montenegro in anticipation of an Allied Landing."[45]

The Partisans, of course, welcomed any assistance the Germans might render in eliminating the Chetniks, although by the spring of 1943 the former were confident that they could deal with Mihailovich's forces on their own.[46] Admittedly this could be done more easily if the Germans allowed the Partisans a free hand to deal with their internal foes. Consequently, in early March, 1943, the top echelon of the Partisan leadership initiated negotiations designed to achieve this end. The stated purpose of the German-Partisan talks that began on March II at Gornji Vakuf was to effect an exchange of prisoners – one of whom was Tito's common-law wife, Herta Has – and to secure German rec-ognition of the Partisans' belligerent rights.[47] However, as Milovan Djilas, a participant in the talks, openly admits in his book *Wartime,* it was understood that Partisan negotiators were free to expand the scope of the talks in an at-tempt to establish a sort of "live and let live" agreement between them and the Germans.[48]

Walter Roberts, who discloses in some detail the substance of these German-Partisan talks, points out that both German and Partisan records confirm that the Partisans specifically offered a cessation of hostilities to the Germans in return for a free hand against the Chetniks, whom they regarded as "their main enemy." Only a few days earlier Mihailovich had made a similar statement about the Partisans, but he had done so in front of Colonel Bailey, who dutifully reported the remark to his superiors in London.[49]

Naturally the Partisan proposal intrigued the Germans, at least at the local level, and on March 17, Siegfried Kasche, German minister in Zagreb, notified Berlin of the nature of the initial talks and suggested that they be pursued in Zagreb. No reply came from Berlin, and consequently on March 25, Djilas and Gen. Vladimir Velebit, traveling under the name of Dr. Petrović, passed through German lines, boarded a German military plane in Sarajevo, and flew to Zagreb to continue the talks with Gen. Glaise von Horstenau. According to Wilhelm Hoettl, who was a senior officer in the Secret Service forces cover-ing southern Yugoslavia, Velebit indicated that Tito was willing to discuss an armistice on the following conditions: "If the Germans would undertake not to attack him inside a certain reserve territory to be agreed upon, he would refrain from extending his revolt to other parts of the Croat State. As an ear-nest of his good faith he was prepared to abstain for an agreed and specified period from all acts of terrorism and sabotage."[50]

In almost every respect these negotiations between the Germans and the Partisans were identical to those conducted between German and Chetnik rep-resentatives. They were motivated by a temporarily adverse military situation and were designed to secure a free hand for pursuit of the civil war. Still, Jozo Tomasevich claims that these talks could not be placed "in the same cate-gory as the systematic and enduring Chetnik collaboration . . . although that collaboration was not based on ideological affinity and was not without res-ervation either."[51] This assertion is challenged in part by evidence given in a postwar interview by Gen. Glaise von Horstenau, who was German Pleni-potentiary General in Croatia. According to von Horstenau, the Germans ini-tiated a prisoner exchange with the Partisans as early as the spring of 1942, and such exchanges continued "until the last" – words that hardly suggest an ephemeral relationship.[52]

Opinion varies as to how much the British may have known about these talks. It is most unlikely, however, given London's growing disenchantment with the Chetniks, that evidence of the Partisan-German talks would have precluded dispatch of the initial SOE missions to the Partisans in the spring of 1943.[53]

In assessing the negotiations with the Germans and his role in them, Milovan Djilas confessed that neither he nor other members of the Communist party's Central Committee had "any pangs of conscience" about their actions. After all, Soviet history offered "an abundance of precedents" for such tactical maneuvering when dictated by the realities of "military necessity."[54]

Tito's apologists have not taken as pragmatic a view of this episode in Partisan history as has Djilas. Louis Adamić, one of Tito's staunchest supporters in the United States, wrote that the Partisans did not avail themselves of deals with the Axis forces because they "were as consistently and unequivocally anti-Fascist-Italian as they were anti-Nazi-German, and as anti-Nedich as anti-Pavelich, while Mikhailovich and his principal lieutenants in 1941–1943 felt differently about the Axis lineup."[55] Phyliss Auty, one of Tito's biographers and ardent admirers, offered a more remarkable, if no less definitive, defense. In a letter to the *Times Literary Supplement* of November 27, 1970, Auty said that she had contacted Tito personally about the alleged negotiations with the Germans and had been told that such reports were untrue. The unsubstantiated denial of the man who, after the war, had Mihailovich executed for allegedly collaborating with the Germans was sufficient evidence for Auty to dismiss the entire matter as a mere fabrication.[56]

Auty's remarks notwithstanding, the fact remains that eight months before the Allies dropped Mihailovich for collaborationist activity between his subordinates and the Germans, Partisan representatives, acting under direct orders from Tito, declared their willingness to forgo further resistance against the Axis forces if they were given a free hand against the Chetniks. The prisoner exchange occurred, but the political and military discussions were not pursued, mainly because the Germans were not interested.[57]

The Partisans subsequently pushed into western Yugoslavia where they profited greatly from the Italian surrender and were nurtured by Allied supplies coming from Italy.[58] By the spring of 1944 they apparently felt confident that they could deal with the Chetniks, free hand or not, and a growing number of reports from agents in the field indicated that they were doing precisely that.

5. The Shape of Things to Come

The most influential report addressing the Partisan-Chetnik civil war came from Maj. Linn Farish, whose views concerning events in Yugoslavia were quite different from those expressed in his initial report some eight months earlier. Farish had reentered Yugoslavia with Brigadier Maclean's party on January 20, accompanied by 2d Lt. Eli Popovich, an American officer of Serbian extraction who was familiar with the Yugoslav people and fluent in the Serbo-Croat language.

Popovich had joined the Army Corps of Engineers shortly after Pearl Harbor, hoping to get into the fighting as soon as possible. The navy had also been interested in him because of his experience in steel construction work. When Popovich found out, however, that the navy wanted to send him to the Canary Islands to build submarine pens, he was not interested. Popovich transferred to OSS in July, 1943, after graduating from Officer's Candidate School at Fort Belvoir, Virginia. He completed his OSS training in the United States and arrived in Cairo in December, 1943, about the time Farish was returning from Washington.[1]

Popovich had never met Farish, though he was familiar with Farish's very favorable report on the Partisans. In time, however, he came to have great respect for the major, whom he described as an easygoing, compassionate man who never attempted to take advantage of his rank. Popovich relished the idea of working with Farish but was not at all pleased about being assigned to Tito's forces.[2]

Farish, Popovich, and Capt. James Goodwin comprised the American component of Maclean's mission, which also included Maj. Randolph Churchill. As soon as the team reached Bosanski Petrovac, Popovich realized that the Partisans were going to take every possible advantage of the fact that Prime Minister Churchill's son had been sent to their forces. Following a brief statement by Brigadier Maclean, a Partisan officer gave a propaganda speech wherein he noted that the presence of Churchill's son was evidence that the Allies were

Members of the Anglo-American mission to Tito's forces: left to right, Lt. Eli Popovich, Maj. Linn Farish, Capt. James Goodwin, and Maj. Randolph Churchill. Courtesy Col. James M. Goodwin (Ret.)

supporting the Partisans and that Mihailovich was a traitor. Popovich translated these remarks for Farish, pointing out that Maclean had said nothing at all about Mihailovich.[3]

After two days at Bosanski Petrovac the mission made its way to Tito's headquarters at Drvar, where Tito himself had invited the mission personnel to be his guests for dinner. During the course of the evening the typical speeches were made about the struggle of the Partisans against the Fascist occupiers and about the great debt of gratitude owed to the Allies—the Soviet Union, Great Britain, and the United States. An awkward situation occurred later when Tito noted that one member of the American mission was of Serbian extraction. The reference was, of course, to Popovich, who was then asked by Tito what he thought of the Partisan movement. Tito used the word *pokret*, which has a political connotation and which Popovich took to refer to the Communist movement in Yugoslavia. The lieutenant replied that in America he had heard only of General Mihailovich's movement and that he had learned of the Partisans only after his arrival in Italy. Tito neither appreciated nor forgot the answer. Some months later when Popovich was supposed to reenter Yugoslavia with another mission, Tito personally intervened to prevent it.[4] In early 1944, however, Popovich found that he had become an unwilling instrument of Partisan propaganda which proclaimed that the arrival of American officers of Serbian extraction was "proof that General Mihailovich was a collaborator and traitor to the Serbian people."[5]

A good example of the way in which the Partisans exploited Popovich's presence occurred in south Serbia in April, 1944, shortly after Farish and Popovich parachuted to Šoroka Planina on their second mission. While they were in this area the Partisans brought a village magistrate from one of the neighboring villages to the American mission and introduced him to Popovich, pointing out that he was an American officer of Serbian ancestry. The old magistrate told Popovich that the people of his village did not favor either the Chetniks or Partisans because they did not want to choose sides in a war where brother was killing brother and father was killing son. Still, he was very much impressed by the fact that the Americans were supporting the Partisans and returned to his village and persuaded all the men there to join Tito's forces.[6] Farish later reported to Bari that the presence of Allied officers with the Partisans had added strength to their recruiting efforts and was "an excellent thing."[7] He further noted that while Mihailovich's prestige remained very high in some areas, "most people are fast realizing that his cause is lost."[8]

According to Popovich the tragedy of the civil conflict weighed very heavily on Farish's mind, particularly when he came face-to-face with the human misery that resulted from the fratricidal struggle. On one occasion as the mission was making its way from one village to another with a Partisan escort, the column came under fire from a group of poorly armed Chetniks. The Partisans, armed mostly with automatic weapons, quickly broke up the ambush and captured many of the Chetniks, including the leader. They brought him to Farish and Popovich, and when he realized that there were American officers in the column, he fell on his knees with his hands clasped together as if in prayer and asked the two Americans, "What are you doing to us?" He said that only a short time ago the Allies were dropping supplies to Mihailovich and now they were supporting the Communists. In despair he told Popovich, "The Germans are killing us, the Bulgarians are plundering our villages, God has forgotten us, and now even you, our allies, are against us. Now who can we turn to?" Popovich translated all of this to Farish, who was obviously moved by the dilemma in which the hapless Chetnik leader found himself, but there was nothing he could do to save him.[9]

This incident and others like it began to take their toll on Farish, as evidenced by some of the signals he sent to his base at Bari. On May 8, 1944, for example, he sent the following message to Lt. Comdr. Edward J. Green, who had assumed command of the base at Bari in February: "We should also like to know whether oss is interested in having us in the center of the Balkans . . . We are well equipped with experience to do valuable work, but feel that oss does not care what we do or where we are."[10] Green, who seems to have been highly respected by all of the officers who knew him, acted quickly to soothe Farish's feelings—and apparently with some success. Only two weeks later Farish advised Green: "Your field report has been received. This is the first time we have felt than any one knows where we are, gives a damn what we are doing, and cares what we think. We doubt if any one ever worked more undirected, isolated, confused, and under unsatisfactory conditions as oss men in Jugoslavia."[11]

The dispirited tone of these messages was out of character for Farish, although his reference to feeling isolated appears to have been a rather common phenomenon experienced by most field personnel from time to time. A more disturbing message that may well have been more indicative of Farish's true state of mind was one that arrived in mid-May, in which he confessed to Green: "Personally I am tired, discouraged, not much interested in future missions or who heads them. This time when I come out, it will be for good. As our British cousins say, 'I have had it.'"[12]

Roughly two weeks after Farish sent this message the Bulgarians launched an offensive in southeast Serbia, forcing the oss team and a number of American airmen who had been rescued by the Partisans to prepare for evacuation. Popovich located a suitable landing zone on June 8 and subsequently notified Bari that the mission was standing by for withdrawal. Bari set the evacuation date for June 15 and dispatched two planes to carry out the operation. The aircraft reached the landing zone shortly after midnight, just hours ahead of Bulgarian units that were only a few miles away. In fact, the planes actually came under fire as they lifted off from the landing strip.[13]

The Linn Farish who now made his way back to Bari was not the same exuberant personality who had parted company with Albert Seitz in Cairo only ten months earlier. He was morose, withdrawn, and visibly distraught over the course of American policy in Yugoslavia—one that in his view he had encouraged by his initial report.[14] Cyrus L. Sulzberger, the famous wartime Balkan correspondent for the *New York Times*, who met Farish after his return to Bari, described him as "frightfully over-tired and wrought up." One evening when Sulzberger and Farish were having dinner in Farish's hotel room, Farish suddenly jumped from his chair "when the moon came up and he grabbed his tommy gun and started to shoot at it." There was no question in Sulzberger's mind but that Farish had "had too much."[15]

These were the conditions under which Farish prepared his last report, which was filed with OSS headquarters in Bari on June 16, 1944. No other document prepared by any observer with either Partisan or Chetnik forces throughout the war so vividly conveys the disillusionment of an American officer who, despite his best efforts, became part of the tragic circumstances surrounding him.

Farish believed and sought to convince others that there was, or should be, a moral dimension to Allied policy in Yugoslavia. He had seen neither heroes nor villains during his last two missions into the country, only victims. In the opening paragraphs of his report, he described the tragic plight of Yugoslavia—a country rent and torn by political, cultural, and religious problems so deeply rooted in the past that "the people themselves do not understand them."[16]

Farish held neither side blameless for the civil war. While he was in the country he had seen and heard direct evidence that both the Chetniks and Partisans considered the other the primary enemy. All of this had led him to conclude that "in this case both sides are speaking the truth. They are their own worst enemies."[17]

Allied intelligence officers as well as Allied airmen, many of whom were wounded and required medical attention, found themselves caught up in the bitter fighting between Chetnik and Partisan forces. Farish reported on the plight of a group of airmen who had been located in the Kakavica Mountains, which had been the site of a recent battle between the two resistance groups. These men told Farish that the Chetniks had rescued them and that despite heavy fighting with the Partisans, a Chetnik doctor had made his way back for several nights at the risk of his own life to care for them. In the process of moving the airmen to the airstrip for evacuation the mission traveled through villages that only a few days earlier had been described as "dangerous Chetnik territory." But Farish wrote:

I could not see any dangerous characters among them. I couldn't tell who was Left or who was Right, who was Communist or Reactionary. Somehow those terms that one hears used so glibly on the outside did not seem to fit the actual circumstances.

What a very peculiar set of circumstances these facts bring out! Rifles stamped 'U.S. Property,' firing W.R.A. Ammunition, flown by American airmen in American aircraft being fired at people who have rescued other American airmen and who were doing everything to make them comfortable and to return them to safety. . . .

If I am confused, what must be the state of mind of the people of Jugoslavia. . . . Is it any wonder that hundreds of them have taken us aside and asked us to tell them what to do, which way to turn.[18]

Farish believed that the United States could and should play an effective role in bringing the Yugoslav civil war to an end and argued that it was morally wrong for his country to continue providing supplies, arms, and ammunition without regard for any other consideration except military outcome. In fact, Farish said that he did not feel that he could continue his work in Yugoslavia unless he could sincerely believe "that every possible honest effort is being made to put an end to the civil strife." He added, "At one time I worried because America was not getting the proper recognition for her participation in supply operations. Now I wonder – do we want it."[19]

Farish then gave eloquent expression to the moral dilemma of every American officer who, regardless of the resistance forces to which he was attached, was dedicated to winning the war while trying to avoid internal political entanglements.

When I have called for aid to the Partisans, and officers with the Chetniks have called for aid to their group, we have had the same person in mind – a barefoot, cold and hungry peasant farmer, a man whose courage and endurance must be observed to be understood. To us they were not Communists or Reactionaries, Partisans or Chetniks; they were merely brave men who looked to us for aid with great confidence that it would be forthcoming. We would have been strange people if we had not responded – we could not have done otherwise, and been American.[20]

In Farish's view the United States could ill afford to remain a disinterested party since he believed that "the issues in Jugoslavia are ones which will have to be faced in many parts of the world." Disillusionment with the present led Farish to paint an equally gloomy picture of what the postwar world might hold: "The Jugoslavians with their wild, turbulent, strong-willed nature, have abandoned Reason and resorted to Force. Is this the shape of the things to come. Are we all of us sacrificing to end this war only to have dozens of little wars spring up which may well merge into one gigantic conflict involving all man-kind?"[21]

Considering the events that have transpired in the four decades since the end of World War II, Farish's question seems far less rhetorical than he might have imagined. Unfortunately, Farish did not live to see the unfolding of those events in the postwar world. On September 9, 1944, he and all of the members of a British mission to which he had been assigned perished in a plane crash near Athens, Greece. Popovich, who had accompanied Farish on most of his missions inside Yugoslavia, was initially assigned to this ill-fated mission, but for reasons never made known to him was pulled from the operation at the last minute and replaced by a British major.[22]

Some have maintained that Farish's last report represented a repudiation of most, if not all, of the conclusions presented in his initial report. Certainly there is a great difference in the general theme of the two documents, but there is little evidence to suggest that Farish had totally reversed himself in the span of eight months. In a message sent to Bari on May 9, 1944, for example, he argued that the only solution to the Partisan-Chetnik struggle was to "strengthen as rapidly as possible the Serb Partisans, thus enabling them to free Serbia with not much aid from the outside."[23] He also continued to send messages from the field in which he charged that Mihailovich's forces had allowed themselves to slip into a collaborationist relationship with the Germans in order to defeat the Partisans.[24]

These messages were consistent with the views Farish had expressed in his second report—actually a series of reports prepared between March 4 and March 9, 1944, while he was at Petrovac. These reports reflect Farish's continued admiration for the Partisans, whom he described as "the most numerous, best organized and by far the most effective in their resistance to the Axis and satellite forces." When Farish spoke of the Partisans, and it is vitally important to understand this, what he had in mind was

a normal, peasant type group of people, unwilling to submit passively to oppression [who] have brought this atmosphere of freedom into being, actually with their bare hands. There may be some whose political aspirations transcend their innate love of liberty, but with the great majority such is not the case. It is these common people, who have served so well and suffered so gravely, that we must consider. Nothing that we can do for them will be out of proportion to their contribution to the common cause.[25]

Farish was not alone in this view. Other American officers supported the Partisan resistance effort without in any way subscribing to the political program of the Communists who dominated the movement. Unfortunately, these officers, Farish included, either misunderstood the dynamics of resistance politics or grossly underestimated the ruthless tenacity with which Tito and his followers would pursue their own political agenda. Whether these failings should be attributed to idealism or simply to naiveté is a matter of speculation. However, one thing is certain. Failure to assess accurately the significance of the

Partisan movement in all of its manifestations – political as well as military –
precluded a fair evaluation of Mihailovich's motives for opposing it.

At the time Farish prepared his celebrated third report, he did not see conditions in Yugoslavia in terms of Tito versus Mihailovich or political versus
military interests. He saw mainly the common people. He depicted the resistance – Chetnik and Partisan – not as servile pawns on some military chess-
board to be manipulated at will by Allied strategists, but as human beings.
And he was concerned less with the strategic results of American policy in
Yugoslavia than with its moral implications. Having seen American weapons
dispatched to the Partisans for use against the Germans turned instead against
the Chetniks, Farish warned that American complicity in a cruel and debilitating civil war could not be covered up by a steady stream of policy statements
that largely ignored reality.

Consistent with Farish's findings, Robert Joyce apprised Donovan of a report from the Political Warfare Executive dated July 26, which concluded that
Tito "is now diverting an increasing proportion of his efforts from the attempt
to expel the Germans from Croatia to the civil war against General Mihailovich's Serbs."[26] The report left no doubt that American and British officers
in south Serbia were "squarely in the business of Yugoslav civil war," confirming what the Royal Yugoslav Government had been saying for months.[27]

oss personnel in different regions of the country also reported that the Partisans were storing away substantial quantities of the supplies they were receiving, apparently for use against their internal enemies. Rex Deane, whose
REDWOOD mission parachuted to Partisan Second Corps headquarters at
Kolašin in Montenegro, found the condition of some Partisan units to be "shock-
ing," which "makes one wonder what is happening to all the equipment the
Allies are dropping in here." Deane added, "In my opinion and concurred with
by Major Hunter and Lt. Green USNR, these people are good merely as a
nuisance value and of some slight use as guerrillas. . . . Like Oliver Twist they
continually ask for more but fail to use what they have on hand."[28]

Lt. Holt Green had parachuted into the Partisan Second Corps area in early
February as head of the RAKEOFF mission and was initially impressed with
what he saw there. In a report filed with Bari in late February, he encouraged
full support for the Partisans, arguing that Allied supplies were being used
to fight the Germans and were not being employed against the Chetniks.[29]

By the time Stephen Galembush joined RAKEOFF in early April as the mission's radio operator, Green's earlier impressions had changed significantly. Both
men began to notice the very poor condition of the weapons carried by most
of the Partisan patrols and became curious as to what was happening to the
supplies they knew were being sent into the area by the Allies.[30] Galembush,
who had become good friends with a young boy named Mischko, learned
through him that the Partisans were hiding supplies in barns throughout the

countryside. Green and Galembush set out to confirm Mischko's story and subsequently discovered numerous barns containing "piles of arms and ammunition of every description." Green ordered all of the supplies to be collected and returned to Second Corps headquarters, where he began distributing them to the Partisans on his own authority. Galembush recalls that when Peko Dapčević, commanding officer of the Partisan Second Corps, was confronted with this evidence "his face reminded me of a youngster caught with his hand in a cookie jar," but he could ill afford to object to Green's orders.[31]

Galembush reported this incident to Bari, but like other intelligence reports from the field that questioned the course of American policy in Yugoslavia, it was largely ignored. On August 10, Reuben Markham of OWI filed a report in Cairo based on intelligence he had seen while in Bari and on personal interviews with American and British officers returning from Yugoslavia. His findings were consistent with much of the information coming out of Yugoslavia at this time, which clearly indicated that contrary to stated policy, Allied supplies were being used by the Partisans in order to consolidate their internal position in the country. The OSS analyst who evaluated Markham's report conceded that it contained "some truth" but largely discounted it on the grounds that "since Markham is anti-communist, anti-Partisan and pro-Mihailovich, his comments cannot be considered very objective."[32] Dan Desich, who parachuted into Slovenia on June 13 and later relieved George Wuchinich as head of the ALUM mission, called attention to this same issue in a report filed with OSS headquarters in Bari. "Where," he asked, "is the best part of the weapons, ammunition, and clothing with which the Partisans have been plentifully supplied? It is believed they are in bunkers, but where and why?"[33]

An OSS report dated August 17, 1944, provided at least a partial response to Desich's queries. It charged that American supplies dropped by American planes under British command were being used to kill Serbs and concluded that the "Partisans have almost ceased fighting Germans and are openly concentrating on the civil war against the Serbs."[34] Secretary of State Cordell Hull had earlier insisted that the State Department would not assent to an "irrevocable decision" to withhold supplies from Serbian forces while "giving support to a forcible penetration of Tito into Serbia."[35]

Hull's declaration was yet another attempt to substitute platitudes for policy. At the very time a steady stream of field intelligence reports was revealing that the Partisans were engaging Chetnik units as much as if not more than the Germans, the Allies were actually preparing to increase the flow of supplies to Tito's forces. On June 1, the Allied High Command created the Balkan Air Force under Air Vice Marshal William Elliot. The primary function of this unit was to provide supplies to those forces in the Balkans that were actively resisting the Germans, and in Yugoslavia that meant the Partisans. A policy statement governing the actions of the BAF made it clear that no supplies would be sent to Mihailovich and "no support will be furnished the Partisans where it is obvious that they will use it not against the Germans, Bulgarians, Ustashi and other definitely accepted Quislings, but merely against the Chetniks." Beyond these considerations, the BAF was to avoid becoming "involved in or a party to purely internal conflicts or domestic issues in Jugoslavia."[36]

Once again, intent and result were far apart. There was some concern within OSS that support of the Partisans "may be extended to include Partisan operations against Nationalist Yugoslav forces, as well as against German and quisling forces."[37] According to David Martin and numerous OSS officers who were inside Yugoslavia during the latter half of 1944, it was.[38] As will be shown, there were specific examples where OSS officers in the field received requests from the Partisans for operational support from the BAF against targets held not by German or Ustasha forces but by Nationalist units. Most of these officers did not have freedom of movement to confirm independently the legitimacy of these requests, and it was only after OSS reestablished a presence in Serbia in August that reports of these operations began to filter back to Bari.

It is not easy to explain how or why OSS appeared to remain oblivious for so long to the manipulation of its personnel and resources inside Yugoslavia. Many of the problems encountered by the agency arose from the constraints imposed on it by virtue of its association with SOE, which had responsibility for implementing a policy often at odds with American views. There is also substantial evidence to suggest the existence within OSS of a group of individuals who, as the outcome of the war became certain, did not hesitate to advance their own political agenda for the postwar period. Lastly, OSS exhibited a great deal of naiveté in its dealings with the resistance effort in Yugoslavia—a trait perhaps to be expected from the young organization, but hardly a desirable one.

A rather ironic situation arose in April, when OSS decided to expand its presence in several countries, including Yugoslavia.[39] The State Department agreed with the dispatch of an enlarged American mission to Tito provided its activities remained military in nature.[40] On the other hand, the department thought it unwise to accept a Partisan mission in Washington as a quid pro quo, since to do so would have political overtones.[41]

The Partisan mission to which the department made reference concerned a request from Tito, which had been pending for some time, that Vladimir Velebit of his staff be allowed to meet with the Joint Chiefs in Washington to discuss certain matters relating to Allied supply operations.[42] Colonel Velebit was already representing Tito in SBS headquarters in Bari, where he was involved in the process of approving certain OSS missions destined for Partisan-held territory in Yugoslavia.[43]

Apparently neither OSS nor the State Department believed that subjecting American military missions to Partisan review might be construed as a political gesture. To be sure, not accepting a mission in Washington on political grounds while sanctioning the dispatch of thousands of tons of supplies to a political-military organization known to be committed to the disestablishment of the existing government suggests that American policymakers had not quite grasped the significance of what was occurring in Yugoslavia. At this point almost any representation to Partisan headquarters had some political implication. As Gen. Henry Maitland Wilson, Allied commander in the Mediterranean theater, pointed out, Tito's headquarters had ceased to be a center of guerrilla activity and had become "sort of a minor political capitol."[44] Likewise, Maj. Franklin Lindsay recalls that before being sent to Partisan forces in Slovenia, he was warned against having anything to do with politics. According to Lindsay, "the mere fact that an American officer was with the Communist Partisans had the greatest political significance. I think it demonstrates in retrospect the naiveté of all of us in dealing with the problem."[45]

Not all of the problems oss began to encounter in mid-1944 and afterwards could be attributed to inexperience and naiveté. Throughout most of the war, a common desire to defeat the Axis powers—particularly Germany—had welded together the disparate political groups that had found a home in Donovan's organization. As Germany's military fortunes began to wane, however, so did much of the cohesiveness with which oss had functioned during the war. Nowhere was this more apparent than among the personnel who were involved with Yugoslav affairs, the focal point of which was sbs headquarters at Bari.

Eli Popovich recalls that the Communist presence and influence in Bari had become so pervasive that oss headquarters there had become known as the "Little Kremlin." So suspicious had he become of the personnel in Bari that he filed the report of his last mission in Yugoslavia with Robert Murphy, American political adviser to the Supreme Allied commander, Mediterranean theater, rather than forwarding it through regular oss channels.[46] Many of the officers who were familiar with the situation in Bari at this time agree with Popovich's assessment. Moreover, there seems to be general consensus among them that Partisan influence began to grow significantly following the appointment of Maj. Francis Arnoldy as chief of the Yugoslav Desk in Bari.[47]

Paul Ceresole, head of the Cairo Desk in Washington, had recommended Arnoldy to Turner McBaine. In his mid-forties at the time he was assigned to Bari, Arnoldy had been born in France and as a young man moved to Russia with his family. He served in the Russian Army during the last two years of the war, after which he worked with the Inter-Allied Commission surveying and establishing borders in the Balkans. Ceresole noted that Arnoldy had spent the past few months in Washington living with the Soviet mission, with whom he was "very much persona grata" despite his earlier service in the Czar's army. Described by Ceresole as quiet, thoughtful, and extremely intelligent,

Arnoldy spoke fluent French, Bulgarian, and Russian, all of which seemed to qualify him eminently for his new assignment in Bari.[48]

According to Arnoldy's own report, he was assigned to Bari by McBaine, whom he describes as chief of si for the Middle East. Actually, McBaine was still in Bari at the time Arnoldy arrived and remained in charge of the base there until late December.[49] In any event, Arnoldy had not been in Bari long before he established contact with Tito's representative, Comdr. Sergei Makiedo, from whom he received permission to recruit Yugoslavs from camps in Italy for his work in Bari.[50]

Among the recruits selected by Arnoldy were twelve women, one of whom was Irene Parent, a young Partisan girl who proudly displayed the red star on her cap even while she worked in the major's office. An organizational chart of Arnoldy's section reveals that Parent had access to all si messages — incoming and outgoing — served as office file clerk, and was typist for the reports officer.[51] In short, Parent had access to more sensitive intelligence than most of the American officers attached to Arnoldy's section, including Capt. John Milodragovich, who was assistant chief of the si section. She not only saw reports that came in from the field, she also knew the attitude of the various officers assigned to operations with the Partisans. During the latter months of 1944, when Tito and members of his staff began to object strongly to the assignment of particular officers to Partisan units and to demand the withdrawal of others, little guesswork was involved in pinpointing those men whom the Partisans wanted out of Yugoslavia.[52]

On one occasion Parent pointedly asked Milodragovich which side he was on — meaning Tito's or Mihailovich's. Not satisfied with the captain's reply that as an American officer he could not take sides in such matters, Parent said, "If you are not with us, you are against us." Evidence suggests that she was quite capable of translating her words into action.

Lt. Joseph Veselinovich, one of the American officers who was withdrawn from Yugoslav operations at the request of the Partisans, filed a report with the chief of the Yugoslav Desk in Bari wherein he outlined the circumstances leading to his recall. He specifically identified Irene Parent and Lidia Medved as two individuals he suspected of playing a role in his being asked to leave the country, and accused both women of being 100% Communist." He contended that "the above people knew me and knew that I was cold to any Communist ideas and showed no liking for me because of that."[53]

Veselinovich's suspicions were probably well-founded. After Holt Green replaced Arnoldy as chief of Y-Section (Yugoslav Section) in early July, he advised the base commander at Bari that certain documents previously in Arnoldy's custody had been either "removed or destroyed." Green also noted that the only other person who had access to the files was Irene Parent, a member

Y-Section S.I.

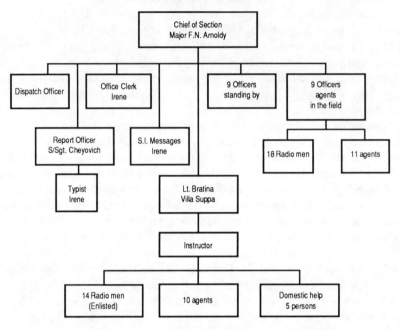

Source: RG-226, E. 165, B. 8, F. 80

of the Partisan movement, who, after Arnoldy's dismissal, had gone to work for the Partisan delegation in Bari.[54]

Rex Deane described Parent as an "ardent Partisan" who "had access to all files in Y-Section, Bari" and who also had the authority to pay the Yugoslav agents who were working for OSS. Deane later reported that while on a mission in Croatia in early 1945, he met a Captain Bogić who claimed to know Parent personally. Bogić told Deane that Parent had been shot by the Partisans because she was no longer of any use to them.[55] Arnoldy later claimed that he had hired Parent because she was fluent in several languages, including English, and could type. Assuming that this was true, one would have to conclude that given the politically charged atmosphere in Bari, Arnoldy exercised poor judgment indeed by placing someone known to be openly sympathetic to the Partisans in such a sensitive position. On the other hand, the major's record as chief of Y-Section would suggest that something more than bad judgment was required to explain some of his actions.

Arnoldy's own account of his work in Bari makes it abundantly clear that the officers who rated highest in his opinion were those who shared his affinities for the Partisan movement. He praised the work of men like Tofte, Huot, Thompson, Hamilton, and Farish but claimed that their efforts were hampered by other oss personnel whom he characterized as "Group B" men. According to Arnoldy, this group consisted of men who were "primarily interested in their own positions, their promotions, their ranks, comfort, safety and then in their work." He accused these men of supporting the "reactionary group in any country" when it was evident that the "national movement" in these various countries was achieving better results.[56]

Two men who obviously fell into the "Group B" category as far as Arnoldy was concerned were Robert Joyce and Edward J. Green. Arnoldy criticized Joyce, who transferred from Cairo to Bari in January, 1944, as chief of si, because Joyce had been associated with the Royal Yugoslav Government and later with the government-in-exile. Arnoldy contended that this former relationship prejudiced the work of oss in Yugoslavia and that the Partisans greatly resented it. In a report filed after he was dismissed as chief of Y-Section, Arnoldy said of Green that "his actions amount to a zero."[57]

Other officers who worked with Joyce and Green in Bari did not share these views. Most of them found the two men to be fair, impartial, and very capable officers who did not allow political bias to color their judgment or influence their decisions.[58] The same could not be said for Arnoldy. George Vujnovich, who was operations officer in Bari while Arnoldy was there, vividly recalls a strong disagreement between himself and the major concerning the reliability of field intelligence reports coming out of Yugoslavia. Arnoldy typically accepted at face value very favorable reports on the Partisans while dismissing equally favorable reports on the Chetniks. On one such occasion, when Vujnovich suggested rather forcefully that Arnoldy should judge all reports by the same standards, the major threatened him with a court martial but chose not to pursue the matter further.[59] Later, however, Arnoldy did recommend that Vujnovich "should be removed from this theater of operations at the earliest possible time."[60]

In the end it was not Vujnovich who was removed from the theater, but Arnoldy. On July 6, Edward J. Green called Arnoldy to his office and advised him that he had been ordered to report to Algiers. This was apparently the result of a request filed by Robert Joyce with Whitney Shepardson, the head of oss-si in Washington.[61] When Arnoldy later asked Joyce about the orders to report to Algiers, Joyce told him that he had not followed the policy of the State Department and that his actions were "definitely pro-Partisan." In a cable dated September 5, Algiers provided Donovan with a list of reasons for Arnoldy's dismissal, among them the belief that the major "was more Partisan than Tito and was really a Partisan representative in Bari."[62]

While Arnoldy may have provided one of the more blatant examples of political bias within the ranks of oss, he was certainly not alone in this regard.

Eugene W. deMoore, who was head of Y-Section (s1) in Cairo from February 15 to July 19, 1944, charged that personnel within the Research and Analysis section there were "leaning strongly towards communism and had openly declared so." He further indicated that some reports from the field were so politically biased that the British had evaluated them as "ridiculous, absurd, and comical."[63]

It was to be expected that oss field personnel would tend to identify with the particular resistance forces to which they were assigned, and in most cases they did. DeMoore was not complaining about the natural camaraderie that develops among men who share together the trauma and hardships of combat. Instead, he directed his criticisms at those whose admiration for the Partisans stemmed primarily from ideological rather than military considerations. Citing only one specific case to support his claim—a report from the head of ALUM mission, George Wuchinich, that he had delivered a speech to a Communist youth organization—deMoore maintained that this type of activity "epitomizes" the problem of "politics in the field."[64]

Wuchinich's political ideas were apparently well-known before he entered the country. In fact, some of the officers who knew him have charged flatly that he was a Communist. John Hamilton, as noted earlier, was another officer who did little to conceal his sympathy for the political program of the Partisan movement. Hamilton spent a good portion of his time between missions in Bari reading Communist literature and propaganda and passing it on to his fellow officers, including Popovich, encouraging them to read it as well.[65] Having already established his reputation as a movie actor, Hamilton undertook in May, 1944, what may have been his earliest attempt at directing. Working in conjunction with the Field Photographic Unit in Bari, he wrote the script and helped select the footage for a short film that was supposed to emphasize the role played by oss in aiding and supplying the Partisans.[66]

Edward J. Green, who knew of Hamilton and of his political views, advised oss headquarters in Caserta, "If, in his enthusiasm to portray the Partisan spirit, anything should be incorporated which might be of questionable nature, this can be deleted by the censors before the film is released."[67] Within eleven pages of script, Hamilton managed to describe the scope of "Allied" assistance to the Partisans in one sentence. He was somewhat more generous in his praise for the Partisan movement, which he attempted to equate with the American Revolution and which, in his words, had "given the world an unequalled example of self-sacrifice and an unconquerable will to smash the common enemy."[68] In short, Hamilton turned a film depicting the role of oss in aiding the Partisans into a propaganda film devoted almost entirely to extolling the virtues of the Partisan cause in Yugoslavia.

Arnoldy had praised Hamilton and other officers who shared his enthusiasm for the Partisans. This same group of men had also found favor with certain officers in the Research and Analysis offices in Cairo and Bari—a fact that may have contributed to deMoore's criticism.[69] In December, 1943, for example, while Operation AUDREY was still in progress, Stuart Hughes, Harvard historian and analyst for the R & A section in Algiers, wrote to Robert Wolff, chief of the Balkan section of R & A in Washington, to advise that shortly after the supply line had been established, "the theatre command was brought over to the pro-Partisan point of view." Huot's removal had complicated matters, and though Hughes was not sure as to the cause for that action, he ventured a guess that it might stem from "the organization back-tracking a bit from Huot's violently pro-Partisan stand." The last part of his message had the familiar ring of Basil Davidson's self-congratulatory exclamation concerning the victory of the "Cairo Partisans" in the spring of 1943. Hughes told Wolff, "The whole development over here has been a striking vindication of the line on Yugoslav affairs you have been taking all along. We all feel that you are to be congratulated and that your consistent effort to present the Partisan case has been instrumental in bringing around the authorities to this point of view."[70]

Another R & A officer, Wayne Vuchinich, who served in the Bari office, wrote to Hughes and Wolff in June, 1944, complaining about the caliber of agents OSS was sending to the Partisans. Denouncing as "an insult to the intelligence of the Yugoslavs" the dispatch of "untrained, uneducated, and frequently unsympathetic men," he indicated that with the exception of Farish, Thompson, Hamilton, and Huot, "the Partisans did not care for any of our agents in the field."[71]

Partisan likes and dislikes were not the best criteria by which to evaluate the effectiveness or objectivity of agents in the field, and any inclination by R & A personnel to do so suggested the existence of a major flaw in the process by which intelligence from the field was analyzed. Especially in Bari, officers who were either critical of the Partisans or sympathetic to the Chetniks ultimately came to feel that their views were not being given fair treatment by R & A personnel, all of whom they regarded as pro-Partisan, if not pro-Communist.[72]

The views expressed in a report by Alexander Vuchinich, also a member of the R & A section in Bari and brother to Wayne, suggest that these suspicions were not altogether without foundation. In the spring of 1943, Vuchinich called for a reexamination of the "Mihailovich Myth," charging that the Chetniks, "led by Mihailovich, have joined the Axis and are fighting for the Axis cause." On the other hand, he claimed, the Partisans, "representing a coalition of groups belonging to various democratic parties," were the only forces actively resisting the Axis presence in Yugoslavia. Comparing Mihailovich to Adm. Francois Darlan of the Vichy regime, Vuchinich wrote, "Mihailovich is not a Darlan, he is worse than the French admiral. Darlan had worked for the Germans and then turned to help the Allies. Mihailovich, who enjoys the blessings of the Yugoslav Government in London, worked for the Allied cause and then turned to help the Axis."[73]

Lieutenant Colonel McDowell, following a visit to Bari during which he had extensive conversations with Joyce and Weil, filed a report in which he charged that "the Research and Analysis section of oss here is controlled by two Americans of Yugoslav origin who are frankly and outspokenly pro-Partisan."[74] McDowell also claimed that on another occasion, after he had submitted a report to his superior that revealed numerous errors in Partisan communiqués, he was told, "Never mind the inaccuracies, the important thing is that we've got to put over Tito."[75] McDowell did not identify the officer who made this statement, though certainly that officer placed a greater value on candor than on discretion. There was after all a sizable group of officers associated with Yugoslav operations, McDowell among them, who did not wish to see Tito placed in power under any circumstances, much less through the influence of a clique of well-placed individuals willing to use their position to advocate such a policy.

It is most interesting to note that when McDowell returned from Mihailo-vich's headquarters in late 1944 and submitted his report, an analyst within the R & A Branch challenged portions of the document on the grounds that its author was a "revisionist historian of pro-German sympathies." Ironically, McDowell described himself as a "lifelong liberal" and was at times labeled "a pink or Communist" by those who knew him. Obviously, the R & A analyst, who chose to remain anonymous, found it more expedient to discredit Mc-Dowell than to subject his report to a fair evaluation.[76]

Joseph Veselinovich was among those officers who, though they served with the Partisans, opposed Tito and his movement – at least the political aspects of it. Based on his personal observations while in Bari and experiences while in the field, Veselinovich filed a report with the chief of Y-Section in Bari that gave succinct expression to the frustrations and suspicions experienced by most, if not all, of those officers in oss who shared his views. In that report, dated February 19, 1945, Veselinovich charged that personnel in the Y-Section of oss-Bari were routinely passing information to the Partisans concerning ongoing intelligence operations in Yugoslavia. He added, "Many things have occurred in the Y Section which leads me to believe that the interests of those American officers are not wholly for the best interest of America but tend to promote communistic propaganda to the extent that their personal feelings, aspirations, and interests are placed before the interests of our nation."[77]

While it is not unheard of for the losing side in any contest to cry foul or attribute its defeat to treachery on the part of its opponents, those claims, at least in this case, have a certain degree of validity. Individuals known to be sympathetic to the Partisans analyzed all intelligence relating to Yugoslavia that passed through R & A channels from Bari through Cairo and ultimately to Washington. Whatever the real impact of this situation may have been, the perception was that these various R & A sections had become so politicized as to render them incapable of fulfilling the purpose for which they were created—specifically, the collection and objective analysis of field intelligence.

Given these conditions, one might better understand Popovich's decision to file his last report through State Department channels or Musulin's reluctance to write a report at all. Indeed, by the time Musulin returned to Bari in May, 1944, the Allies had abandoned Mihailovich and committed themselves to supporting Tito, whose grip on the country was, according to most accepted intelligence reports at least, virtually unbreakable. Events would soon show just how tenuous that grip was and in so doing would cast doubt on the judgment of those who had consistently presented such an optimistic appraisal of Partisan strength.

On the morning of May 25, some elements from German air and ground forces participating in the Axis Seventh Offensive—code named Rösselsprung or Knight's Move—initiated an operation aimed at capturing Tito and his staff near the village of Drvar in Bosnia. In this instance Ultra provided a vague hint that the Germans were preparing an operation of some kind but offered no conclusive evidence that the objective of the undertaking was Tito's headquarters.[78] Lacking a clear picture of German intentions, the British chose not to issue an advance warning to their mission at Drvar for fear of arousing German suspicions as to the security of their Enigma codes.[79] Actually, Lt. Col. Vivian Street, acting head of the mission in Maclean's absence, recommended moving the headquarters into the hills outside Drvar after noticing an increase in German reconnaissance flights over the area.[80] This precautionary measure, timely though it was, proved barely sufficient when German paratroops and glider-born forces, some of whom landed only three hundred to four hundred yards from the mission, began their assault.[81]

Tito, his staff, and members of the various Allied missions, with less than a thousand troops available to hold off the Germans, had precious little time to effect their escape. Fleeing into the hills in small groups, they left the Germans with little to show for their efforts except Tito's uniform, which was later put on display in the Military Museum in Vienna.[82] Over the next few days, Tito's party, with no supplies except what could be dropped to them by air, found itself locked in a deadly race with pursuing German forces that had been reinforced following the attack on Drvar. Street, who had somehow managed to salvage his radio set, established contact with British authorities in Bari, informed them of the desperate circumstances he and the others were in, and requested immediate evacuation.[83]

At this point Tito and those with him were almost totally dependent on Allied air strikes to keep the Germans at bay long enough to find and secure a suitable landing zone from which to be evacuated. From May 25 to May 31, the Mediterranean Allied Air Force (M A A F) flew approximately one thousand sorties against enemy troop concentrations and supply dumps in addition to continuing its air supply operations to the Partisans. On May 29, General Wilson informed the British Chiefs of Staff that in the aftermath of the Drvar attack "maximum air support was being given and all targets asked for by Tito have been attacked."[84] According to Deakin, the air support given to Tito's forces, particularly during the week immediately following the attack, was "decisive."[85] Still, by June 1, the Germans had nearly succeeded in cornering their elusive prey in the Prekaja Mountains southeast of Drvar.[86]

With Tito's fate hanging precariously in the balance, Allied planners in Bari hastily prepared a large-scale operation in the islands off the coast of Yugoslavia in an attempt to relieve some of the pressure from the beleaguered Partisan leader. Capt. Robert Houlihan, whose Operational Group (o G) of 140 men was part of the four-thousand-man force assembled for this operation, vividly recalls the sense of urgency that accompanied preparations for the attack. It would be some time later before he would learn the reason behind this undertaking, but he knew that it was the largest operation in which the o Gs had participated. There was one other difference—a rather troublesome one to those in the assault craft who were conspicuously making their way across the moonlit waters of the Adriatic on the evening of June 2. According to Houlihan, "Most of our operations were done in the dark of the moon, but this one was done in moonlight and I'll never forget us seeing these ships approaching the island of Brač. In the middle of the night, in the moonlight, you could see them all, see the island, see the roads and the beaches."[87]

By June 4, Operation F L O U N C E D had been completed and the forces involved in the attack had begun to evacuate to the island of Vis. The American o Gs, among the last to be withdrawn, suffered only one casualty in the fighting, the brunt of which had been borne by the Partisans.[88] It is difficult to say to what degree the Brač operation may have contributed to Tito's escape. However, it should be noted that he and most of the Allied personnel traveling with him managed to slip through the German lines on the evening of June 3 and make their way to Kupresko Polje, from which they evacuated late that same night.[89]

Tito, Street, and members of the Soviet mission were the first to be evacuated by a Soviet plane—actually an American DC-3 made available to the Soviets through the Lend-Lease program—which had taken off from Bari, without orders, in advance of the other aircraft. American C-47s also based in Bari evacuated other Allied personnel. In fact, evacuation operations continued until the evening of June 5–6, when the last of the Partisan wounded were picked up just hours before German forces captured the landing strip.[90]

The picture of Tito being routed from his headquarters and unceremoniously chased around the countryside by a relatively small German force appeared inconsistent with intelligence reports that as early as September, 1943, had credited the Partisans with dominating most of Yugoslavia. Indeed, Tito might well have been captured and his movement seriously jeopardized or destroyed had the Allies not provided an air umbrella that protected and sustained his hard-pressed troops until the force of the German offensive was spent. The Partisans thus survived the last major German effort to crush them, and Tito escaped, temporarily at least, from the hazards of the battlefield to the more sedate, if no less treacherous, world of high diplomacy.

The attack on Drvar also set off a new round of charges concerning the manipulation and/or misuse of intelligence information for political purposes. On this occasion, however, the accusing finger pointed at those regarded as supporters of General Mihailovich. On June 12, the British Chiefs of Staff wired Middle East Headquarters: "We have received information via SOE sources that prior to recent attack on Tito's headquarters, information of location of headquarters obtained by Colonel Knezevich cabled by him to representative in Cairo. . . . Request you investigate possibility of leakage of information from M's representative in Cairo to the enemy."[91]

The Joint Staff mission in Washington also received this message and replied later the same day that "we have no evidence that there has been a leakage concerning Tito's present whereabouts."[92] A partial investigation conducted by OSS officials in Washington suggested the possibility, at least, that information concerning the location of Tito's headquarters might have been passed to the Germans, but no one was ever formally charged with having done so. Within OSS, Lt. Col. Oliver Sands, deputy director of Intelligence Services, became a primary suspect because of his known sympathies for Mihailovich and his close association with officials in the Royal Yugoslav Embassy who were strong supporters of the general. Although Sands was subsequently cleared of any wrongdoing, doubts lingered for some time concerning the activities of certain embassy personnel.[93]

Assuming the Germans did receive secret intelligence informing them about Tito's location, it had very little, if anything, to do with the near success of their attack on Drvar. British intelligence knew from reading the Ultra traffic that the Germans routinely reported on the location of Partisan formations, their receipt of Allied supply drops, and even the nature of the signals by which they would identify themselves to Allied pilots. One intercept dated December 27, 1943, for example, clearly indicated that the Germans knew of Tito's dropping zones at Gugonjo, Mliniste, Petrovac, and Drvar. Furthermore, an intercept of December 14 repeated details of a planned supply drop which had been sent to Partisan units near Kolašin on the previous day.[94] While the possibility of a security breach within OSS was not a trivial matter, it is most likely that any information that may have been passed to the Germans merely confirmed what their own intelligence sources had told them.

Whatever else the German action at Drvar may have accomplished, it resulted in an unexpected opportunity for the British to have direct discussions with Tito about Yugoslavia's political future. Harold Macmillan echoed the sentiments of many of his colleagues when he suggested that Tito's presence in Italy might be helpful "because it should increase our hold over him."[95] The British seemed to be holding a winning hand at this point, but Ivan Šubašić, the newly appointed Yugoslav prime minister, was obviously not the man to play it. His first meeting with Tito on the island of Vis in mid-June resulted in Tito's consenting to the formation of a united government consisting of members of the government-in-exile and his own National Liberation Committee. Tito refused, however, to commit himself to supporting a return of the monarchy, arguing that that question should be decided by the Yugoslav people after the war. Šubašić agreed to recognize the program adopted by the AVNOJ in November, 1943, and to assist in organizing support for Partisan military efforts inside the country.[96]

In Washington, Secretary of State Hull criticized the Tito-Šubašić accord, characterizing it as "essentially an arrangement between the British and Tito" that represented an almost unconditional acceptance of Partisan demands. Hull further denounced the agreement for excluding Serbian interests and, as noted earlier, insisted that the State Department would not agree to withhold supplies from Mihailovich while supporting Tito's movement into Serbia.[97]

Having urged support for Tito on military grounds, Churchill decided that he would fly to Italy, meet Tito face-to-face, and confront the Partisan leader with Allied concerns over his employment of Allied military aid for political purposes. Not surprisingly, Tito denied any intention to impose communism on Yugoslavia by force and reminded Churchill that he had publicly stated his position on this question on more than one occasion. As well as anyone and perhaps better than most, Churchill knew the current market value of public statements and found very little comfort in Tito's assurances.[98]

The prime minister returned to London visibly distraught over his meeting with Tito and sent a note to Anthony Eden lamenting "our responsibility for supplying Tito with arms with which he could subjugate Yugoslavia." Eden, who felt that Churchill had disregarded his advice on Yugoslavia for many months, pointed out in a note to the Foreign Office that "the Prime Minister had indeed persistently championed Tito despite our warnings."[99]

Churchill had good cause to be pessimistic. The Tito-Šubašić agreement, though "made between two Jugoslav parties which at that moment could literally not have eaten one meal except by the grace of H.M.G. [His Majesty's Gov-

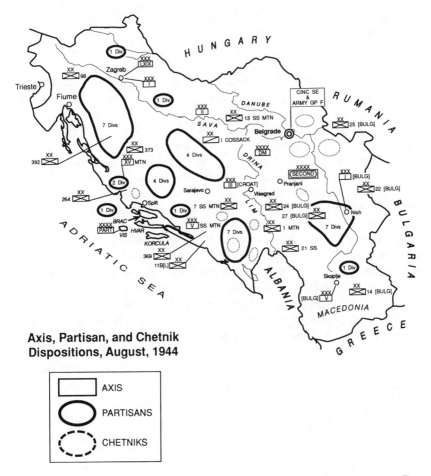

**Axis, Partisan, and Chetnik
Dispositions, August, 1944**

- AXIS
- PARTISANS
- CHETNIKS

Source: *German Anti-Guerrila Operations in the Balkans, 1941–1944.* Department of the Army Pamphlet, August, 1954. Composite drawing prepared by Greg Taylor.

ernment]," offered little hope that the prime minister's goal of restoring the monarchy after the war would be achieved.[100]

While it is true that Tito had been forced to negotiate under less than favorable circumstances, he was not exactly without influence at the bargaining table. With Germany's defeat virtually assured, her forces would soon be compelled to withdraw from Yugoslavia. The Partisans, though temporarily on the defensive, remained a significant military force with both the capability and determination to fill the void created by the German withdrawal. Lastly, having been accorded recognition by the Big Three as the only resistance force in Yugo-slavia and generously supplied by the United States and Britain, Tito's well-armed Partisans were sufficiently prepared to eliminate their chief internal rivals, the Chetniks, when the time came.

With Soviet and British missions accredited to his headquarters, Tito also learned prior to his meeting with Churchill that the United States was at last prepared to dispatch its own independent mission into the country. Donovan met with Tito on August 11 and introduced him to Col. Ellery Huntington, newly appointed head of the Independent American Military Mission (IAMM) to Partisan headquarters, then situated on the island of Vis.[101] Huntington, who had been an All-American quarterback at Colgate, had known Donovan during their law school days at Columbia. He also served in France during World War I and, like Donovan, had returned to practice law in New York City. Prior to being named head of the IAMM he had served in Washington, briefly succeeding Col. Preston Goodfellow as chief of Special Operations, and later in Italy.[102]

The Joint Chiefs of Staff (JCS) order of June 9 approving the IAMM stipu-lated that all American personnel then assigned to Maclean would be trans-ferred to Huntington's command. Huntington would have authority to approve all additional personnel assigned to him and would be advised of all OSS per-sonnel operating outside his command.[103] Huntington took very seriously the prerogative of selecting his own personnel and so informed Colonel Toulmin after Toulmin had deigned to recommend an executive officer for the mission. Taken aback by the vehemence of Huntington's protest, Toulmin responded, "God knows I am not (and was not) trying to saddle you with anything you don't want. . . . I personally wish you would not be so touchy – we are all friends in the same cause."[104]

There were a number of compelling reasons for OSS to have an independent mission at Tito's headquarters, not least of which was the persistent demands of the Partisans themselves for such representation.[105] Maclean had continued to represent American interests at Partisan headquarters after Weil's departure, but this had become an undesirable situation for two reasons. First, OSS found itself almost totally dependent on Maclean for intelligence, the accuracy of which was suspect because of "political bias and personal ambition." Appar-ently some British military authorities shared these suspicions and had en-couraged the Americans to establish a mission with Tito to, among other things, "provide a check on McLean's [sic] reports."[106] Secondly, Donovan saw the establishment of an independent mission as the best means of divorcing OSS from British political policy, the implementation of which, he believed, rested primarily with Brigadier Maclean.

Robert Joyce confirmed these views when he informed Donovan that Brit-ain was advocating "all-out support for Tito" despite disagreement from cer-

Leaders of the Partisan movement in Macedonia: Gen. Mihailo Apostol-
ski, seated at center of table, and "Tempo" Svetozar Vukmanovic to right
of star. Courtesy Steven Bizic

tain members of the Foreign Office and "many British liaison officers who had served in Yugoslavia." Joyce concluded that "England has placed its bets on Tito and will do all possible to see he comes out on top."[107]

Donovan emphasized to Huntington that the United States expected the people of Yugoslavia to work for their own liberation and that oss would support their efforts with all possible military assistance. Noting that Britain and the Soviet Union might have political interests in the Balkans that the United States could not support, Donovan stressed that there was to be no separate American "policy" insofar as the prosecution of the war was concerned.[108] Thus briefed, Huntington prepared to move his mission to Vis, where the team's new headquarters had been selected and prepared by an advance party consisting of Lt. Timothy Pfeiffer, Sgt. Walter Muselin, and Pvt. Louis Freund.[109] The arrival of the IAMM on Vis in mid-August meant that oss was once again in step with its British and Soviet counterparts, or so it seemed.

6. Their Return Overrides All Objections

High above the rugged snow-covered terrain of southern Serbia, the crew of a crippled B-17 returning from a raid on the marshaling yards in Sofia, Bulgaria, had to abandon its aircraft. Among those who bailed out of the plane was Sgt. Gus T. Brown, a twenty-one-year-old flight engineer from Luling, Texas. Drifting beneath the canopy of his open parachute, Brown knew that in a matter of minutes he would be in enemy-occupied territory. Once on the ground he would have to avoid the Germans and Bulgars while attempting to establish contact with friendly forces, and it was not at all clear as to what groups might be regarded as friendly. He recalled the warning of the briefing officer that hostile resistance elements were operating within Yugoslavia and therefore every effort should be made to contact Partisan forces. The officer had explicitly warned that the forces of General Mihailovich were not considered friendly. Brown remembered Mihailovich's name from a film he had seen in 1941 that portrayed the Chetnik leader in a very favorable light, but apparently many things had changed since then.[1]

Landing in a waist-deep snow drift on the side of a mountain, Brown quickly buried his chute and went in search of other members of his crew. He found only Richard Hobby, and with darkness closing in the two men decided to make their way into the trees on the side of the mountain. They would spend the night there and continue their search in the morning. At approximately ten o'clock that evening, Brown and Hobby saw what appeared to be a German patrol coming down the mountain toward them. Although the men were carrying lanterns, they did not see the two airmen huddled behind a snowbank only thirty feet away. As the patrol moved on, Brown and Hobby discussed their situation and decided that they must either surrender or face the prospect of freezing to death. At that point Brown "saw a light across the valley and started yoo-hooing and heard an answer. Someone called 'Amerikano?' we turned and said 'yes' and they hollered back 'Chetniks.' They came running down toward us and we hollered with joy, so they started kissing us and we started kissing them, beard and all."[2]

While Brown and his crew may have been the first American airmen to fall into Chetnik hands, many such meetings took place in Yugoslavia during 1944 and early 1945. From the Bulgarian border in the east to the Adriatic coast in the west, Mihailovich's bands scoured the countryside in search of Allied airmen who had been forced down in their territory, provided constant protection for them, and played a vital role in their safe evacuation. To many of the airmen the treatment they received at the hands of the Chetniks was a pleasant surprise since they, like Brown, had been advised that Mihailovich's forces were hostile to Americans.[3]

Richard Felman first learned during a predawn briefing before a raid on Ploesti in early July that Mihailovich was "no longer the guerrilla darling of the free world." The briefing officer told the men that if they went down in Yugoslavia they should look for "the guerrilla fighter with the red star on his hat" and avoid the Chetniks, who, on the basis of recent intelligence reports, were cutting off the ears of downed American airmen and turning them over to the Germans.[4]

Prior to the Ploesti mission Felman and the crew of "Never a Dull Moment" had flown twenty-three missions against different targets in southern Europe, and after the last of these missions had counted 212 flak holes in their ship. The men had joked about their apparent invincibility, but on this particular morning there was noticeable anxiety among the crew. Ploesti was one of the most heavily defended targets in Europe, and for those crews which survived the attack there was the prospect of returning to base over enemy-occupied territory wherein there allegedly operated guerrilla bands with an affinity for collecting ears. All things considered, there was very little to be jocular about as the plane rumbled down the runway at five-thirty in the morning with Ploesti as its destination.[5]

None of the crew could have known it then, but once her wheels lifted off the ground, "Never a Dull Moment" was airborne for the last time. She took a tremendous pounding over the target area, and the crew had to abandon her over Yugoslavia. Felman had time to reflect on his dilemma as he floated toward an open field below. Once on the ground he immediately tried to get out of his harness, only then discovering that he had been hit and could not move his leg. Then he realized that he was "surrounded—by about 20 peasants, men, women, and children. The bearded men kissed me. The women and children kept an awed distance. No red stars. Chetniks! Instinctively the words of the briefing officer came to mind. I reached for my ears to protect them. They didn't want my ears. They raised me up on their shoulders and carried me about 500 yards to a group of three cabins and laid me comfortably in a small room."[6]

O ss authorities in Bari knew as early as February, 1944, that Chetnik forces were holding some American airmen for evacuation. Mihailovich had told Musulin in late January during the Saint Sava Congress that some American airmen had been picked up by Chetnik forces – possibly Brown and his crew-mates. Musulin relayed the information to Bari, along with a request that he be allowed to remain in the country to assist in the evacuation of those and other fliers who might fall into Chetnik hands. Musulin's request arrived while the British were clamoring for a complete break with Mihailovich and gave Roosevelt a legitimate basis for maintaining at least a token o ss presence in Chetnik territory had he been inclined to take it. Unfortunately, the president chose not to do so, and Musulin eventually evacuated in May. Thus, o ss was unable to provide independent intelligence reports on events in Serbia, and American airmen in the area were left with no immediate prospect of evacuation.

As the number of American personnel in Chetnik hands grew with each passing week, it became increasingly difficult for the United States to make no effort to effect their evacuation, whatever the British might say. Farish, who was involved in the evacuation of airmen from Partisan territory, stated the case rather well when he informed Bari that "if internal conflict and political matters prevent the evacuation of our personnel, our war effort will be impeded. Our airmen might as well be prisoners or hostages."[7] In much the same vein, Frederick T. Merrill, a Foreign Service officer on the staff of Robert Murphy, wrote to his superior on June 20, 1944, that if the value of each crew were considered in nothing more than "crude dollars and cents terms," their worth was about $250,000 and that alone would justify their return. Merrill continued, "I conclude and Norden concurs – the lives of American airmen and the military advantage to be gained by their recovery overrides any objections the British might have on political grounds."[8]

Musulin, who after his return to Bari had continued to insist that American airmen in Chetnik territory were due the same consideration as those who happened to go down in Partisan areas, had the opportunity to meet with Farish and Popovich to consider how this problem might be resolved. Nelson Deranian, chief of s o-Bari, sat in on these discussions, which resulted in a general agreement that the United States could not, for the sake of any political understanding with the British, allow its airmen to remain indefinitely in Yugoslavia without making some attempt to evacuate them. Shortly after these discussions, o ss representatives arranged a conference with Gen. Nathan Twining, commanding general of the Fifteenth Air Force, at which Musulin and Farish reiterated their position.[9] The efforts of Musulin, Farish, Popovich, and Deranian bore fruit when on July 14, 1944, Lt. Gen. Ira Eaker, commander of the Mediterranean Allied Air Force (M A A F), signed the order creating the Air Crew Rescue Unit under the command of Col. George Kraigher.[10]

The A C R U was established as an independent American unit under M A A F and attached to the Fifteenth Air Force in an attempt to separate it from the intelligence-gathering and special-operations functions of OSS. Charged with the responsibility of locating and evacuating airmen throughout the Balkans, ACRU initially had two B-25s at its disposal but could, when circumstances required, call upon either BAF or Fifteenth Air Force for additional aircraft.[11] The men best suited by training and experience to carry out the task assigned to ACRU were OSS agents, who were familiar with the Balkan countries to which they had been assigned and the various resistance elements operating in those countries. In fact, rather than having its own separate communications link, ACRU simply used OSS communications at Bari.[12]

As expected, the British did object to the dispatch of OSS personnel to Mihailovich's forces, viewing the ACRU as a thinly veiled attempt by Donovan to reestablish an American presence at Chetnik headquarters. Their suspicions were not altogether unfounded, but in supposing that Donovan would be content to slip only an ACRU into Serbia now that the door had been wedged open, the British woefully underestimated the resourcefulness and persistence of their American colleague in secret warfare.

Only five days after the ACRU came into existence, Donovan informed Toulmin and Green that Mihailovich had contacted the Yugoslav Embassy in Washington advising authorities there that approximately one hundred American airmen were under the protection of his forces and were awaiting evacuation at the earliest possible time. Donovan then added an urgent admonition: "You are requested, therefore, to act on this soonest, using this chance as a means of establish [sic] a clandestine intelligence team in Yugoslavia. In order that our colleagues may not take advantage of our present position, you must act soonest. Mihailovich has offered us the use of the radio facilities he has with the Embassy in Washington, but unless you cannot otherwise reach him, I would rather not use them."[13]

Thus was planted the seed that would be nurtured in strictest secrecy and in time germinate as the RANGER Mission under Lt. Col. Robert McDowell. For the present, however, OSS officials in Bari were putting together the first ACRU team that would be dropped into Serbia to assist in evacuating the airmen to whom Donovan had alluded. Obviously, George Musulin was the logical choice to head the mission, code-named HALYARD. He was known and respected at Mihailovich's headquarters, had been the last American officer to return from Chetnik territory, and, as Deranian suggested, possessed "the rugged character required to meet the hardships involved."[14] M/Sgt. Michael Rajacich, borrowed from SI for this particular assignment, and Arthur Jibilian, the mission's radio operator, rounded out Musulin's team. Jibilian had earned the reputation for being a very effective radioman, having served with Farish and Popovich during their last mission into Yugoslavia between April and June, 1944.[15]

Since HALYARD technically functioned as an SO team on loan to Fifteenth Air Force as ACRU-I, Musulin received his orders from Lieutenant Commander Green, who specifically enjoined the members of the unit from making "any military or political commitments on behalf of the United States of America or other Allied nation, or to make any commitments or promises for the furnishing of supplies or other material aid to any political or military group."[16] Thus advised, Musulin and his team began making preparations for entering Yugoslavia – an undertaking greatly complicated by an undependable radio link with Mihailovich and British obduracy.

Without direct radio contact with Chetnik headquarters, the HALYARD team would have to make a "blind drop" near the area where the airmen were being held. Musulin and his team were prepared to assume this risk, but the British succeeded in reestablishing contact with Mihailovich through the Villa Resta link – the code name given to all of Mihailovich's messages sent in the code Hudson had provided in late 1941. Having revived Villa Resta, the British advised Mihailovich of plans to send in the HALYARD team and received confirmation, presumably from Chetnik headquarters, that his forces would stand by to receive the mission at Čemerno Planina between July 15 and July 20.[17] On the basis of information provided in this message about ground signals and confirmation signals from the plane, Musulin's party made its first attempt to enter the country on the night of July 19–20. This initial sortie proved unsuccessful, however, when no ground signals were observed over the drop zone.[18]

Subsequent events served to convince Musulin that the British were engaging in a bit of sabotage of their own in an effort to prevent his team from reaching Mihailovich's headquarters. Having experienced one failure because the pilot had received the wrong coordinates for the drop, Musulin, on his fourth attempt, asked the pilot to give him the coordinates for the mission. When the pilot read out the position, an astonished and angry Musulin replied that his men were not going to be dropped at that location since it was in Partisan territory. When he asked the pilot about his briefing, the latter indicated that he had been briefed by BAF personnel who were, of course, under British command. Then to make matters worse, Musulin noticed a Partisan soldier sitting in the back of the plane and asked the pilot why he was going on the mission. When the Britisher responded that he was to act as the mission's dispatcher, Musulin, never one to mince words whether angry or not, told the pilot that "no son of a bitch of a communist" was going to push him and his men out of any plane and then aborted the mission on his own authority.[19]

While Musulin and his team were becoming increasingly frustrated at their inability to get into Yugoslavia, the airmen who were waiting at Pranjani airfield for the arrival of the promised rescue unit were growing very apprehensive about their chances of getting out of the country. Finally in late July a group of the airmen received permission from Mihailovich to use a field radio station in an attempt to establish direct contact with Bari. With no codes to use, the airmen had to broadcast in the clear, greatly increasing the possibility that the Germans might intercept their messages and use the transmissions to pinpoint their location. However, it seemed likely that an extended stay in the same area might produce the same result. Accordingly, Lt. T. K. Oliver, operating under the call letters "TKO," sent the following message to Italy on July 26: "(1) Mudcat Driver to CO, APO 520 (2) 150 Yanks are in Yugo (3) Shoot us workhorses. Ask British about job. (4) Our challenge first letter of bombardiers name, color of Banana Nose Benigos Scarf. (5) Your verification last letter of Chief Lugs name color of fist on club wall. (6) Must refer to Shark SQDN 459 Gp for decoding. (7) TKO 0-25855 Flat Rat 5 in lug order."[20]

Oliver's own explanation of the code is as follows:

(1) My airplane was named the Fighting Mudcat. APO 520 was the 15th Air Force in Italy. (2) The Germans knew this. The 15th Air Force did not; so I felt it was just as well to come right out with it. (3) The workhorse of World War II was the C-47, of course. (4) The first letter of my bombardier's name would be known to the 15th Air Force, but not to the Germans, "Banana Nose" Benigno was a pilot in our squadron who always wore a white scarf. (5) Col. Munn, who commanded our group at one time wrote on the wall of our officer's club in Italy, "All lugs in the 459th Group sign here. M. M. Munn, Chief Lug." Considerably further down the list I signed myself as Thomas K. Oliver, Flat Rat 5. There was a red mailed fist painted on the club wall. (6) My squadron had painted shark's teeth and mouths on our B-24's (7) My initials, serial number, and reference to the writing on the officer's club were an attempt to prove authenticity.[21]

Assuming that air force personnel in Italy would soon confirm the information provided by "TKO," Oliver and his colleagues next had to find a way to advise their base as to their location without giving themselves away to the Germans. This they did by sending the names of three of the airmen to Italy along with a series of numbers which, when subtracted from the serial numbers of the identified fliers, provided the coordinates as well as the confirmation signals to be flashed from ground to air when the rescue party arrived. This message was received in Italy at approximately four-thirty in the afternoon of August 2 and once decoded was sent to Bari where the HALYARD team was impatiently waiting for another chance to get into the country.[22] Having been on virtual standby since the unit was activated, Musulin and his men responded quickly to this new information from Fifteenth Air Force and, shortly after midnight on August 3, found themselves descending over the target area where a large party of American airmen anxiously awaited their arrival.[23]

Richard Felman, who was at Pranjani, recalls the scene when the mission actually arrived at the airfield: "The one who was in the lead was the center of a mob of Chetniks – they were kissing him and cheering him with tears in their eyes. He was in an American uniform and was one of the biggest chaps I'd ever seen. He walked over to us and put out his hand. 'I'm George Musulin,' he said."[24]

After the mission personnel collected their personal equipment and the medical supplies that had been dropped with them, Musulin arranged a meeting with a committee of the airmen to discuss the preparations that would need to be made before evacuation could take place. He discovered that there were approximately 250 airmen divided into six groups and housed within a ten-mile radius of the airstrip. Musulin established a courier service between the mission and the various groups in order to provide daily news on the progress being made toward evacuation. He also distributed funds to enable the airmen to purchase needed supplies. At the same time General Mihailovich assigned the First Ravna Gora Corps to provide security for the operation.[25]

The most critical problem facing the HALYARD team was lack of an adequate airstrip to accommodate the air force's C-47s. Employing three hundred laborers and some sixty ox carts, Musulin had the landing strip widened to 75 yards and lengthened to 630 yards – barely sufficient for aircraft that would be loaded with airmen when taking off. Better airstrips were found but were some fourteen hours walking distance away – an impossible trip for many of the airmen who were either sick or wounded. Thus Pranjani, with all of its shortcomings, offered the best chance of success.

By August 8, work on the airstrip had been completed and Jibilian notified Bari: "Pranjane Field Improved for Night Evac. Ruts Filled, Strip in Good Condition, Surface hard but not rough. . . . Inform if planes will come on ninth and how many also ETA . . . Will be prepared to receive as many planes as you wish to send."[26]

Bari responded that same day, advising Musulin that the evacuation would begin on "nine August and continue each successive night until completed. Expect eight planes each night first of which to arrive approximately 2000 hours Greenwich." Bari also recommended that Musulin prepare for a daylight evacuation "on short notice – if it becomes necessary."[27] Bari feared, as did Musulin, that the increase in activity around Pranjani and the evacuation itself, once underway, might prompt a response from the Germans that could jeopardize the entire operation. Those fears appeared to be well-founded when, on the afternoon of the ninth, three German planes unexpectedly appeared over the area – one returning for a second look. Although no German action resulted from this reconnaissance, it definitely increased the tension and anxiety of those assembled around the Pranjani airstrip that night hoping that the first sound of approaching aircraft they would hear would be the familiar roar of the C-47.

Although the experience of each airman was unique, most would have agreed with John E. Scroggs, who would later reflect on the relationship that existed between the airmen and their Chetnik protectors:

It is of profound significance to realize that, although these people had never seen us before, and they had little in the way of material possessions, they enthusiastically placed everything they owned at our disposal. They attended us hand and foot. Damn few Americans would do that. I felt quite sorry for myself one night sleeping on a blanket over a dirt floor in a hut, until I awakened to see the peasant father, mother, and little kids curled up in a goat pen outside.[28]

Although the overwhelming majority of airmen evacuated from Mihailovich's territory had nothing but praise for his Chetniks, there were, as with the Partisans, a few exceptions. Second Lieutenant Raymond Smith, whose plane went down about one hundred miles north of Banja Luka, Serbia, reported that he suffered a broken ankle after bailing out of his aircraft and received no medical treatment at all during a week-long stay with the Chetniks. After joining the Partisans, however, he received immediate attention.[29] First Lieutenant Lewis M. Perkins, who, with the rest of his crew, bailed out approximately ten miles west of Podgorica, reported a more serious case of mistreatment. According to Perkins, he and his men were shot at during their descent, presumably by Chetniks since they appeared to be the only people in the area. These forces picked his crew up on July 28 and, from then until September 15, made no attempt to evacuate them from the country or even to move them to an evacuation site. On September 15 the airmen joined Partisan forces and were evacuated in less than ten days.[30]

Cases such as these were obviously the exceptions—a fact borne out by the Escape and Evasion reports of the returning airmen as well as by the testimony some of them gave before the commission of inquiry in New York after the war. One such airman was Robert N. Vlachos, who was with the Chetniks for just over two months after his plane went down south of Belgrade on June 2, 1944. He told the commission that "having spoken with men who had been rescued by the Partisans and the Chetniks," he had concluded that "by far the better treatment had been received at the hands of the Chetniks."[31]

In many instances American airmen found themselves indebted to the Chetniks for considerably more than hospitable treatment. When Lt. Merrill Walker and his crew crash-landed in the hills roughly forty miles south of Belgrade on June 6, their plane attracted a German and a Chetnik patrol, leaving the Americans in the middle of a small but fierce skirmish. Although under fire, Lt. Bora Kacarević and two of his men crawled to the plane and began hacking away at the side with an axe to make an opening. Inside the plane the Americans had no way of knowing what was happening and naturally feared the worst. They were greatly relieved that "the first head through the door belonged to a small man with a big beard and bulging eyes whose chatter and gestures made no sense to the Americans"—thus, not a German.[32]

When Walker and his men emerged from the plane they were greeted by "a ragamuffin band of soldiers dressed in various pieces of uniforms scavenged from various sides in the war." Their weapons, which did not match, appeared to have been acquired the same way. Nevertheless, they had been sufficient to drive off the Germans. Walker later noted that while the Chetniks were armed with rifles, machine guns, and hand grenades, "the guns were of all makes and caliber, many being in such poor condition that they were dangerous to fire." Equipped in this fashion, the Chetniks did not routinely go in search of an enemy whose firepower was vastly superior to their own. They did, however, fight it out with the Germans, and on occasion the Partisans, when the rescue of American airmen was involved.[33]

Sgt. Karl Smith reported that the Chetniks who rescued him were at the time under fire from Partisan forces, and even after he and his men joined the Chetniks, the firing continued unabated. Sgt. Leon W. Hoadley had a similar experience when "the Partisans and Germans made several attempts to take men away from the Chetniks causing pitched battles." During one such battle the Allies dropped supplies to the Partisans, causing Hoadley "quite some worry as to the Chetnik reaction."[34]

The experiences of Thomas C. Richards closely paralleled those of Hoadley. According to Richards, the "Partisans and Germans engaged in combat with us and tried to effect our capture anytime the opportunity was presented to them. The Partisans were unfriendly and would attack us even when Chetniks and Germans were engaged in combat."[35] Robert D. Fulks was another airman who found himself inadvertently caught up in the civil war. After his plane went down on September 3, south of Lapovo, Fulks was taken by an English-speaking Chetnik to a small village where he remained for a few days awaiting an escort to the evacuation point. While he was there, Partisans attacked the village. From their hiding place in the attic of a home, Fulks and his Chetnik companion witnessed the execution of five pro-Chetnik peasants by Tito's forces.[36]

Some of the airmen who managed to avoid the civil war between the Chetniks and the Partisans found themselves in the company of Chetnik units that were actively involved in sabotage operations against the Germans. Mihailovich apparently had many informants among the railroad workers throughout the country who apprised him of important supply shipments or troop movements by the Germans. On one such occasion the general was given details about a supply train that was to leave for Rumania on the following day. That night a group of Chetniks, accompanied by Richard Felman, made their way into the yard, boarded the train, and placed some hollow chunks of coal filled with TNT in the bottom of the coal box. It was the type of operation for which the Chetniks would probably not receive credit, but neither would the Serbian peasantry be subjected to German reprisals.[37] William K. Callam, whose plane went down northeast of Belgrade on June 15, 1944, joined Chetnik forces that would ambush German convoys or attack German barracks in some of the smaller towns and would then beat a hasty retreat into the mountains.[38]

Ironically, other airmen managed to survive inside Yugoslavia because of the "live and let live" policy that governed Chetnik-German relations in some parts of the country.[39] James Inks, who was in the country for approximately ten months, kept a diary in which he confessed his complete bewilderment at the strange circumstances in which he and his men found themselves. No doubt he echoed the feelings of many other airmen when he wrote, "How the Germans can remain allied with two groups who fight each other, or how the Chetniks can be allied with the Germans and still be on our side is quite beyond all of us."[40]

By far the most trying experience for Inks and his men came in late September when, disguised as Chetnik soldiers, they joined a retreating German column that was making its way out of the country. As the column wound its way through a German roadblock, Inks passed a German guard and "looked straight in his eye. He returned my stare and my heart began a maddening thumping. But he said nothing, and I walked on past without saying a word."[41] Detection by the Germans was not the only danger Inks and his crewmates faced. Beginning in early September, Allied air units, working with Partisan forces inside the country, launched a concerted effort aimed at impeding the withdrawal of German units from the Balkans and inflicting as many casualties on the retreating Axis forces as possible – Operation RATWEEK. Inks noted in his diary, "This is one hell of a lesson for a bomber crew, to be down on the ground among the civilians who are getting it from their buddies."[42]

The bombing also proved to be a source of great embarrassment to Inks and his crew, particularly in the aftermath of an Allied air raid on the town of Podgorica in early October. Inks found it difficult to face the Chetnik commander, who told him, "The Partisans are using you to kill us. They know there are no Germans in the town, only Chetniks. But they have told your headquarters it is full of Germans and asked for the bombing."[43]

Nothing could better illustrate the great advantage that accrued to the Partisans as a result of the Allied decision to withdraw all intelligence missions from Mihailovich's territory. The United States had repeatedly stated, as if repetition alone would make it so, that its support of Tito was exclusively military in nature. Washington, however, had denied itself the means to determine whether or not the intent of its policies was being carried out in Yugoslavia. As a result, Tito not only used Allied supplies to prosecute the civil war against Mihailovich, he also harnessed, on occasion, the considerable might of Allied air power to serve political rather than legitimate military ends. Although Inks and his men witnessed this subversion of Allied assistance, they did not leave the country until May, 1945, by which time their information was of greater value to the historical record than for any other purpose.

Of course, the airmen assembled at Pranjani awaiting evacuation represented a potential source of intelligence, particularly concerning Serbia. They had witnessed the civil war between Chetnik and Partisan forces and had experienced the full range of Chetnik-German relations, from open hostility to wary tolerance and at times accommodation. They had seen Chetnik soldiers give their lives to save them from capture and had been protected and well-treated by Mihailovich's forces and by the Serbian peasantry. Indeed, their very presence at Pranjani under Chetnik protection was in itself clear evidence that Mihailovich remained well-disposed toward the United States and was no collaborator in the true sense of the word.

Lastly, it should be noted that the parents of many of the airmen who went down in Serbia were first notified that their sons were safe, not through regular military channels, but through telegrams received from the Yugoslav Embassy in Washington. Mihailovich communicated the names of the airmen and the addresses of their next of kin to Constantin Fotitć in Washington, the Yugoslav minister (later ambassador) to the United States, who sent telegrams to those families informing them of their sons' status—this from the man who had been labeled a collaborator and accused of turning over American airmen to the Germans for money.[44]

As the airmen began to filter in from the hills around Pranjani, many small reunions took place among crewmates who had been separated after entering the country. There were also farewells as the airmen said good-bye to the Chetniks who had been their companions and protectors over the past weeks and months. These things done, there was little to do but to sit and wait for the arrival of the promised aircraft. It was well past the designated time when the first faint engine sounds were heard, setting off a ripple of apprehension that did not subside until the men were certain that the C-47s had found their target. The cheers of a brief celebration gradually melted away into an almost prayerful silence as the first plane made its approach, its landing lights groping through the darkness in search of the makeshift runway below.[45]

As soon as the plane touched down, Musulin had his men ready to board— only twelve per plane, however, due to the short runway. As the airmen climbed into the plane they began taking off their shirts, pants, and shoes and throwing them to the Chetniks who were standing outside the aircraft. It seemed to be at once the least and the most they could do.[46] Forty-eight airmen were evacuated during this initial phase of the H A L Y A R D operation, after which Musulin advised Edward Green in Bari that Mihailovich had increased his security force to about one thousand men and wanted to place two hundred to three hundred of these under American supervision with the idea that they could be supplied arms and ammunition.[47]

On the following day the HALYARD team carried out its first daytime evacuation. The team now included Lt. Nick Lalich, who had arrived the previous evening. Lalich, a graduate of Ohio University, had entered the service in February, 1942, and later transferred to OSS from the Army Signal Corps. He served as traffic control officer for this particular operation, which involved 177 American airmen and a number of Allied personnel including eight Yugoslavs from Mihailovich's headquarters.[48]

HALYARD's success prompted a quick response from Bari. Green radioed Rajacich that "good old Col Kraigher is still floating around in the air four feet above the ground." Still, Green could not promise that arms and ammunition could be sent to the Chetniks "even for the purpose of guarding the airstrip from which the Americans were being evacuated."[49]

Green and Joyce were reluctant to approve the dispatch of arms to the Chetniks, even on the limited basis called for by Musulin, fearing that to do so might further upset the British. They soon discovered that Musulin had taken care of that when he allowed a Yugoslav delegation aboard the second flight of planes during the morning of August 10. When Mihailovich's representatives arrived in Italy, British security intercepted them and notified Philip Broad, British Foreign Office representative in Bari. According to Joyce, Broad became "exceedingly excited" over this matter and showed American officials a telegram he intended to send to Harold Macmillan. In this message, which Joyce characterized as "somewhat hysterical in tone," Broad charged that the Americans, particularly Musulin, had exceeded their authority during the air rescue operations. Moreover, he feared that Tito, who was in Italy at the time for discussions with Churchill and Šubašić, would never believe that the mission had been sent without Allied approval.[50] Joyce subsequently advised Toulmin that the Yugoslav delegates, who arrived in Italy under the impression that their mission had been approved by Allied authorities, had been taken to an apartment in Bari where they were being held incommunicado until Caserta could reach some decision about their disposition.[51]

In the meantime, Kraigher informed Musulin that the "situation caused by arrival of Jug delegation is so extremely delicate all available information must be presented," and ordered him to return to Bari on the first available plane. Musulin replied that Mihailovich had authorized inclusion of the Yugoslav delegation and that refusal to send the representatives or a decision to return them "would cause a most unpleasant situation and hinder future evacuations."[52]

When Kraigher refused to cancel Musulin's evacuation orders, Rajacich appealed to Deranian, pointing out that the success HALYARD had enjoyed was in large measure attributable to Musulin and the work he did in Yugoslavia

during his first mission. According to Rajacich, Musulin was known throughout the area as "George the American" and had become almost a legend among
Mihailovich's forces. Rajacich expressed hope that Musulin would be able to
return to the country after completing his report, adding that "we, as well as
the people here will miss his presence tremendously even if it will be for a
few days."[53]

Already greatly disappointed by the treatment Mihailovich was receiving
at the hands of the Allies, Musulin became furious at being recalled over what
in his view was a very minor incident. He made no attempt to conceal his
anger when he sent the following message to Kraigher on August 20: "I wish
you would make up your minds. Waiting around here on airfields 4–5 hours
each night with boys who are sick and injured isn't pleasant. We have no gas
and batteries are down. If you don't hear from me you will know reason. Doctor has no medical supplies. Why let down at your end."[54]

A week of waiting did not improve Musulin's disposition. On August 26
he radioed Kraigher, "In view of your fumbling indecision and broken promises would strongly request day evacuation. Waiting for evacuation 49 Yanks,
2 Polish, 2 Russians, 16 Italians, 2 British. No planes as usual last night."[55]

Planes did arrive late in the evening of the twenty-sixth to evacuate the airmen and to bring in McDowell and the members of his RANGER mission.
Musulin's last official function as commander of the HALYARD team was to
provide a reception for the RANGER team, the arrival of which quickly created
a storm of controversy with the British and Partisans so intense as to over-
shadow the incident with the Yugoslav delegation altogether. Musulin reluctantly boarded the last aircraft and while standing in the door of the plane
yelled out instructions over the roar of the engines to Lalich, who was now
in command of the HALYARD operation.[56] It should be noted that when
Kraigher first informed Musulin that he was being recalled, the man under
consideration as his replacement was John Blatnik. At that point Lalich, who
had been trying to get into the country for some time, presented his case to
George Vujnovich. In his capacity as operations officer, Vujnovich insisted on
the right to name Musulin's successor. Green and Joyce agreed, and Lalich
got the assignment.[57]

After returning to Bari, Musulin prepared a report on the HALYARD operation, but no one at OSS headquarters ever debriefed him.[58] In his report, Musulin generously praised those who had played a role in HALYARD, including
General Mihailovich and his forces. These accolades were undoubtedly de-
served, but the moving spirit behind the establishment of the ACRU and more
particularly the success of the HALYARD mission was George Musulin himself. In the words of Nelson Deranian, "The success of the Musulin project
inspired ACRU to expand its activities."[59] General Donovan recognized Musulin's contributions to the HALYARD mission when he presented him with

Col. George Kraigher, far left, Capt. Nick Lalich, fifth from left, and Capt. George Vujnovich, far right, shown here with a group of airmen returning to Bari from Yugoslavia. Lalich assumed command of HALYARD after Musulin was recalled and was the last American officer with Mihailovich's forces. Courtesy George Vujnovich

the Legion of Merit. His work in Yugoslavia, however, was at an end. Some ten days after arriving in Bari, he was told that he would be allowed to return to the states to visit his parents and then would receive additional training for his next assignment, which would take him to China.[60]

Musulin's removal from the theater left Lalich in command of HALYARD, which was reduced to a two-man operation following Rajacich's transfer to the McDowell unit.[61] Nevertheless, Lalich and Jibilian continued to conduct evacuations until late December, well after RANGER had completed its brief but controversial stay in Yugoslavia.

7. No Excuses or Apologies to Tito

For Donovan, the arrival of the RANGER mission at Mihailovich's headquarters represented the culmination of an effort that had been ongoing since May, 1944, when Musulin was forced to evacuate from Serbia. Roosevelt's decision to order the withdrawal of OSS personnel from Mihailovich's forces at Churchill's insistence forced Donovan to implement a policy with which he did not agree and one he set about to reverse almost immediately. The director took his case directly to General Wilson, arguing that a mission dispatched to Mihailovich for the sole purpose of gathering information—as opposed to one designed to assist his forces from an operational standpoint—would not place Britain and the United States at cross purposes in Yugoslavia. Wilson agreed, and Donovan so informed the president in early July, pointing out that "it is a very difficult task to turn off and on intelligence work, and information of Central Europe is badly needed."[1]

Roosevelt agreed with his intelligence chief, and in early August, Donovan advised the Joint Chiefs of his conversation with Wilson and of the president's verbal approval to send intelligence missions into Yugoslavia and other Balkan countries to gather information and to assist in air rescue operations. By this time, of course, the ACRU was operational and Donovan had alerted Bari to be prepared to move quickly to establish an intelligence mission in Serbia.[2] Robert Joyce regarded the proposed mission as having the "utmost significance" since it would give OSS direct contact "with a group which is playing and will play a vital role in the post war organization of Yugoslavia." Equally important to Joyce was the fact that it represented a clear-cut departure from British policy.[3]

Precisely for that reason, and on the assumption that Churchill would again intervene to prevent their reestablishing contact with Mihailovich, OSS officials proceeded with their preparations in strictest secrecy. Dr. Stephen Penrose, chief of SI, OSS-Washington, advised Joyce, "If there are leaks to any of these (bt. or pzns.), we face the possibility of jeopardizing our works in the Partisan areas, of running into the same blockade which hit us when the mission was proposed before, and of having the whole works royally ruined before it gets in operation."[4]

Penrose suggested that the team assemble in Cairo, rather than Bari, "into which town the mission should never go," and then be sent to Brindisi. Reiterating the need for secrecy, Penrose recommended to Joyce that he "discuss with no one, and I mean no one, who has or will have connections with Partisans. They should be able to deny any knowledge of our plans."[5] Joyce, aware of what would happen if the British got wind of the proposed Mihailovich mission, took great pains to carry out the wishes of his superior. In fact, when he discovered that a routine progress report covering the period from August 1 to August 15 contained a brief reference to the mission, he bracketed the information and ordered it sent under separate cover marked top secret.[6]

Apparently these precautions sufficed for only a brief period of time. On August 8, Joyce informed Donovan that "we must assume that it is an open secret that we are planning to dispatch Lt. Colonel McDowell to Mihailovich's Headquarters." Joyce predicted that Tito would react unfavorably to the idea and might choose to take action that would jeopardize the success of the Huntington mission.[7]

At first it seemed that Joyce might have been unduly pessimistic in his analysis. When Donovan met Tito in Caserta and informed him of the McDowell mission, the Partisan leader merely remarked that he thought the plan rather "maladroit in the present situation."[8] However, after the mission actually arrived in Serbia, Tito made a prophet of Joyce, lodging a series of strenuous objections to McDowell's presence at Mihailovich's headquarters and restricting the activities of personnel attached to Huntington's mission.

McDowell's work before and during the war appears, in retrospect, to have been designed specifically to prepare him for the critical and delicate mission for which he had been chosen. He had served with British military intelligence in World War I, after which he lived in eastern Europe and the Near East for a number of years. After returning to the United States he entered the University of Michigan, where he earned his Ph.D. and later taught modern Balkan history.[9] Shortly after the United States became involved in World War II, McDowell gave up his position at Michigan and entered the army. Not surprisingly, he served with an intelligence unit in the North African Theater and later joined the Joint Intelligence Collection Agency (JICA), Middle East. Both assignments allowed him to monitor events in the Balkans and to maintain contact with Allied personnel who were responsible for covering the countries of that region, including Yugoslavia.[10]

McDowell was apparently among those officers whose missions to Chetnik forces had been canceled in the spring on Roosevelt's orders. Convinced that the withdrawal of OSS personnel from Serbia was a serious mistake, he out-

lined a compelling case for reestablishing contact with the Chetniks and submitted it to JICA and Air Force intelligence on June 6, roughly one week after
Musulin's first evacuation. McDowell desired to be more than just an advocate
for such a mission, adding that "in view of the contacts which the undersigned
has already established, he volunteers his services for this purpose."[11] When
Gen. Thomas Roderick, McDowell's superior, agreed to release McDowell from
his duties at JICA for the Mihailovich mission, OSS believed that it had found
the right man to head the RANGER team.[12]

In addition to Rajacich, who as noted earlier transferred from HALYARD,
McDowell's team included Capt. John Milodragovich, Sgt. Michael Devyak
(the mission's radio operator), and 1st Lt. Ellsworth Kramer, who entered the
country on September 4.[13] Milodragovich had previously served as Arnoldy's
assistant at the Y-Desk in Bari, where he was known to his friends as the "Ranger
from Montana"—he had earned a degree in forestry from the University of
Montana and had worked with the United States Forestry Service before entering military service. He carried the nickname with him when he joined Mc-
Dowell's unit, which later bore the code name RANGER.[14]

McDowell and his men arrived at Mihailovich's headquarters just a few
days before the beginning of Operation RATWEEK, a joint Allied-Partisan undertaking aimed at destroying German forces retreating from Greece and Yugoslavia into Austria.[15] Furthermore, Mihailovich had designated September 1
as the date for general mobilization, calling all men between the ages of sixteen
and sixty to join his forces.[16]

Within a matter of days after Mihailovich called for mobilization, Ultra
revealed a noticeable increase in Chetnik activity. Nationalist forces cut railway lines in the Dubrovnik area and also severed the lines connecting Višegrad,
Sarajevo, and Doboj.[17] A report from the Fifth SS Corps indicated that "Cetniks in entire eastern and central Bosnian area (two five thousand [25,000]
men) had opened hostilities against Germans." With their supply convoys also
coming under attack from the Chetniks, the Germans had good cause to fear
that the "loyalty of Cetniks and carefully fostered cooperation" was in jeop-
ardy. Apparently the situation was not quite so critical in neighboring Hercegovina, where, according to Ultra, the "Hercegovinian Cetniks were loyal to
Germans."[18]

Amidst this flurry of activity, and in an attempt to secure as much direct
intelligence as possible, McDowell dispersed his personnel, choosing to concentrate his own efforts in western Serbia and Bosnia. He sent Rajacich into
the area around Belgrade and Kramer into eastern Serbia in the Morava Valley
region.[19]

McDowell's team had not been in the field long before it began to uncover
irrefutable evidence that the Partisans, particularly after September 1, were
engaged in a systematic effort to break the back of the Nationalist movement

Members of the RANGER mission to Mihailovich's headquarters: left to right, Lt. Mike Rajacich, Lt. Col. Robert H. McDowell, Capt. John R. Milodragovich, and Sgt. Michael Devyak. Courtesy J. B. Allin and M. Mike Sujdovic

Members of the HALYARD and RANGER missions conferring with General Mihailovich: left to right, Rajacich, Mihailovich, Lalich, Musulin, and McDowell. Courtesy George Vujnovich

in Serbia and were using Allied supplies and air power for this purpose. Mission personnel observed American planes "strafing areas held not by Germans but by the Nationalists," and American pilots who had been shot down stated that they had been told that "everything was 'enemy' North of the Partisan lines in the Zap Morava Valley."[20] Following an attack on the town of Čačak on September 2, McDowell informed Bari that the only damage done to the Germans was the destruction of a small quantity of gasoline. The Chetniks and civilian population were not as fortunate. McDowell continued, "We strafed train loaded peasants market bound and outside town column nationalist troops headed front, causing casualties both attacks. Nationalist troops displayed panels Yugoslav colors. This attack constitutes misuse and waste our planes."[21]

On one occasion Milodragovich witnessed a battle between the Partisans and Chetniks in which the latter came under a withering barrage of mortar fire by Tito's forces. After the battle he discovered that the Partisans had been using American firing tables for their 81-mm mortars.[22] Worse still, McDowell and his men witnessed Nationalist forces going into battle with antiquated rifles and little ammunition "to face American and British mortars and automatic weapons" and then sat alongside these same men at night and listened while American transports flew in "to drop further weapons and munitions into the Partisan lines for the morrow's battle."[23] Milodragovich found that the Partisans were receiving so many supplies from the Allies that they were actually having to store them—information consistent with the findings of Green, Galembush, and Desich alluded to earlier. On the other hand, some Chetnik forces went into battle with no weapons at all, hoping that they would be able to arm themselves with the rifle of a fallen comrade or with guns taken from the enemy.[24]

Naturally, the Allies were supplying the Partisans in the belief that the latter were concentrating their efforts against the Germans. However, from mid-September until his team was evacuated from the country in early November, McDowell provided a steady stream of intelligence to Bari which clearly indicated that the Partisans were directing the bulk of their forces and supplies against the Chetniks.[25] Walter Carpenter, an OSS medical officer sent to Mihailovich's headquarters on September 3 to attend to the medical needs of the American airmen, confirmed these conclusions. After approximately two weeks in Yugoslavia, Carpenter returned to Italy and filed a report in which he wrote, "Here we see American weapons and bullets being furnished by the British daily to kill the enemies of Germany."[26] On the basis of his own personal observations and those of his men, McDowell concluded that through August and September "the Partisan Army made no serious effort to fight Germans or hinder their retreat, but concentrated on attacking Nationalist troops who in some instances were occupied in attacking Germans."[27]

General Wilson shared this view and urged Tito, with limited success, to attack German forces as they retreated through Bosnia. Tito's explanation that he had to fly to Moscow to consult with Stalin concerning the taking of Belgrade failed to satisfy Wilson, who wrote, "The Russians would have taken Belgrade anyhow, but where planning and cooperation were really wanted to bring off a success, namely in the Bosnian mountains, they were allowed to go by default."[28]

Kramer's experiences in eastern Serbia were quite similar to those reported by McDowell. Through September and part of October he observed the Partisans concentrating their forces against the Nationalists, while at the same time a steady stream of German traffic moved through the Ibar Valley to Kraljevo with no opposition whatsoever. He also saw German troops of the Prince Eugene Division pass through Partisan lines to attack Chetnik forces without a shot being fired. He observed the same pattern in Bosnia, where Partisan units attacked the Chetniks but allowed German rail and highway traffic to continue uninterrupted between Sarajevo and Doboj.[29]

McDowell's team interrogated several Partisan prisoners and discovered that all of them had repeatedly engaged Nationalist forces, but none had seen action against either the Germans or Ustasha. In addition, none admitted having seen either American or British liaison officers in the vicinity of any engagements, though some knew of the presence of Allied personnel at rear headquarters. Based on his own observations and the official reports of other officers who had reported on the civil war, McDowell concluded that "the principal concern of the Partisan leadership has been, not to destroy Germans, but Nationalism in Yugoslavia and in the Balkans."[30]

The RANGER mission also found conclusive proof that the Partisans had been falsifying and were continuing to falsify military and political information on a grand scale when it suited their purposes to do so. Just before his departure from Italy, McDowell examined a situation map prepared by the British from Partisan sources that showed much of western Serbia in Partisan hands. After arriving in Yugoslavia he "diligently sought for evidence of Partisan liberated areas between the Morava and the Drina and found that there were none and had been none."[31]

In late August, when a Partisan radio broadcast identified three towns in north central Serbia that had been liberated by their forces, McDowell sent Rajacich into the region to verify the claim. When he reached the area in early September and investigated the report, Rajacich found that the towns were actually controlled by Nationalist forces. McDowell happened to be in east Bosnia September 26–29 when a Partisan broadcast announced that that region had risen in support of the Partisans, but found that "there was absolutely no trace of a local Partisan rising."[32]

Members of the RANGER team also found other Partisan claims to be false. The charge that Dragutin Keserović had broken with Mihailovich and denounced him as a collaborator was untrue. The alleged capture of some of Mihailovich's staff along with his archives was never confirmed. Lastly, the mission discovered that the Partisans claimed and had erroneously been given credit for the sabotage of the Gračanica-to-Doboj railway in east Bosnia. After investigating these and other incidents, McDowell charged that Partisan leaders were following "a deliberate policy of falsification of news and documents to suit their own needs."[33]

The fact that McDowell had held and voiced such views before entering Yugoslavia may have provided those who were inclined to challenge his conclusions with a plausible basis for so doing. Ellery Huntington, for example, forwarded some excerpts taken from messages that passed between McDowell and Bari to his executive officer, Stafford Reid, requesting that he check the accuracy of the information with certain Partisan officers. The irony of attempting to refute McDowell's claims, most of which attacked the probity of Partisan information, with intelligence gleaned directly from Partisan sources appears to have escaped Huntington. Still, he wanted the study completed because, in his words, "I may wish to dispute the veracity of MacDowell's [sic] statements."[34] Ironically, as will be shown in the following chapter, officers attached to Huntington's mission actually corroborated many of McDowell's conclusions.

Tito, of course, had no interest in sparring with McDowell over his facts. He wanted the RANGER mission out of the country and forcefully conveyed that message to both Maclean and Huntington, warning that McDowell's continued presence at Chetnik headquarters could jeopardize Partisan relations with Britain and the United States.[35]

When Maclean informed Churchill of Tito's complaint, the prime minister immediately took his case directly to Roosevelt, seeking once again to secure the withdrawal of American officers from Mihailovich's territory. Writing to the president on September 1, Churchill took Roosevelt to task about the McDowell mission and pointed out that if the United States and Britain backed different sides in Yugoslavia "we lay the scene for a fine civil war." The prime minister concluded his protest by charging that Donovan was "running a strong Mihailovich lobby, just when we have persuaded King Peter to break decisively with him."[36]

Our salient point Churchill chose to overlook was the fact that a civil war was already raging in Yugoslavia. An OSS report originating in Algiers and later sent to Donovan was far more candid in its appreciation of conditions inside the country than the prime minister had been. This document claimed that in supporting Tito for the purpose of resisting the Germans, the British had also insured that he would win the civil war. Furthermore, the United States was underwriting British support of Tito by providing arms to the British that they in turn were giving to the Partisans. It was, the report concluded, "an impossibility to confine the use of American supplies to resistance forces in the Balkans to operations against the enemy while a bitter civil war is being fought."[37]

McDowell's messages coming out of Serbia may well have been the basis for this report. Certainly they confirmed its conclusions and demonstrated the wisdom of Donovan's insistence on having an intelligence-gathering mission in Mihailovich's area. Unfortunately, the president did not take these matters into consideration before responding to Churchill on September 3. The fact that he replied only two days after receiving the prime minister's note clearly suggests that principles relating to strategic intelligence did not exercise any influence on his decision. Without assessing the value of McDowell's mission or the contribution his findings might make toward evaluating American policy in Yugoslavia, Roosevelt simply replied to Churchill, "The mission of oss is my mistake. I did not check with my previous action of last April 8th. I am directing Donovan to withdraw his mission."[38]

This is an amazing statement when one considers the lengths to which Donovan had gone to inform the president of the McDowell mission and the subsequent actions taken by Roosevelt himself. As noted earlier, Donovan had advised the president in writing about the proposed mission on July 4 and had discussed the idea further with him two days later, at which time Roosevelt approved the plan. On August 5, two days after Donovan notified the Joint Chiefs of Staff that Roosevelt had verbally agreed to dispatch the mission, the president rescinded his April objection to the infiltration of teams into Mihailovich's area.[39] Obviously, then, the McDowell mission was not the result of an oversight, as Roosevelt implied, but rather of an informed policy decision that the president quickly disavowed when challenged by Churchill.

Roosevelt would have been well within his right to have informed the prime minister that the RANGER mission was not supporting Mihailovich's forces in an operational sense and was in Yugoslavia solely for the purpose of gathering intelligence with the knowledge and consent of the Allied theater commander. That is precisely what Wilson told Tito after the latter complained about the American mission and suggested that the Allies were sending supplies to the Chetniks. In a message fairly bristling with indignation, Wilson told Tito that he took "strong exception" to his allegations and informed the Partisan leader that he (Wilson) was "perfectly competent to take care of the situation." Wilson also reminded Tito that he had been apprised in advance concerning both American missions to Mihailovich's territory; Wilson did not suggest that either was a mistake or should be withdrawn.[40]

In late October, Maclean again advised Wilson of Tito's continuing objections to the McDowell mission and attempted to add a little levity to the situation by pointing out that "Mihailovich is, as you know, subject which makes Tito and his followers see even redder than usual and they are quite unable to grasp that there could be any adequate reason why UNITED STATES Govt is now retaining Mission with Cetniks." Wilson was not amused and told Maclean to advise Tito to pay less attention to Mihailovich and concentrate more "on the important task of preventing enemy Northward movement."[41]

Roosevelt chose not to take issue with Churchill over the McDowell mission, evidencing no desire to test the bonds of Anglo-American unity or his personal friendship with the prime minister on a matter occurring within a theater that was tangential to American interests. Donovan saw things differently. In his view, the president had for the second time in six months bowed to pressure from Churchill and, on both occasions, had compromised the legitimate intelligence-gathering functions of OSS. In a sharply worded memorandum to the White House, Donovan's deputy director, Charles Cheston, pointed out to Roosevelt that the British were sending personnel into "Chetnik areas" at the very time they were insisting on the withdrawal of American officers. Cheston argued that such action clearly revealed the need for "independence in the field of intelligence where a change of mind on the part of the objecting party alone may give that party a monopoly of first-hand information."[42]

The reference to British personnel in Chetnik territory was based on a memorandum from Robert Murphy, who reported that Maclean had gone into Chetnik territory a few days earlier and informed Allied Forces Headquarters (AFHQ) that the Chetniks were "aiding the Germans actively and are keeping the Partisans from making the most just now of German confusion."[43] The great disparity between Maclean's statement and McDowell's observations, supported by a substantial body of intelligence developed by OSS officers attached to Partisan forces, provided a compelling argument for allowing RANGER to remain in Serbia. Unfortunately, Roosevelt refused to rescind his evacuation order.

Accordingly, on September 14, Green advised McDowell that "due to circumstances beyond our control or yours and pursuant to instructions for [sic] high authority, your complete unit is ordered to come back to Bari soonest." Green assured McDowell that every effort would be made to keep the evacuation order secret until the mission had returned to Bari. In a separate communication to Glavin, Green recommended that Huntington be instructed not to inform Tito of the status of the McDowell mission.[44]

Confusion now arose as to whether or not the president's order extended the Lalich and Jibilian, whose mission had been approved prior to and independently of RANGER. Kraigher interpreted the order to include members of the HALYARD team, who were contacted by radio on September 19 and instructed to return to Italy as soon as possible. Although Bari repeated these orders on October 10 and 24, Glavin and Joyce sent a message to McDowell on October 22, suggesting that he consider the possibility of a separate evacuation, leaving the ACRU to collect the remaining airmen.[45]

According to Donovan, oss personnel in Washington did not realize that Fifteenth Air Force had operational control of HALYARD and therefore included it in the evacuation order.[46] In any event, Lalich interpreted the message from Glavin and Joyce to mean that he and Jibilian could remain in the country and continue their efforts to evacuate Allied airmen.[47] Only McDowell's team was therefore under orders to leave the country, which it eventually did, but not until November 1.[48]

McDowell claimed that certain personnel changes in Bari and "technical" problems associated with coordinating an evacuation combined to delay the departure of his mission.[49] Resolving the question of HALYARD's status took some time, as did Kramer's unsuccessful attempts to rejoin the team. In the course of trying to overcome these obstacles, oss officials in Bari received a steady stream of complaints from Tito and from American officers attached to his forces, charging that McDowell's continuing presence at Mihailovich's headquarters was having a most detrimental effect on American-Partisan relations.[50] One American officer who had been told by the British that there were oss missions with the Chetniks asked Bari for confirmation, adding, "Our position would be hopeless if this fact is true."[51]

Robert Joyce, who had attached such great importance to the McDowell mission, greatly resented the fact that Churchill's intervention and Roosevelt's obsequious response to it had resulted in RANGER's untimely recall. With patience and tact in short supply, Joyce soon had his fill of Tito's complaints. He fired off a terse message to Huntington telling him that if Tito or his staff "continue to harp on our intelligence unit in Nationalist Serbia," Huntington should reaffirm Donovan's position that the United States was within its right to send the team into the country and was withdrawing it now that it had completed its mission. Joyce emphasized that Huntington was not to "adopt" an "apologetic attitude" in this matter and that oss was "making no excuses or apologies to Tito."[52] Only a week later, Huntington informed Bari that Tito had imposed restrictions on the movement of American personnel inside his territory that would remain in effect as long as McDowell remained in the country. Joyce immediately ordered Huntington to protest this action, adding, "We repeat Donovan's opinion that we have no excuses to make and will not be dictated to in connection with our right to obtain military intelligence wherever we can."[53]

Donovan and Joyce were obviously doing all they could to defend a principle, even in the midst of losing another battle. In the meantime, McDowell continued preparations to leave the country despite the fact that Kramer had not been able to rejoin the mission, nor had he been heard from since mid-October.

As noted earlier, Kramer had entered the country on September 4, a little more than a week after the RANGER team had arrived, and was then assigned

Members of the RANGER mission: Lt. Ellsworth Kramer, left, McDowell, third from left, and Fifteenth Air Force medical officer Capt. Jacques Mitrani, shown here with Mihailovich. Courtesy J. B. Allin and M. Mike Sujdovic

to eastern Serbia. He left Pranjani on September 9, en route to Col. Dragutin Keserović's headquarters near the town of Kragujevac in the Morava Valley. Though he had no way of knowing it at the time, Kramer had embarked on one of the most difficult and bizarre odysseys undertaken by any OSS agent during the war.[54]

While traveling to Keserović's area, Kramer's party was attacked once by the Partisans and also had to make several detours to avoid German convoys. He reached the Chetnik commander's headquarters on the thirteenth, explained the nature of his mission, and soon thereafter found himself thrust into the middle of the civil war. After hearing Keserović's complaints that the Partisans were attacking his men whenever they attempted to engage the Germans, Kramer sent a courier to the local Partisan commander as the first step toward negotiating a truce between the two groups. The Partisans beat the courier, denied that there was an American mission in Serbia, and launched an attack on the Chetniks the following day. In the course of the fighting a number of Partisan prisoners fell into Chetnik hands. From them, Kramer learned that two Partisan officers, Col. Ljubo Vučković and Lieutenant Colonel Burić, had given their men specific orders to kill or capture "the American officer with the Chetniks."[55]

This revelation was but one of many Kramer experienced as the Partisans and Chetniks continued to fight one another. He saw German convoys moving through the region, unchallenged by either side. In exchange, the Germans aided both resistance groups. On one occasion when the Chetniks were running low on ammunition, they discovered a pile of Italian arms and ammunition left by the Germans along the roadside early one morning and immediately rushed it to the front. Reports also indicated that while the Partisans and Chetniks fought each other, German tanks joined the battle, killing troops on both sides. In another instance Kramer might well have become a casualty himself had it not been possible for his bodyguards to convince the Germans that he was actually a Chetnik commandant traveling to the front to engage the Partisans.[56]

On October 9, Keserović asked Kramer if he would enter the German-occupied town of Kragujevac to speak to a large group of Serbs in an attempt to relieve their anxiety about the approaching Russians. Kramer agreed, and while Chetnik and Nedić troops, under conditions of a truce, provided protection from the Germans, he told an assembly of about one thousand people that they had nothing to fear from the Russians, who were Allies of the United States and Britain. After Kramer finished his speech, a German tank officer approached him to determine what guarantee of protection the American officer could grant if the German garrisons of Kragujevac and Kraljevo surrendered. Kramer explained that since this was now a Russian zone of operations, he could do no more than advise the nearest Russian commander that the garrisons had capitulated and the towns could be occupied by Russian troops. Minutes later a tank departed in the direction of Kraljevo, apparently carrying the gist of this conversation to the German forces there.[57]

In Kragujevac, fighting broke out in the railroad yard and at the airport when Chetnik forces attempted to steal some arms and ammunition from the Germans. However, Kramer noted that on the following day, Chetnik and German soldiers were "walking about the streets paying no attention to each other." He also saw a Chetnik truck loaded with arms and supplies leave the town without being challenged by German troops who were standing nearby. Obviously, with the Russians only twenty kilometers away, the Germans had more pressing concerns than the loss of a truckload of supplies.[58]

The Russian advance also created problems for Kramer. Cut off from McDowell, he realized that he would have "to choose between being captured and killed by the Partisans, being a prisoner of the Germans for the duration of the war, or relying on the mercy of the Russians as an ally." He chose the latter and sent a message to the nearest Russian officer, suggesting that he had information about the German garrison in Kragujevac that might prove useful. On the following day, October 14, a Russian officer arrived at Keserović's headquarters to meet with Kramer, who turned over the information as promised. Before the Russian could leave, however, Knei, the German commander in Kragujevac, arrived unexpectedly. Knei had previously met with Kramer to discuss how his troops might surrender without becoming prisoners of the Russians, but was not satisfied with the rather vague terms the American offered.

While the Russian waited outside the house wearing a Chetnik hat and a raincoat over his uniform, Knei asked Keserović in Kramer's presence if the Chetniks would defend him and his men. Keserović replied that he had promised to fight the Partisans, not the Russians, whom he regarded as allies. He warned Knei that he would have only thirty minutes in which to decide whether or not to surrender, after which time the Chetniks would take the town by force. Knei left immediately, promising to fight, and Kramer, accompanied by the Russian officer who had been waiting outside, quickly made his way to the Russian commander to inform him of Keserović's plans. The Russians promised that they would not shell the town and would not allow the Partisans to interfere with the Chetnik attack. Under these conditions, Keserović's men launched their attack, quickly defeated the German garrison, and took possession of the town before the Russians arrived.[59]

Keserović and the Russian commander delivered speeches to the people of the town, but this show of unity was short-lived. Russian troops subsequently disarmed the Chetniks and placed Kramer under armed guard. After being held for a brief time, he was escorted to see the Russian general who had assumed command of Soviet troops in Kragujevac. A Russian colonel questioned Kramer regarding the nature of his mission in Serbia and then dismissed him, though he remained under armed guard. Kramer subsequently traveled from Kragujevac to Paracin, where a Russian intelligence officer interrogated him further concerning his mission and the location of Mihailovich's headquarters. Still under guard, Kramer left Paracin in the company of two German officers and a Russian lieutenant colonel and traveled across the Yugoslav border into Bulgaria.

Although the Russians repeatedly told Kramer that he was not a prisoner, he could not help but notice that he and the Germans were being treated much the same way. This changed rather dramatically on the morning of October 17, when Kramer was notified that he would be picked up by a Russian officer but was given no details as to his destination. He was taken to the Russian mission in Sofia, where he was told that the American mission had been informed of his arrival and was sending someone for him. Kramer finally walked into the American mission around 10:45 P.M. and was immediately recognized by J. B. Allin, who happened to be in Sofia after having returned from Yugoslavia, where he had been sent to cover the RANGER mission for the Field Photographic Branch.[60]

Kramer reached Bari during the afternoon of the eighteenth, reported to SBS (Special Bari Section) headquarters, and then proceeded to get the first complete night's sleep he had had in seven weeks. He soon found, however, that he might still be in some danger. American officers in Bari informed Kramer that while the Partisans had promised to protect the lives of the officers with the McDowell mission in Serbia, they had issued a death warrant in the field to have him (Kramer) killed. Kramer needed to hear no more. Taking the advice of his comrades, he boarded a plane that afternoon for the relative safety of Caserta and some much needed rest.[61]

Bari requested that Kramer prepare a report for transmittal to Washington as soon as possible and notified McDowell that the lieutenant had returned to Italy. McDowell acknowledged this transmission, suggesting that Bari defer judgment on whether or not Kramer had deliberately disobeyed orders to rejoin the mission until all relevant information had been reviewed.[62]

Only a few days later, McDowell found himself answering charges relating to his own alleged activities in Yugoslavia. The British had apparently picked up a German broadcast that quoted McDowell as having cleared Mihailovich of collaboration and as indicating that the general would receive American Lend-Lease aid.[63] Donovan thought that McDowell ought to have a chance to comment on the charge—which he did, dismissing it as "entirely false."[64] This incident proved to be only one in a series of accusations leveled against McDowell, all of which persisted well after he had been withdrawn from the country.

Adding to the controversy was the long delay in the evacuation of the RANGER mission, which Bari suspected might have been caused in part by in-

terference from Mihailovich.[65] Huntington had recommended that McDowell
be evacuated through Partisan territory, a proposal Bari rejected since it did
not wish to "provide Tito with propaganda material which he is certain to use
in a manner deleterious to our prestige."[66] Bari had likewise turned down a
similar suggestion made earlier by James Klugmann (SOE-Cairo), who had argued that RANGER's chances for safe evacuation through Partisan territory
would be about 95 percent, but only 40 to 50 percent with the Chetniks. In
this connection it is most interesting to note that McDowell did receive orders
from Bari, the authenticity of which he questioned, instructing him to "surrender" to the nearest Partisan field headquarters. This he refused to do because the Partisans had, in earlier radio broadcasts, threatened his life if he
entered the country.[67] Kramer's experience certainly suggests that McDowell
was well advised to take these threats seriously.

RANGER finally evacuated on November 1, setting off a new round of charges
by the Partisans that Mihailovich had evacuated with the American mission.
Bari flatly denied the charge, characterizing it as nothing more than a rumor,
but this failed to satisfy the Partisans.[68] Finally, when Mitar Bakić, a member
of Tito's staff, continued to pursue the issue, an exasperated Robert Joyce wrote
to Col. Charles Thayer, who had succeeded Huntington as head of the American mission to Partisan headquarters: "We are not in the business of making
formal denial of rumors. . . . If Bakic still insists rumors are true in spite of
my denial, in your discretion you might indicate to him that we are heartily
sick of this business and if he has no confidence in our denials we are no longer
interested in making them."[69]

OSS officials in Bari considered the possibility that Mihailovich might
evacuate with either McDowell or Lalich but concluded that such a decision
could not be made unilaterally by the United States. William Maddox, who
had been chief of the SI Branch in London before coming to Caserta, advised
Joyce, "We should not take the responsibility of Mihailovich's fate. We ought
to give aid only if higher American or political or military authorities order
us to do so." Maddox believed that Washington might well take the position
that in Mihailovich's case, the British must "assume complete responsibility
or at least their share."[70] According to McDowell, General Wilson did send
a "very courteous message" to Mihailovich inviting him to evacuate with the
RANGER mission, but the Chetnik leader declined, saying that he would prefer to die in his own country than to live as an exile.[71]

Approximately three weeks after returning to Italy, McDowell submitted
his report to OSS headquarters in Bari, requesting that copies of it be sent to
G-2, AFHQ, JICA, Air Force Intelligence, General Wilson's headquarters –
including the American and British political advisers – and the British minister resident.[72] Given the controversy that continued to swirl around McDowell
and the political nature of his report, Bari initially restricted its dissemination

to Donovan, Robert Murphy, and David Bruce, chief of oss-London. oss imposed similar restrictions on the reports of Milodragovich and Rajacich.[73]

Before completing his report, McDowell discussed his findings with a small number of senior American and British officials, including Harold Macmillan, who described the colonel as "a charming American professor dressed in uniform." Macmillan's assessment of McDowell and his mission, though not shared by many of his colleagues, is both interesting and amusing: "Round the innocent head of this sweet old man has raged a tremendous storm. He has been the oss mission to Mihailović. . . . Broad (at Bari), Air Vice-Marshal Elliot and all the real Tito fans (urged on by Brigadier [Fitzroy] Maclean) have ascribed the most sinister causes to this episode. But I feel sure that the dear colonel was not a very mysterious or dangerous force."[74]

The storm to which Macmillan alluded showed no signs of subsiding quickly. Consequently, when McDowell and his team completed their reports, which Bari noted were "at variance" with British reports on conditions in Serbia, the colonel was whisked off to Washington under orders to discuss his mission with no one until he had met with either Donovan or his representative.[75] McDowell later contended that the treatment he received was similar to that experienced by other Allied officers who had been associated with Mihailovich's movement. He complained that Allied officers who had been associated with Mihailovich's forces were effectively "muzzled" after reaching Allied headquarters, while officers coming from the Partisans enjoyed complete freedom to express their views. In McDowell's words, "My turn came in November, 1944, after my return from Yugoslavia, when after a few days of free, frank and very friendly conversations with top level British and American personnel at Allied Headquarters I was cut off abruptly from all contacts; my report on the situation within Yugoslavia was limited to two copies with no circulation through channels; and for a short period I was placed under wraps in Washington."[76]

On the whole, McDowell's report was an eloquent and well-reasoned defense of Mihailovich and his Nationalist resistance forces. Noting that the political dynamics of the Partisans and Chetniks were diametrically opposite, McDowell argued that different standards or means of evaluation had to be employed in analyzing the intelligence gathered on the two organizations. It was a valid argument, but to British and American analysts the most important criterion remained which group was, or appeared to be, killing the most Germans.[77]

Against this background McDowell considered the evidence he was able to collect, which touched upon a number of important issues, chief among them being the question of collaboration. He acknowledged that "certain Serbs have collaborated with the Axis forces in varying degrees" but challenged the assumption that the guilt of some impugned the entire Nationalist movement, including Mihailovich. McDowell charged that the Partisans had attempted, with some measure of success, to place Mihailovich's forces beneath the "Chetnik" umbrella, thereby blurring the legitimate distinctions between his movement and those of other Serb leaders that were, in fact, collaborationist. Reiterating a theme he had emphasized before entering the country, McDowell quickly pointed out that "the Partisan leadership, with its patent hatred for Mihailovich and its record in respect to the falsification of information, should not be taken too seriously in its role of accuser."[78]

Furthermore, McDowell argued that the Partisan effort to destroy the Nationalist movement in Serbia, of which there was ample proof, was largely responsible for what he termed "a semblance of collaboration" between some of Mihailovich's commanders and the Germans. Kramer witnessed this kind of ambivalent relationship when Keserović's men found themselves hard-pressed by constant Partisan attacks in mid-September. Viewed in isolation from all other circumstances, this type of activity might be regarded as outright collaboration. However, McDowell insisted that fairness required the evaluation of such activity in light of Mihailovich's earlier resistance to the Germans, his continuing opposition to them in east Bosnia, his unquestioned loyalty to the Allies, and his threatened extinction by the Partisans. In concluding his findings on the collaboration issue, McDowell wrote: "All the evidence, including much collected earlier by British and American liaison officers, cries out against the hypocrisy and dishonesty of the Partisan effort to destroy the Nationalist movement by labelling it collaborationist or quisling. By this attack they have only succeeded in depriving the Allies at this moment of the services of well seasoned troops, eager to attack the Germans if only relieved of the pressure of Partisan attacks."[79]

According to McDowell, the Partisans did not confine their efforts to undermine the Nationalist movement to the battlefield. Both he and Rajacich developed information from Chetnik and German sources which indicated that the Communists were working with the Gestapo to identify and apprehend Mihailovich's undercover agents who were working in Belgrade. Rudi Stärker, the German representative with whom McDowell met on two occasions, suggested that the ss and Gestapo had employed such methods in Yugoslavia, and indeed, throughout the Balkans. McDowell did not consider the charges to be "substantiated" but did think them worthy of further investigation.[80] Compelling evidence, apparently accepted by the British, suggested that Partisan and Ustasha units were cooperating in joint attacks on the Chetniks and that known Ustasha criminals who had taken part in the massacres of great numbers of Serbs in 1941 had joined the Partisans to escape punishment for their deeds.[81] As will be shown, American officers attached to the Partisans confirmed this latter charge, adding more weight to a growing body of evidence suggesting that on the issue of collaboration or accommodation the Partisans were not exactly blameless.

McDowell became personally involved in the Partisan attempt to depict Mihailovich and his movement as collaborationist when charges began to circulate that the general had arranged and attended McDowell's meeting with Stärker. Noting that he had been ordered by his superiors at Bari to make contact with Hermann Neubacher, the German special ambassador for Southeastern Europe, as part of general Allied policy to encourage early surrender, the colonel categorically denied that Mihailovich played any role whatsoever in this episode. As McDowell pointed out, "General Mihailovich not only had no opportunity to meet Stärker but had vehemently opposed any contact on my part with the Germans while I was attached to his headquarters lest it lead, at it did, to further false charges of Nationalist collaboration."[82]

McDowell notified Bari on September 4 that Stärker had contacted him and proposed that the Americans and British allow all German troops to withdraw north to the Sava-Danube line without interference "in return for German engagement to use troops against Russians." McDowell refused to pursue the conversation further along these lines but suggested that talks aimed exclusively at bringing an end to German resistance in the Balkans might continue in a few days.[83]

On the following day, Joyce sent McDowell a set of guidelines developed by the Combined Chiefs of Staff to govern all negotiations with the Germans concerning the possibility of early surrender. These directives prevented McDowell from making any commitments to the Germans, whose surrender had to be unconditional and subject to any terms that might later be imposed by the Allies.[84] Although McDowell and Stärker met for a second time, the talks broke down over Stärker's insistence that no German forces surrendering to the British or Americans would be turned over to the Russians—a guarantee that McDowell could not give. When Neubacher, Stärker's superior, was questioned after the war by a special State Department team, he provided a version of the McDowell-Stärker talks that varied significantly from McDowell's. According to Neubacher, the appearance of Russian forces in Yugoslavia surprised McDowell, who urged Mihailovich to ask for German assistance against the Partisans.[85]

Another controversial issue raised after the war concerned charges that McDowell made personal statements and commitments to Mihailovich that were contrary to established Allied policy in Yugoslavia. In this instance, however, the allegations came not from Partisan sources but from Mihailovich himself. Testifying in Belgrade during the course of his own trial, Mihailovich stated that McDowell told him that "Germany has lost the war, your fight against the Germans does not interest us. You have to keep your position among the people." Furthermore, Mihailovich testified that McDowell assured him that the United States was "exclusively" helping him and his movement in Yugoslavia.[86]

McDowell emphatically denied these charges in the press and through a sworn statement given to the Commission of Inquiry. When asked specifically about his alleged statement to Mihailovich that the United States would aid only his movement, he replied, "I definitely did not tell General Mihailovich that the United States would aid him and his government exclusively. To have done so would have been to convict myself as both liar and fool. It was painfully obvious to all of us around the General that no American or British aid was available for his cause, while nearly every night we could see or hear American planes coming over to drop supplies and munitions to the Communists."[87]

Capt. John Milodragovich, McDowell's executive officer, concedes that the colonel thought the Allied decision to stop all supply shipments to Mihailovich was a mistake. He remains convinced, however, that McDowell did not, as a result of this belief, make commitments to Mihailovich that were contrary to American policy. Milodragovich served as interpreter for conferences between McDowell and Mihailovich and would therefore have been privy to any promises of exclusive American aid that the colonel was alleged to have made.[88]

Some twenty-five years after all of these events occurred, McDowell characterized his mission to Mihailovich as a "failure." That would seem to be an unduly harsh indictment when one considers that RANGER did all that OSS asked of it and in so doing restored some degree of balance to the historical record.[89]

When McDowell and his men finally withdrew from the country on November 1, 1944, Lalich and Jibilian remained as the only official link between Mihailovich and the Allies, and efforts were unremitting to sever even this last tie. Bari ordered the two men to evacuate through Partisan territory and advised them that no further supply drops would be made to them so long as they remained in Chetnik territory. Frustrated that his superiors in Italy either could not or would not understand the difficulties involved in traveling over rugged terrain with men who were sick and wounded, Lalich repeatedly requested that food, clothing, and medical supplies be dropped to his position. All such requests were denied.[90]

In early December, Kraigher again ordered Lalich to withdraw through Partisan territory and warned that "you will be required to explain reasons for your delays in obeying orders."[91] At one point Lalich considered the possibility of trying to join up with Partisan units, but he decided that since OSS and the Fifteenth Air Force had sent him into Serbia to evacuate downed airmen, they could come to Serbia to get him.[92] Weary of sending explanations that had no effect, Lalich made no further attempt to defend his actions. He simply notified Bari that "it is a shame and very embarrassing to have Ameri-

Capt. Nick Lalich, left, and Sgt. J. B. Allin, center, taking advantage of a rest to converse with Mihailovich. Allin was a member of the Field Photographic Branch who provided film coverage of the HALYARD mission. Courtesy J. B. Allin and M. Mike Sujdovic

can airmen without proper clothing and eating what little these people have to offer."[93]

Lalich finally agreed to make his way to the airstrip at Boljanić in Bosnia from which McDowell and his team had been evacuated. Mihailovich and a sizable force of Chetniks accompanied him for a while, during which time Lalich came to know the general quite well. Although Mihailovich had made it clear that he would not leave his country, Lalich asked if he ever came to the United States what part of the country he would like to see. Peering at Lalich through his thick spectacles, Mihailovich thought for a moment and then perhaps recalling a conversation he had had with a young American airman almost a year earlier, replied that he would like to see Texas. Undoubtedly, Gus Brown would have been pleased.

On December 11, in the town of Srednje, north of Sarajevo, Lalich and Mihailovich bade one another farewell. Mihailovich gave Lalich a ceremonial dagger for himself and one to take back to Bari for George Vujnovich. Lalich kissed Mihailovich on both cheeks, unshouldered his carbine, and presented it as a gift, saying, "Well general you didn't receive any guns from America. I guess this is more of an adventure for me than anything else, and I will never forget it." It was a difficult parting for both men. In fact, Lalich really did not want to leave the country at all. Nevertheless, with a Chetnik escort the OSS team and some twenty airmen set out for Boljanić.[94]

Only after Lalich and his party reached the airstrip at Boljanić did Bari dispatch the badly needed supplies for which ACRU had been calling for some time. Appropriately the drop was made on Christmas Day, prompting Lalich to radio Bari, "Thanks for Merry Christmas! Now believe in Santa Claus. Morale high. Drop huge success. Happy new year to Kraigher—Green—Ross—Vujnovich—Joyce. . . ." That night, around a crudely decorated tree, there was plenty to eat and drink, Christmas carols were sung, and in Lalich's words, "we had a wonderful Christmas." Two days later planes arrived to evacuate the OSS team and the airmen who were with them. These aircraft also brought in supplies, obviously not for the airmen, but for the Chetniks who had protected them and provided security at the airstrip. Lalich gave Vujnovich credit for sending in the supplies, which he was certain was done "without one-hundred-percent authorization."[95] When Lalich and his party reached Bari on the afternoon of the twenty-seventh, Vujnovich was there to greet them. Operation HALYARD was over.

After returning to Italy, Lalich prepared two reports on his activities inside Yugoslavia. The first, dated December 31, was submitted to Colonel Kraigher and dealt almost exclusively with the various evacuation operations carried out by HALYARD. In this report Lalich stated that the ACRU team had, between August 9–10 and December 27, conducted seven evacuations in which 417 personnel had been evacuated from Yugoslavia. Of this number 343 were American airmen, 8 were British, 17 were Russian, 9 were French, 11 were Yugoslav, 24 were Italian, 2 were Polish, and 3 were American civilians.[96]

Lalich reported that Mihailovich always cooperated fully in every phase of the evacuation operations. Chetnik forces provided the labor necessary to clear the airstrips, provided security around them, and brought the airmen to the landing zones for evacuation. Lalich described the scenes which took place before a group of airmen left the country:

The people would fill up baskets of meat, fruits, bread, cakes, etc, for the airmen to eat on their way back to Italy, also brandy to drink. Souvenirs of all kinds were presented to the yanks, everything from knives, native shoes and trinkets, wood water cans, insignias, everything that Americans usually try to collect. Also when leaving, airmen would be showered with flowers. People would cry with joy. Nothing was too good for our boys and I and everyone of them appreciate every moment with these people and will never forget them.[97]

Lalich submitted a second report dated January 10, 1945, that focused more on intelligence matters than on ACRU operations. He placed Mihailovich's strength at eighty thousand men, noting that while morale was high, these men were poorly armed, lacked adequate supplies of ammunition, and faced critical shortages of food and clothing. The Chetniks were carrying out sabotage operations against the Germans, including numerous attacks along the important Višegrad-Sarejevo road, but BBC continued to give the Partisans credit for these operations.[98]

Like McDowell, Lalich found evidence that the Partisans were diverting Allied aid to their struggle against the Chetniks. He also witnessed the flight of many peasants sympathetic to Mihailovich from the advancing Partisan army to German-held cities where they felt more secure. Aside from the continuing threat posed by the Partisans, Lalich discovered that Mihailovich was having to contend with a number of serious internal problems as well. This became apparent when Col. Zaharije Ostojić approached Lalich asking for assistance in establishing independent communications with the Allies and insisting that Mihailovich not be told of his request. Lalich and Jibilian agreed to meet with Ostojić and others on the pretext of cooperating with them. Actually, they gathered as much information as they could and presented it to Mihailovich, who seemed to be aware that some of his officers were conspiring against him. Ostojić later canceled his plans but never offered any explanation to Lalich for his strange proposal.[99]

Despite these problems, Lalich believed that Mihailovich and his forces were far more effective than the Allies were willing to concede. "General Mihailovich," he wrote, "is much stronger than the general public is led to believe — he is a force to be reckoned with." The Allies may not have been convinced of this, but Tito was. For some time he had been preparing to deal with Mihailovich, who, now that the HALYARD team had been withdrawn, was completely isolated from the Allies. McDowell had reported earlier that the Nationalists had complained to him that the Allies no longer wanted to know what was happening in Yugoslavia. They would not let Mihailovich's representatives out to report, nor would they send officers in to observe. The Nationalists feared that they had been "sealed off as thoroughly as Jews in a German gas chamber—and for the same end." They knew, as did Tito, that the long-awaited reckoning was at hand.[100]

8.   Kicking against the Pricks

The RANGER mission, more so than HALYARD, had been dispatched to Serbia as part of a plan by Donovan to chart a more independent course of action for OSS in Yugoslavia. Likewise, Huntington's mission to Tito was another manifestation of this same policy. Unfortunately, circumstances forced Donovan to undertake these initiatives at a time when the civil war had begun to take precedence over resistance to the Germans. Consequently, his men, whether assigned to Chetnik or Partisan forces, found themselves caught up in the vortex of a civil war that grew more intense as German influence diminished.

In all of this, however, Huntington enjoyed one advantage denied those officers who had been sent to Mihailovich. The British accepted and supported his mission. Indeed, when Donovan advised Maclean that all American personnel currently serving with British missions in Yugoslavia would remain on detached service with those missions but would come under the exclusive command of Colonel Huntington, the brigadier replied, "That is splendid and is what should be done." In a subsequent conversation with Maclean and Tito on the same day, August 10, 1944, Donovan emphasized that Huntington's mission was purely military in character and would "serve no political ends." It was being sent to the Partisans to aid their efforts against the common enemy, Germany, and to facilitate the infiltration of OSS intelligence teams into contiguous enemy countries.[1]

At the time Huntington assumed command of the Independent American Military Mission to Tito's headquarters, there were ten OSS missions or submissions operating in Yugoslavia. Three of these, RELATOR, FUNGUS, and ALTMARK, were in Bosnia. The CUCKOLD, FLOTSAM, ALUM, and DARIEN missions were in Slovenia. Two missions, SPIKE and ABBEVILLE, were operating in Serbia. And the DEPOSIT mission was located in Montenegro.[2] Farish and Popovich, two of OSS's most experienced officers, had been placed under the operational control of the Balkan Air Forces to do aircrew rescue work and therefore did not come under Huntington's command.[3]

T/Sgt. Steve Bizic (labeled A in photo) and members of SPIKE mission take a rest from the rigors of a forced march, *pokret.* Courtesy Steven Bizic

On September 1, approximately two weeks after Huntington arrived on the island of Vis to assume the duties of his new command, Donovan sent a message to Roosevelt advising the president on the current status of oss operations in Yugoslavia. The general emphasized that oss had adhered to a policy of noninterference in political matters within the country, "although the fact of delivery of supplies by British in which our supplies to British were included may be construed as refutation of this and that in fact such action constitutes material and political support." Beyond this, however, American interests in Yugoslavia had been concerned with prosecuting the war against the Germans and using the country as a base for infiltrating intelligence teams into central Europe—a matter of great importance in Donovan's opinion. The oss chief noted with some degree of pride: "We have done this so far without incurring hostility of either Tito or Mihailovich although each one feels that we should not in any way be working with the other. However within Yugoslavia itself an American soldier can still move without fear of harm in Partisan or Chetnik territory."⁴

At the time Donovan wrote to the president about the relative safety American agents enjoyed in Yugoslavia, his statement was essentially correct. Within a matter of days, however, oss personnel attached to Tito's forces experienced a dramatic change in attitude among the Partisans and found themselves subjected to even stricter limitations on their freedom of movement and access to information.⁵

There was nothing new about Partisan efforts to restrict the freedom of action of Allied intelligence officers operating in their territory. As early as February 1, 1944, Holt Green, then commanding the RAKEOFF mission, complained to Bari that "the only items of enemy intelligence we are in a position to get are those which funnel through Partisan Headquarters; and of course this would apply to a large extent if you are in the field."⁶

At first, oss viewed the restrictions imposed in early September as a reaction to McDowell's arrival at Mihailovich's headquarters, and, indeed, there was a connection between the two. Tito wanted McDowell and his men out of Serbia for the same reason he restricted the movement and freedom of action of those officers attached to his forces—he wanted no witnesses to his campaign against the Chetniks as he carried his movement into Serbia. On September 5, Tito ordered his corps commanders: "Keep in mind that the basic aim of this whole operation is to liquidate the Chetnik forces of Draza Mihailovich and the Nedic forces as well as their political and administrative apparatus. Do not allow Mvich to carry out mobilization and to take people with him."⁷

Huntington advised Donovan that Tito felt that "the Civil War is all but in the bag" and obviously did not want American and British officers free "to observe and report development of his plans to consolidate his military victory in the political and economic field."[8] Donovan forwarded Huntington's assessment to Roosevelt along with details of Tito's orders which stipulated that no Allied missions could operate with units smaller than a corps and no Allied personnel could travel inside Yugoslavia without Tito's written permission. He also noted that the British had responded to all of this by temporarily canceling further supply drops and suspending the evacuation of Partisan wounded.[9]

Tito's policy obviously strained relations between his movement and the Allies, drastically reduced the morale of Allied officers attached to his forces, and reduced their ability to collect and report meaningful intelligence to near zero. Capt. Charles B. Grimm, whose WILLOW team reached Serbian Partisan headquarters during the second week of September, complained that after mid-October, when his men were allowed contact only with Partisan sources, "our presence in Yugoslavia as a military mission was utterly worthless."[10]

From Slovenia, Lindsay reported that the Partisan staff was doing a very poor job of supplying information on operations and complained that "the information we have received has been inaccurate, incomplete and several days late."[11] Goodwin, also in Slovenia, reported that nearly all intelligence coming out of his area was given to the Allied missions in a "daily Partisan sitrep [situation report] made by the most inefficient and biased Partisan intelligence branch who insist that all intelligence we send out come through them."[12]

Capt. Charles O. Fisher, whose work in Slovenia was in part related to OSS efforts to infiltrate agents into Austria, filed a report in early December in which he concluded that "there's one thing about working with the Partisans that may as well be made clear once and for all. There is no such thing as freedom of movement." Fisher charged that every attempt he made toward securing Partisan assistance for the movement of agents into Austria was "met by hearty agreement, promises to help in every way, but then delay—delay—delay."[13]

Maj. Scott Dickinson, who headed the SPIKE mission in Serbia, reported one specific instance in which the Partisans obviously exceeded the limits of polite obstructionism. In early December, Dickinson and some of his men drove out to view a large power station near the town of Skoplje. During the course of their inspection a young secret police (OZNA) officer arrived, confiscated the mission's camera and film at gunpoint, and forced the British driver to take the men back to headquarters. Although Dickinson and his men later received an apology for this treatment, the Partisans made it clear that they saw no need for the continued presence of an Allied mission in their area.[14]

In early October, Lt. Dan Desich, who had replaced Wuchinich as head of the ALUM mission in Slovenia, complained to Huntington about the restrictions that had been imposed on him and his men by the Partisans. Huntington lodged an energetic protest with Partisan headquarters, informing Tito that the limitations placed on Desich were "in direct contravention of the under-

Maj. Scott Dickinson, commanding officer, SPIKE mission. Courtesy Steven Bizic, T/Sgt., member of SPIKE mission to Macedonia

standing arrived at between yourself, General Donovan, and myself." Huntington also reminded Tito that Arnoldy had previously cleared Desich's entry into the country through Partisan representatives in Bari.[15] Huntington's exertions had no effect. On October 11, Desich informed the colonel that he and his team had been confined to headquarters and that he had been "ordered by Partisans to cease all radio communications" until written permission was received allowing him to continue.[16]

When Huntington received this message he was in Valjevo, where he had been for five days waiting to see Tito. Finally, on October 16, with the Desich matter still unresolved and other complaints filtering in from different parts of the country, Huntington sent a strongly-worded message to Tito that said in part, "If my own stay here in Valjevo is any indication of what is happening in other areas, I can well understand the feeling of our various representatives throughout Yugoslavia that they are serving no useful purpose and could better contribute to the war effort elsewhere."

Having apparently decided that he had stated his position forcefully enough, Huntington (though presumably someone else could have done so) deleted the following sentence from his message: "I would prefer to be busy in my own homeland than to remain, an idle visitor, in this delightful land."[17]

Despite Huntington's intervention, Desich continued to be confined to his room for the most part and could leave only when accompanied by a Partisan "courier." On one occasion Desich was "literally pulled away" from an American airman with whom he was talking and was forbidden to have further contact with the man. So vehemently did Desich protest this restriction that the Partisans relented and allowed him to have contact with all American airmen passing through the area.[18]

At times the Partisans went beyond restricting the flow of information to and from American agents and actually demanded their expulsion from the country. Tito had made it clear that American officers of Yugoslav descent were no longer desired, and an OSS field report directed to Nelson Deranian suggested that it would be unwise to send any agents into Yugoslavia "who have refused to become completely partial to the Partisan point of view."[19] In early October the Partisans gave substance to these reports when Gen. Arso Jovanović, Tito's chief of staff, submitted a formal request to Huntington for the recall of Capt. George Selvig "because of unloyal statements made by him about representatives of our Army in Croatia."[20] Deranian saw the matter differently and charged that the Partisans were ordering out of the country an American officer who "dared to exercise his freedom of speech in a manner which apparently was inconsistent with Tito's program for domination of Yugoslav politics."[21]

Selvig, it will be recalled, had entered Yugoslavia on December 3, 1943, and had shortly thereafter joined the British RELATOR mission headed by Maj.

John Henniker-Major and attached to the Partisan Eighth Corps. In early April, he left the Eighth Corps in Bosnia and in the company of Randolph Churchill traveled to Croatia where, through the FUNGUS mission, he coordinated supply drops and distribution to Partisan forces operating in that area. Acting largely on his own initiative, Selvig oversaw construction of a much-needed airstrip at Gajevi near the towns of Vrgin Most and Topusko. This strip soon became a major landing zone for supplies coming out of Italy and for the evacuation of American airmen and Partisan wounded. In fact, while Selvig was in Croatia, approximately 150 airmen, 900 Partisans, and 600 refugees evacuated from this airfield.[22]

Gajevi was also the site of a tragic plane crash in which a number of Allied officers lost their lives and others, including Randolph Churchill, barely escaped. The incident occurred on July 16, 1944, as the prime minister's son, with a number of British and Russian officers, was returning to Partisan Croatian headquarters. Apparently the pilot of the aircraft, realizing that his approach was going to overshoot the runway, pulled the plane too sharply into a climb and caused it to stall. The plane then went into a dive, flattened out into a glide, and crashed. According to Lt. Nels Benson, another American officer who had joined Selvig on June 12, the plane was fully enveloped in flames by the time those on the ground could reach it. Selvig credited the Partisans with pulling the survivors from the burning aircraft, which may well have happened in some cases. However, Benson reported that Churchill, Evelyn Waugh, and others had managed to escape through a crack between the door and the floor of the plane.[23]

Randolph Churchill subsequently replaced Selvig as head of the FUNGUS mission on September 10, although Selvig remained in the country a month longer. In his final report, Selvig made no mention of any specific incident that might have prompted the Partisans to request his removal from the country. In fact, in his written report he seems to have been far less critical of the Partisan movement than many of his fellow officers. Selvig did note in his report the extent to which the peasants gave support to the Partisans in return for the protection of the "army." In his opinion, this was "not of great importance, because the army always runs from the enemy on an offensive and the poor peasant either stays behind and gets shot, or goes on the move and loses all of his worldly goods."[24] One might understand how Partisan sensibilities would be offended had Selvig openly associated himself with such views while in the country. Although many other OSS personnel who were familiar with Partisan military tactics agreed with his analysis, it was not a flattering characterization of a movement that would later claim to have liberated Yugoslavia.

Joseph Veselinovich, who joined the American mission at Croatian headquarters in mid-December, 1944, discovered less than two weeks later that the Partisans had canceled his permission to remain in the country. When Veselinovich attempted to determine why he had been recalled, he found himself being questioned by the commissar of the town of Kistanje as to why the Americans still had a military mission with the Chetniks. When Veselinovich replied that there was no mission with Mihailovich, the commissar said sarcastically that he knew a mission was continuing to operate with the Chetniks and that if he "ever got hold of Nick Lalich, he would never come out alive." He made a similar threat concerning five American airmen in the town of Knin, whom he suspected of being a mission of Mihailovich's forces.[25]

Veselinovich left Kistanje the following day and traveled to the town of Topusko, where he reported to Major Lindsay, who had been in Slovenia until December.[26] Lindsay confirmed that Veselinovich had been recalled but could offer no explanation for the decision. Bad weather made it impossible for Veselinovich to leave Topusko until January 14, when Lindsay gave him a jeep and a driver, Sgt. Joseph Bradshaw, with orders that the lieutenant be taken to Split. The two Americans reached the town of Gračac on the sixteenth and remained there for two days because of extremely heavy snowfall. It was at this point that Veselinovich and Bradshaw first began to suspect that they might actually be in some danger.[27]

On the morning of the eighteenth the two Americans found themselves under armed guard and were told that orders had been received from Eleventh Corps instructing them to travel to Knin. Unable to confirm the authenticity of these orders, which were in conflict with those issued by Lindsay, Veselinovich protested the treatment he and Bradshaw had received and demanded to go to Lovinac. Not until Veselinovich threatened to leave Gračac even if arms were used against him did the Partisans allow the two men to continue their journey—still under armed guard. Upon arriving in Lovinac, Veselinovich and Bradshaw drove their jeep to the British mission, rather than to Partisan headquarters as they had been ordered to do, and informed Allied officers there that they were being held as virtual prisoners. They then proceeded to Partisan headquarters, reported in, and returned to the British mission to try to determine why Veselinovich had been recalled and by whom.[28]

While at the British mission, Veselinovich received additional orders from Partisan Eighth Corps instructing him to proceed to Knin, which he did on the following day. En route, he passed through the town of Obrovac, where he met Gen. Petar Drapšin, Commander of the Partisan Eighth Corps. Drapšin introduced Veselinovich to several senior staff officers who were present, by saying, "This is Lt. Veselinovich, our Serbian blood, but to our great sorrow has let us down and is one of the men who must leave this country." Surprised by these words, Veselinovich sought an immediate explanation from Drapšin, who replied that the matter would be discussed more fully in Knin the following day.[29]

The subsequent meeting with Drapšin was more congenial, if not more illuminating. The Partisan commander could offer no reason for Veselinovich's recall except that he had received orders from Belgrade to that effect. Veselinovich was struck by the fact that Drapšin mentioned by name a number of high-ranking officers of the Sixth Corps who had been killed in the past six months, which led the Partisans to believe that "some type of gestapo organization" was working against them in that region. In this vein, Drapšin also questioned Veselinovich about two Allied officers, Lt. Robin Nowell (oss) and a British captain named Owen, who had expressed anti-Partisan views. When Veselinovich suggested that there must be some mistake, particularly concerning Nowell, Drapšin assured him that the information had come from sources in Bari and was correct. Perhaps it should be noted here that Veselinovich had previously served with Nowell on the joint oss-soe geisha mission in Slovenia from May to October, 1944. Interestingly enough, one of the conclusions Nowell reached and included in his final report was his belief that the entire Army of National Liberation was "shot full of German spies."[30]

Capt. Robert Weiler, whose walnut mission operated in Drapšin's area between September, 1944, and March, 1945, noted in his report a rather strange incident that might account, in part, for Drapšin's almost obsessive concern for security. According to Weiler, the British had succeeded in establishing undercover agents in Hungary and were maintaining contact with them through Partisan channels. Apparently, one of these agents had been captured and "sweated" by the Germans because a package, sent to the British mission through regular channels, contained a bomb that exploded and killed Colonel Malinković, Drapšin's chief intelligence officer, as he opened the container.[31]

Drapšin's comments and the certainty with which he made them, particularly those relating to Nowell, convinced Veselinovich that the Partisans had infiltrated oss-Bari to such an extent as to be privy to secret intelligence reports and even the privately expressed views of Allied officers who had been in the country. He suggested in his final report that an investigation of the activities of certain "American officers of Jugoslav descent" would "correct the recent irregularities and . . . bring to light certain conditions which have been overlooked during the past year."[32]

The "irregularities" to which Veselinovich referred took a more sinister turn in the case of Maj. Franklin Lindsay. After moving south from Slovenia into Croatia, Lindsay received a message from Bari that two agents would soon be dropped to him and that arrangements must be made for their infiltration into Austria. Having requested no additional men and really having no way of maintaining them even for a brief period of time, the major requested that they not be sent, but to no avail.

About a week after the men arrived, the Partisan political commissar, with whom Lindsay had become well acquainted, approached him and revealed that one of the agents—an Austrian by birth and member of the American Communist party—had proposed doing away with Lindsay and operating the mission on his own. Deciding that if he shot the man, which he "had no particular stomach to do," he would be "replying to investigations from then on," Lindsay sent the agent into Slovenia and informed Bari about the incident. In Lindsay's words, "I received no acknowledgment, or further questions about it. It just disappeared."

Three years later when he was with the Central Intelligence Agency, Lindsay asked to review his OSS message file, hoping that it might reveal some evidence relating to this strange matter. There was no record of the incident, nor was Lindsay's initial message reporting on it found. It was as if the whole thing had never occurred.[33]

Perhaps the most bizarre case arising out of Partisan efforts to restrict the movement of American officers in Yugoslavia—and a well-documented one—involved Capt. Temple Fielding, who had entered the country in mid-August with the Huntington mission, to which he was assigned as morale operations officer.

On November 19, Fielding traveled to Split where he met with General Drapšin to discuss a number of questions relating to propaganda operations his mission might undertake. The meeting lasted slightly more than an hour and ended in some rather casual conversation, all of which suggested to Fielding that this particular mission was going to be somewhat routine and uneventful. It proved to be neither. What follows is an intriguing account of Fielding's six-day ordeal (November 19–24) taken mostly from a journal he maintained throughout the entire episode. As Fielding himself points out, "Some of the notes of the final night are incoherent, emotional, and disconnected. They were written by flashlight, candle light, and the light of a small bonfire, at a time when my life was in great danger."[34]

To begin, Fielding noted on returning to his room on the evening of the nineteenth that his luggage had been thoroughly searched. Nothing had been taken, but every item had been examined and returned to its place. At this point, he obviously thought the search had been carried out by enemy agents—German or Ustasha—and confessed to his journal that "this is one city I'd rather not see again, until Jerry is licked for good."[35]

Early the following morning Fielding was called to the Allied Liaison Office, where he was questioned by a Partisan officer the British suspected of being an OGPU (Unified State Political Directorate) agent. The Partisan officer demanded to know the nature of Fielding's business in the Eighth Corps area, why he was traveling in the area without a pass, and how he had gotten into the area without one. Fielding indicated that he had arrived in Split with a British officer for the purpose of meeting with General Drapšin and was unaware that he needed a pass for that purpose. The Partisan official insisted that Fielding give him the name of the British officer who had transported him to Split, but the captain refused. At this point the Partisans told Fielding that he must return to Dubrovnik on the first available boat and was not to leave the township of Split until his departure.[36]

After notifying members of the British mission of his instructions, Fielding went into Split where he spent the afternoon—obviously under surveillance. During the night, actually about one o'clock in the morning, he was awakened by someone on the balcony outside his window attempting to force his way into the room. In Fielding's words, "this was too much. First some one had been through my baggage—and found nothing. Then I had been followed. They knew that I carried my papers with me, and they were out to get them another way."[37]

On the morning of the twenty-first, reflecting on the events of the previous day, Fielding confided to his journal:

In one sentence, Partisan sentiment boils down to this: they are tremendously suspicious of Britain and America and they do not want us in Yugoslavia. That's the essence of it. Because we give them hundreds of thousands of tons of food, clothes, ammo, guns and sundry supplies, and because we bomb for them and lend them ships and transport, and other necessities, they must tolerate us—but if they were able to shift for themselves, we would be out on our ear, without delay.[38]

On the twenty-third, Fielding left Split by boat, hoping to reach Dubrovnik. However, the boat on which he sailed broke down and had to put in at Korčula. That evening in the dining room of the hotel where he was staying, Fielding noted the arrival of a "powerfully-built thug wearing a Partisan private's uniform" and carrying two suitcases, but he attached no particular significance to this even when the man entered the room adjoining his. Later that night, at approximately eleven o'clock, Fielding was awakened by the clicking sound of a bolt on an automatic weapon coming from that room. Upon examining the two large cabinets or wardrobes next to the head of his bed, he discovered that one was merely a false front and could be entered from the adjoining room. Hurriedly shaping the pillows in his bed to resemble a human form, he grabbed his submachine gun and moved to the corner of the room. Shortly thereafter he heard the door in the adjacent room open and realized that two people had entered the cabinet.[39]

He pushed his bed against the cabinet to form a partial barricade and then draped the mattress and covers over the top of the cabinet for further protection. Over all of this he placed medicine bottles that would fall at the slightest disturbance, thus providing a warning in the unlikely event that he might fall asleep. Even under these conditions, Fielding continued to write in his journal: "This is the most dangerous moment of my life. My room in this house has a trick closet, which I discovered—there are two thugs in the next room, who have been in that closet. It is 1 A.M.—I took benzedrine, and now I have barricaded the closet with the bed and the mattress. I am sitting on the floor, with my gun in may lap, and these two trying to find a way in."[40]

At approximately 2:20, Fielding thought he heard one of the men creeping down the stairs, possibly going for help. Writing now in bold print on the assumption that his tormentors might soon be reading his journal, Fielding wrote: "The best part of this is that the British and Americans know what happened, if I don't show up – Read that, you Bastards!!!"[41]

Two hours later, Fielding sensed that he was completely surrounded. His candle was gone, and he had built a fire out of a wicker basket and a book to throw some light on the closet. The men in the next room had begun punching holes in the wall to allow them to see into his room, but he spotted these with his flashlight almost as quickly as they were made and plugged them.[42]

Six hours into his ordeal, Fielding's fear had begun to turn into anger. He wrote: "The only way they can get me is to come and take me, the sons of bitches. They might try a grenade. I have put a tabletop against the window for this contingency. It's 5:05, and I'm still master of them, the dirty filthy bastards. I hope they come soon – I'm going to shoot that big thug, so help me God."[43]

About an hour later, he said, he began shooting out the window again and spelling his name aloud repeatedly, hoping that someone would remember it and tell the British and Americans that he had been there. Just as he finished, Fielding heard a voice from the courtyard below which said three of the most comforting words he had heard in what seemed like an eternity, "I'm British, lad." Fielding heard the words with guarded optimism, fearing that this might be yet another trap. In a few moments the Britisher was standing outside his door answering a series of questions ranging from rugby to British army rations in an attempt to authenticate his identity. Finally, when the British soldier slipped his pay card under the door, Fielding felt that "at last my savior had come." His savior in this instance was Bernard H. Bridges, a "cocky, capable, red-faced British Sergeant, as typical of England as John Bull."[44]

While Fielding gathered his belongings, Bridges inspected the rooms to verify his story. At this point the two men who had harassed Fielding all night came upstairs to get their gear. As they started to leave, one of them turned to Fielding, smiled and said, "Zdravo! Bono homo!" With a pistol in hand, Fielding shouted back, "Don't Zdravo me, you son of a bitch! If I ever see you again, I'll kill you!" Bridges and Fielding cautiously made their way to the dock and boarded the schooner that was to take them to Dubrovnik. As the vessel slipped out of the harbor at Korčula, Fielding knew that his work in Yugoslavia was over. He confided to his journal, "As far as Yugoslavia and I are concerned, I have had it. I am of no further value to anyone here, and it might mean my life, as it so nearly did last night, if I stayed."[45]

After reaching Dubrovnik, Fielding filed his report with the American mission there and was examined by a British doctor who found him to be "in complete control of his senses and of sound mind." Sergeant Bridges also filed a report that confirmed the details of Fielding's story concerning events of the night of November 23–24. When these formalities were completed, Fielding returned to Italy never having solved the mystery of why he had been threatened by Partisan agents.[46]

Admittedly, Fielding's case represented an extreme example of what could happen in Yugoslavia as relations between the Partisans and Allies began to break down beneath the weight of mutual suspicions and mistrust. The degree to which restrictions applied to oss personnel appears to have varied somewhat depending on location, time, and the attitude of individual Partisan commanders. In general, however, Donovan's men were confined to corps headquarters where they were spoonfed only the information the Partisans wanted them to have; they were denied access to the civilian population or to prisoners; and, in some cases, they were limited in the contact they could have with American airmen. Furthermore, the intelligence the Partisans did supply was usually characterized as being untimely, incomplete, inaccurate, highly exaggerated, or obviously false – all of which Weil had said six months earlier.[47]

Of course, six months earlier the Partisans were not anticipating the imminent arrival of Soviet forces on the borders of Yugoslavia – a factor that undoubtedly contributed to worsening relations between Tito's forces and the western Allies. oss officers had for some time complained that the Partisans seemed to hold the Russians in far greater esteem than either American or British representatives, despite the vast amount of aid provided by the Western powers. As Rex Deane put it, "Russia of course is the Savior here. We are tolerated to supply the goods with constant inquiries as to why we aren't doing more." Deane also noted that speeches given at Partisan political rallies made frequent references to Stalin and the "glorious Red Army," while "occasionally there would be a reference to England and America, but very seldom."[48] Capt. Eugene O'Meara claimed that most Partisans were not aware of the extent of American aid to their movement, but he agreed that in terms of prestige, the United States lagged far behind the Russians.[49]

The Partisans seemed to have maintained this almost reverential attitude toward the Russians despite a rather inauspicious beginning occasioned by the arrival of the first Soviet mission in February, 1944. The man selected to head the Russian team was Lt. Gen. N. V. Korneyev, a line officer who had seen action on the Russian front at the time of the German invasion and had later played a role in the defense of Stalingrad. His second in command, Maj. Gen. A. P. Gorshkov, had been involved in the defense of Moscow and had subsequently served with Russian Partisans behind enemy lines for approximately eight months. The Soviet team, described by oss sources in Cairo as having had "substantial experience in the field," landed at an airfield near Bosanski Petrovac in Horsa gliders furnished by the British.[50]

According to Eli Popovich, who was in Drvar just before Korneyev arrived, Partisan enthusiasm for their Soviet comrades had begun to wane even before the mission reached the country. The Russians apparently sent word in advance to the Partisans that they wanted a house in which to locate the mission, specifying the number of beds they would need and insisting that each bed was to have a mattress and sheets. According to Popovich, "This was quite a shock to the Partisans when they heard this, because there we were sleeping on a wooden bench on straw in our sleeping bags and nobody complaining and here these so-called liberators of the masses coming into the country requesting sheets and mattresses and having their rooms painted white."[51]

A few days later when the Russians arrived at Bosanski Petrovac, they informed the Partisans who were there to greet them that they should dispense with their clenched-fist salute and must recognize the rank of Soviet officers when addressing them.[52] This preoccupation with rank prompted D. L. Rider of ASH team to consider wiring Bari to request a dozen assorted medals just to keep up with the Russians.[53] A number of American officers were struck by and commented on the almost blatant condescension that characterized the Russians' attitude toward the Partisans. George Selvig thought that the Russians seemed "not very much interested in getting their feet muddy so to speak," and acted toward the Partisans "like somebody from the city meeting their country cousin and not enjoying it at all."[54] According to Dan Desich, however, the Partisans failed to impress the Russians because there were "too many speeches and not enough action."[55]

With few exceptions, American and Soviet liaison officers got along well enough, though it is clear that some OSS personnel resented the preferential treatment afforded the Russians by the Partisans.[56] Russian liaison officers were not subjected to the same restrictions as those imposed upon American and British officers and appeared to have easier access to certain information as well as to upper-level Partisan officials. Furthermore, at Partisan political rallies, of which there were many, the Russians always spoke immediately following the Partisan speakers, and the Russian national anthem usually preceded the American and British anthems.[57]

American and British officers quite naturally resented this sort of treatment since OSS and SOE had been primarily responsible for supplying the Partisans with arms and munitions while the Russians had done virtually nothing in this regard. Rex Deane undoubtedly expressed the sentiments of many American officers when he voiced this resentment at the distrust and "open hatred" expressed by the Partisans while they were receiving tons of supplies from the western powers every night.[58]

The matter of supply had been and, to some extent, continued to be a source of contention between the American and British missions. oss officers were concerned that the Partisans did not appreciate the extent to which the United States was supporting their movement and that they may not have been aware that a large part of the "British" supplies they were receiving was actually American in origin.[59] In reality, the Partisans, at least staff personnel at corps level and above, knew that much of their supply was coming from the United States and queried American officers as to why it was controlled by the British. They even attempted to exploit the situation by promising certain favors – information or material assistance – to the side that provided the most aid.[60]

Commenting on the problems that arose at times between the British and Americans over the supply issue, Huntington expressed resentment that the rank and file of the Partisan movement were constantly complaining about the lack of American aid. Most high-ranking Partisan officials knew the truth, as did the chief of the British mission, whom Huntington credited with being "generous and fair in recognizing the American contribution." Huntington complained, however, that other British officials "insisted on the fiction of undiluted British aid – a fiction which in no wise does justice to the perspicacity of the Jugoslav."[61]

By this time, of course, the Americans had accepted the fact, not necessarily with enthusiasm, that Yugoslavia was in a British theater of war and therefore British wartime and postwar interests would be best served if the Partisans regarded Britain as their chief benefactor. To Britain, supply was somewhat like an umbilical cord by which she could sustain and nourish the resistance with the hope of being rewarded by the birth of regimes well-disposed to her in the postwar period. Since the United States had consistently denied having any such ambitions in the Balkans, it seemed unwise to hinder British efforts in this regard. After all, only the Soviet Union stood to gain from the diminution of British influence in the region.

Precisely for that reason, American officials refused to accept passively the steady flow of Partisan propaganda apotheosizing Soviet supply efforts. According to Dan Desich, Partisan crews that received supply shipments at landing zones in Slovenia had been ordered to say that the supplies and the planes delivering them were Russian. The fact that markings and emblems on the planes clearly identified them as either British or American made absolutely no difference.[62] To counter this sort of propaganda, Eli Popovich made it a point to go to the landing zone while supplies were being brought in and wave to the pilots, whom he pretended to know by name, in an attempt to prove the supplies were coming from the West.[63]

In January, 1945, it appeared that Tito had fallen victim to his own propaganda. During the course of a conference with oss representatives in Belgrade, the Partisan leader chided the Americans for their lack of support for his movement and the "paucity" of supplies they had sent. When the Americans responded by pointing out that over half of the Partisan army had been supplied by the Allies, Tito flatly denied it. At that point the OSS officers produced a complete list of the supplies that had been sent to the Partisans. Reviewing it, Tito appeared "surprised" and "gave the impression that he had never comprehended the full extent of Allied aid."[64]

Not all American officers wanted the United States to assume credit for supplies sent to the Partisans, for by so doing the United States must acknowledge at least some responsibility for the manner in which those supplies were used. OSS officers attached to Chetnik forces, particularly McDowell and other RANGER personnel, had argued convincingly that from early September the Partisans had begun to divert the bulk of their supplies to operations against Mihailovich's forces rather than the Germans. OSS officers with Tito's forces corroborated these charges, and some suggested that continued support of the Partisans would merely insure the defeat of the Chetniks and the consolidation of Tito's political position inside the country. Capt. Charles Grimm actually recommended that "no further war supplies, other than small arms be sent to Tito, unless we wish to strengthen the Partisans in case of a civil war and assure a Communistic victory."[65]

There was also evidence that the Partisans were continuing to store supplies, perhaps anticipating that their war with the Chetniks might extend beyond the point when the Allies would continue to supply them.[66] Rex Deane, who was for a while attached to the Partisan Second Corps, reported that "any fighting spirit here at HQ is non-existent. There are generally 4 to 6 Generals sitting around drinking coffee all day. . . . There is a complete lack of organization here and altho tons of ammo and demolition equipment have been dropped, no use has been made of same."[67]

Huntington alluded to none of these problems either in his final report or in an earlier report entitled "The Jugoslav Army of National Liberation: Its Potentialities for Allied Use." In the latter, he suggested that Tito could provide between sixty thousand and one hundred thousand men for operations aimed at impeding the retreat of German forces through western Yugoslavia and closing their escape route at Ljubljana. On paper, Huntington's proposal seemed realistic enough. With an army of three hundred thousand—Huntington's estimate—at his disposal and Russian forces advancing into eastern Yugoslavia, Tito could, by all appearances, well afford to assist his Anglo-American allies in this undertaking against the common enemy. Unfortunately, the potentialities to which Huntington referred remained largely that.[68]

This is not meant to imply that the Partisans ceased operations against the Germans, for certainly they did not. They continued to attack smaller German units and to sabotage transportation and communications lines when possible. Between September and December, 1944, Ultra credited the Partisans, whom the Germans regarded as a much greater threat than the Chetniks, with many such actions.[69] Likewise there were several references to German forces encountering resistance from "strong" and "well-equipped Tito guerrillas" in different parts of the country.[70]

Under these circumstances the Germans attempted to hold the key transportation and communication centers, abandoning less critical areas to the Partisans. An intercept dated December 12, 1944, for example, describes the territory around Bihać as being weakly held by the Germans, and the area to the south as "purely Partisan territory."[71] There were also occasions when the Partisans attempted to block the withdrawal of enemy forces altogether. One such instance occurred in early November when German troops in Sibernik found their line of retreat blocked by Partisan units and "expected severe losses during break-out."[72]

However, at no time during the German withdrawal did the Partisans bring to bear the levels of manpower and firepower of which they were capable. Having apparently decided that the Germans were a spent force, the Partisans saw little wisdom in expending men and resources to kill them when Allied military pressure was forcing them to leave the country as quickly as possible. In Vojvodina, for example, the Germans and Partisans had obviously adopted a "live and let live" policy toward one another. Don Rider of ASH team reported that on more than one occasion he accompanied Partisan columns that passed within one hundred yards of German tanks and bunkers and neither side fired on the other.[73]

Dickinson reported that in late October he and his men tried to persuade the Partisans to destroy railroads and bridges that were being used by the retreating Germans. Although the Partisans argued that they were not adequately prepared to confront the Germans directly, Dickinson suspected that they simply did not want to destroy the facilities in question. When he argued that the Germans would destroy them in any case, the Partisans "paid no attention to this advice and made only feeble and temporary attempts to stop the Germans." Dickinson later concluded: "From the extent of the German movements it was clear that the Partisans were permitting them to get out and were occupying towns and villages as soon after the Germans left as possible."[74]

By late 1944, German forces in Yugoslavia were engaged in a desperate defensive struggle, not to hold on to the country but to extricate themselves from it. If, under the guise of anticommunism and through the promise of material support, they could neutralize or gain support from particular Chetnik formations, they were inclined to do so. Likewise, if the Chetniks could gain arms from a defeated enemy to use against another foe – the Partisans – they would do so.

Was Mihailovich in any way responsible for cultivating this almost symbiotic relationship between his forces and the Germans? The Germans certainly thought that he was, but there is no evidence to show that this belief served to ameliorate relations between the two groups. When Hilter finally gave his consent to the arming of certain Nationalist groups, he ordered Field Marshal Maximilian von Weichs to supply only those "Cetnik formations which had so far proved reliable." Furthermore, von Weichs was to employ these units for "limited undertakings" in Serbia under German command and control. Thus did the German High Command hope to insure that weapons provided by Germany would not "in changed circumstances turn against her." As a further precaution, Neubacher, not Nedić, was to decide which Chetnik formations would be supplied.[75]

Neubacher assumed that as Tito's strength grew, hard-pressed Chetnik forces, even those with ties to Mihailovich, would approach the Germans for support against the Communists. An intercept dated September 16, 1944, mentions the need to maintain contact with Bačević in an effort "to get him to follow the common fight against communism."[76] Two months later when other Chetnik officers were "again endeavoring to obtain arms and ammunition from Germans," Bačević came to the Germans with an offer to subordinate "all Mihailovic formations to Germans."[77] Whether or not Mihailovich knew of this particular offer is not clear. It is almost certain, however, that he knew of and reluctantly approved initiatives similar to Bačević's. An entry from the OKW *War Diary*, quoting a "reliable source," indicated that "Mihailovich ordered his non-commissioned officers to work together with the Germans" but avoided direct participation because of the "sentiments of the people."[78]

Although Mihailovich's critics regard these actions as proof that the general was a collaborator, the Germans never saw him in that light. Neubacher, who knew the details of the German-Chetnik "treaties" perhaps better than anyone, characterized Mihailovich's attitude toward Germany as one of unremitting hostility. Mihailovich and his Chetniks fought the Germans when they could, avoided fights when they had to, and reached accommodations in order to survive and resist the Partisans. In all of this, however, Mihailovich never sought to advance the goals of German policy in Yugoslavia, nor did he consider cooperating with the Germans against the Allies as did the Partisans.[79]

Franklin Lindsay also complained that Tito's forces did far less than they could have to harass the Germans or impede their withdrawal, particularly after September, 1944, "when the Partisans almost completely failed to hold the initiative."[80] According to Deane, the Partisans "seemed content to keep out of the Germans' way and let them get out of the country. No concerted effort was made to stop them or ambush them in any way." The primary concern of each corps commander seem to be to pass the Germans on to the next corps. As far as Deane could tell, the Partisans were far more interested in attacking the Chetniks and their supporters than in fighting the Germans.[81]

The British encountered similar problems when some of their troops landed at Dubrovnik as part of a plan to interdict the German withdrawal through that area. When Partisans forces refused to cooperate in the operation, the British commander declared bitterly that "they all should be court-martialed for letting the Germans escape."[82] In Slovenia, Desich reported that the British officer in charge of the SOE mission there, a Colonel Moore, had become so disenchanted with the Partisans that "rather than wait for favorable weather for evacuation by plane, he broke all records by walking to the coast to get to London as soon as possible." When Desich last saw Moore in January, the colonel said that "he had had it as far as the Partisans were concerned, and regretted that Britain had given its support to such people."[83]

Moore was obviously not alone in this opinion. As early as September 1, Joyce reported on a conversation with Harold Macmillan during which Macmillan "discussed with considerable cynicism the activities of Brigadier Maclean, head of the British Mission to Yugoslavia." According to Joyce, Macmillan thought Maclean "should have sold his shares on Tito at the peak of the market some months ago."[84] At about the same time, Anthony Eden told Dr. Ivan Šubašić, then prime minister of the Yugoslav government-in-exile, that "we would not have abandoned Mihailovich if we had known Tito was going to behave like this."[85]

In early October, Donovan informed Roosevelt that Churchill had sent a "sizzling telegram" to Tito, telling him in no uncertain terms that the British government had sent arms to him "to fight the enemy and not to fight his own people."[86] Lt. Col. Charles Thayer, who assumed command of the IAMM on November 13, advised Joyce, however, that most observers in Belgrade believed that Churchill was simply "kicking against the pricks."[87]

By early October, Churchill had good cause to be disillusioned with Tito. The Partisans had imposed such severe restrictions on British liaison officers as to render them largely ineffective; cooperation on military matters, when given, was proffered grudgingly; and Allied supplies were being diverted to wage a civil war against the Chetniks. These things were happening in spite of the fact the British had gone to great lengths to provide for the comfort and security of Tito and his staff on Vis following their evacuation from Yugoslavia in the aftermath of the Drvar attack. Tito appeared to make the transition from guerrilla fighter to statesman with little difficulty and soon found himself rubbing elbows with a procession of political and military personalities, including Churchill himself.

Understandably, Tito's unannounced departure from Vis on the night of September 18 in a Russian plane was regarded by Churchill as a personal affront—one not soon forgotten. In mid-November, for example, he told King Peter, "You know I do not trust Tito. He surreptitiously flew to Moscow to meet with Stalin before my arrival in London. He is nothing but a Communist thug, but he is in power and we must reckon with that fact."[88]

The Western Allies had for some time regarded and dealt with Tito as the real power in Yugoslavia. Their support had been instrumental in allowing him to achieve and consolidate his position within the country, though by it they had not acquired any great influence over his military or political policies. Churchill's statement represented a candid admission that while the Western powers might not agree with the course of events in Yugoslavia, there was little, if anything, they could do about it.

By mid-September, however, Tito was not primarily concerned with the unsolicited encroachments of Anglo-American influence. The steady advance of the Red Army convinced him that the time had come to reach an understanding with Stalin concerning the status of Soviet troops in Yugoslavia and the relationship that must exist between the Soviet army and his own Army of National Liberation. Moreover, the understanding would be negotiated directly between him and Stalin, thus avoiding any misunderstanding as to where real power lay in Yugoslavia.

American officers noticed that the enthusiasm with which the Partisans had anticipated the arrival of the Red Army waned rapidly after Soviet forces entered the country. According to Rider, "Before the arrival of Russian troops, the Jugoslav Partisans continually referred to the Red Army in the most magnanimous of terms, but after seeing them, the Partisans became very silent on the subject, except to give weak apologies for the Russians."[89]

Grimm reported that the hostility the Partisans had exhibited toward the British and American missions diminished considerably after the Partisans "had their first glimpse of the glorified Russians." As Grimm noted, "It took only a few days for the Partisan Officials to realize the blunder they had commited [sic] in their propaganda, as an army depending on American trucks, jeeps, medical aid, food, etc, would be definitely unable to supply another nation with like items."[90]

Partisan disenchantment with the Russians did not result in a general reconciliation with the Western Allies. Tito and his advisers seem never to have been convinced that the West, especially Britain, would accept the establishment of a Communist regime in Yugoslavia. Churchill's efforts to salvage some degree of British influence in the country and to secure, if possible, the return of the monarchy may have convinced the Partisans that their suspicions were correct. Furthermore, on October 9, only a few days after warning Tito about his diverting supplies to fight the Chetniks, Churchill flew to Moscow to meet with Stalin and discuss, among other things, British-Soviet relations in the Balkans.

The two leaders agreed in what Churchill later termed "an offhand manner" that their countries would share equal interests in Yugoslavia after the war, with Russia having a controlling influence in Rumania and Britain retaining her dominant interests in Greece. Deakin suggests that the famous penciled note outlining the division of the Balkans was "simply a balloon put across the table" — an effort on Churchill's part to get some idea as to where the Russian army was going to stop. The prime minister later informed Roosevelt of the understanding, indicating that in light of the existing military situation it was probably "the best possible solution."[91]

According to Vladimir Dedijer, the Partisans learned of the agreement as a result of some intemperate remarks by Randolph Churchill and naturally received the news as further evidence of Western hostility to their movement. As a result, they continued to impose severe restrictions on Allied missions attached to their forces and viewed with increased suspicion any Allied initiatives that had not been fully explained to and approved by the Partisan High Command. While reaction to Stalin's involvement in the percentages agreement was neither as obvious nor as immediate, there can be little doubt that this incident was a major factor contributing to the 1948 split between Moscow and Belgrade.[92]

During the course of the propaganda war that followed in the wake of Tito's break with Stalin, both sides claimed credit for having liberated Yugoslavia.[93] The politics of the Cold War favored Tito in this battle of words with the Soviet dictator, particularly in the West where even a maverick Communist could become a hero of sorts by standing up to Stalin. Unfortunately, what was initially accepted largely on the basis of political expediency came, in time, to be endowed with the mantle of historical respectability. Thus was born the myth that the Partisans liberated Yugoslavia.

The operational files of OSS contain overwhelming evidence refuting the long-held view that Tito's Army of National Liberation was the instrument by which Yugoslavia was freed from the yoke of Nazi oppression. OSS field reports, even those filed by officers having genuine admiration for the military contribution of the Partisan movement, clearly indicate that areas designated by the Partisans as liberated simply referred to territory in which the Germans chose not to conduct operations. When the Germans did decide to move through these regions, there was little the Partisans would or could do to stop them. Capt. John Blatnik admitted that "it is not only possible to have our liberated areas overrun or cut thru by the enemy, but it could be done quite quickly."[94]

Beginning in the summer of 1944 and continuing until they withdrew from the country, the Germans ceased to conduct any further offensives against the Partisans. Instead, they chose to hold certain key cities and the communications lines linking them, which they defended when attacked. Otherwise, they were content to allow the Partisans to occupy large but strategically unimportant areas throughout the country — which the Partisans, of course, regarded as liberated territory.[95]

Furthermore, many towns and cities that the Partisans claimed to have liberated were actually occupied by them after Axis forces had withdrawn. Reporting on Partisan efforts to take the town of Nikšić, which fell on September 20,

Rex Deane observed that "the Germans decided to get out and the Partisans entered. This I found was always the case during the summer campaign."[96]

Most American officers would have agreed with Capt. Eugene O'Meara, who reported that in Dalmatia the Germans could have controlled any area they wished but simply lacked the troops to do so.[97] Obviously, the Partisans claimed to have liberated much territory that either fell to them by default or was never contested at all by the Germans.[98] Dan Desich concluded that "with regard to liberating particular towns or areas, I doubt very seriously that the Partisans could do it. It is true that the Partisans have a large liberated area in Slovenia, but I believe it is only because the enemy has stayed out rather than having been forced out."[99]

What was true for Slovenia was generally true for Yugoslavia. Although the Partisans continued to attack smaller German units when the numbers were in their favor and to sabotage roads, bridges, and railroads, their actions were in no way sufficient to force German troops out of the country.[100] The steady advance of Soviet forces, which threatened to close all escape routes from the Balkans, was the decisive factor in forcing German troops out of Greece and Yugoslavia. Tito had positioned himself well to take advantage of this situation, moving with alacrity to insure that Partisan influence quickly filled the political and military vacuum created by the German withdrawal. His actions, however, reveal the deft hand of a highly skilled political opportunist, not the strong arm of a sword-wielding liberator.

Of all the reports that touched upon the issue of liberated territory, the one filed by John Hamilton is the most interesting. Regarded by those who knew him as a consistent "champion of the Partisans," Hamilton's admiration for the Partisan movement, as expressed in his earlier reports, had known no bounds. Such views were conspicuously absent in the report he filed on September 28, 1944, after returning from Croatia – Partisan Tenth Corps – where he had been in charge of an ACRU mission code-named HACIENDA. Charging that "the Partisan movement is not an expression of the people's will," Hamilton characterized Partisan claims of holding "liberated territory" as "pure bunkum." He continued, "Partisan territory is 'free' simply because the enemy does not care to use it at the time. When the enemy wants to, he marches in and the Partisans take to the hills. This leaves the farmer holding the bag. The Germans, or local Fascists, plunder his farm, rape his women, burn a few homes and move on. Then the Partisans return and the cycle is ready to commence anew."[101]

To portray the Partisans as the liberators of Yugoslavia requires one to shape and force together bits of evidence so incongruent in nature as to defy otherwise the emergence of a coherent picture. By the fall of 1944, for example, most OSS reports credited Tito with having at his disposal an army of over three hundred thousand men, tested in battle and well equipped – perhaps better equipped than many Soviet troops. Still, there is virtual unanimity among American intelligence officers that the Germans could, up until they actually left Yugoslavia, move at will through any region of the country—even those areas considered to have been liberated by the Partisans.

Through the summer of 1944, the Partisans had been the object of no fewer than seven German offensives, all of which had failed because the guerrillas eluded, rather than repelled, the forces deployed against them.[102] To maintain that within a matter of weeks these same guerrillas began successfully to do what they had never done before—confront the German invader and hound him from their soil—is to suggest a transformation with few, if any, parallels in the annals of military history.

The preponderance of evidence gleaned from OSS field reports simply does not support this version of Yugoslavia's liberation. Instead, American intelligence officers attached to both elements of the resistance indicate that at the very time when German forces were most vulnerable to the types of operations the Partisans could employ against them, the Partisans had their attention riveted on Serbian and Mihailovich. As a result, Tito denied to the Allies considerable assistance that could have been rendered by his forces and those of General Mihailovich as well. According to Rex Deane, many German forces escaped unchallenged from Yugoslavia because the Partisans were "too busy evening up old scores with Chetnik families in the neighborhood rather than fight Germans."[103] In other words, after September, 1944, Tito was doing precisely what Mihailovich had been accused of doing earlier—tailoring his resistance policies to accommodate political objectives. That he succeeded where Mihailovich had failed was due in part to his own political abilities and to the policies the Allies had adopted toward his movement. With German forces withdrawing and Chetnik strength waning, Tito's military supremacy in the country was unchallenged. And though none had done so with any great degree of enthusiasm, Churchill, Stalin, and Roosevelt had, by their actions, tacitly recognized Tito as the sole political authority in Yugoslavia.

It was, in fact, under terms of the agreement concluded between Tito and Stalin in Moscow that Soviet troops entered Yugoslavia on October 1. Within three weeks, these Red Army units, in conjunction with Partisan forces, knifed through relatively weak German opposition and liberated Belgrade—the last German resistance being crushed by October 20. Four members of the American mission, including Huntington, joined the Partisan First Corps on October 9, during its advance through western Serbia, and observed the actual liberation of the capital. Within a matter of days, the IAMM established its headquarters in the newly liberated capital, where it soon became apparent that the team would no longer function exclusively as a military mission.[104]

On November 5, Huntington turned over command of the mission to Maj. Stafford Reid and returned to Italy. Reid headed the IAMM about a week before

Maj. Basil Davidson (SOE), left, and Capt. Donald Rider (OSS), ASH Team, right, pictured with an unidentified Russian soldier shortly after the liberation of Belgrade. Courtesy Don Rider

relinquishing command to Lt. Col. Charles Thayer, who had previously served as the mission's political intelligence officer. Thayer, a West Point graduate with more than eight years of diplomatic experience in Germany and Russia and a personal friend of Maclean's, seemed well suited to head the mission during the transition from military to political affairs.[105]

Thayer soon found himself confronting many of the same problems that had plagued Huntington during his tenure as head of the IAMM, particularly the degree to which mission personnel were restricted by the Partisans. Only five days after assuming his new command, Thayer informed Joyce that as far as the status of his mission was concerned, the word "independent" was being ignored by the Partisans.[106] He later admitted that his team had been able to collect only a "small percentage" of available intelligence because of the "consistently uncooperative attitude of Partisan officials." Thayer also found himself caught up in the propaganda struggle, protesting, as had Huntington and others, and with about as much success, that the Partisans were not giving due credit for the support rendered to them by the United States and Britain. He later reported that while American assistance was not given "one-tenth the publicity accorded Russian, or even Bulgarian, aid, it is occasionally noted in the newspapers."[107]

Thayer had to deal with other and more serious problems. Never, for example, did the Partisans abandon their obstructionist tactics aimed at thwarting OSS efforts to infiltrate teams into countries contiguous to Yugoslavia. Donovan had planned to use Tito's territory as a springboard for infiltrating missions into Austria, Germany, Czechoslovakia, and Hungary, and he emphasized to Huntington the importance of beginning these operations as soon as possible.[108] The difficulties Huntington faced while attempting to carry out this policy have already been noted. Thayer fared no better.

The experiences of the ORCHID team provide a good example of the kinds of problems OSS encountered from the Partisans, whose help was crucial to the success of the northern penetration effort. On August 26 eight men, making up TUNIC, FERN, ROSE, and ORCHID teams, entered Yugoslavia under the auspices of the OSS Labor Desk. While traveling northward through Slovenia, the men met Lindsay and discussed the nature of their missions with him. Neither Lindsay nor his British counterpart held out much hope that the Partisans would cooperate in the effort. This discouraging news prompted five of the men to return to Bari, where they reported that attempts to penetrate northward through Slovenian headquarters would be "difficult if not impossible." The three men who remained – ORCHID team – did succeed in moving northward into Austria where they operated for a brief period of time under the protection of a Partisan battalion commander, but the intelligence they gathered fell far short of what OSS had expected.[109]

Members of the ORCHID team offered numerous reasons for the disappointing results achieved by their mission—all of which had a familiar ring to them. The men reported that "at no time was it possible to effect an arrangement through which the normal flow of intelligence concerning either military of political developments would be turned over to the team as a matter of routine." On the other hand, much information that was provided reflected "a passion for exaggeration and a state of major unconcern which almost approached disdain for routine details." The Partisans never denied requests for assistance in conducting the penetration operations; they simply responded with a series of interminable delays.[110]

New and potentially more serious problems arose as Soviet forces began to move into the regions targeted for penetration by OSS. Although the Russians had agreed in principle to the operation of OSS teams in central Europe, that spirit of cooperation dissipated quickly as it trickled down to local Soviet military commanders. The OSS-SI team operating from Sofia, for example, found it impossible to reach any sort of understanding with the Soviet command there and finally agreed to leave the area in order "to forestall being arrested and the chance that an incident would be caused." Gen. Jacob Devers, Deputy Supreme Commander, Mediterranean Theater, urged Gen. George C. Marshall to secure blanket authorization from the Soviet High Command allowing OSS teams the freedom to continue with their work.[111]

Marshall pursued the matter but found that the Soviets had retreated from their initial position. Gen. P. D. Fitin, chief of Russian Secret Intelligence, notified Gen. John R. Deane, head of the American Military Mission to the Soviet Union, that OSS teams would not be allowed to enter countries occupied by Soviet forces without approval of the Soviet Foreign Office. At this point, Deane suggested that OSS might outflank the intransigent Soviets by attaching its teams to the American component of the Allied Control Commission. Donovan liked the idea and recommended it to the Joint Chiefs of Staff for approval. By means of this bureaucratic circuitousness, Donovan adroitly bypassed the Soviet roadblock and succeeded in sending OSS teams into Rumania, Bulgaria, and Hungary.[112] A direct confrontation with the Russians had, for the present, been avoided but in a manner hardly compatible with the ideal of Allied harmony.

There was one area in which the Partisans continued to support OSS efforts despite the lack of cooperation elsewhere, and that was the evacuation of American airmen. Actually, Partisan assistance went beyond merely facilitating the evacuation of these men. At times they, like the Chetniks, fought German units to rescue downed air crews, and frequently they suffered casualties in the process.[113] Of course, Mihailovich and his men had been abandoned by this time, while the Partisans continued to be well supplied by the Allies. As of October 1, 1944, official air force statistics reveal that of 1,088 airmen evacuated from Yugoslavia, 732 were credited with assistance from the Partisans.

OSS Coverage, 1945

Missions with Partisan forces

1. IAMM
2. SPIKE
3. DURAND
4. ARROW/ACRU
5. DEPOSIT
6. DUNKLIN
7. ALUM
8. MAPLE
9. ORCHID/LABOR TEAM

Source: RG-226, L-55365

Subsequent evacuations raised this number appreciably, although Partisan claims to have been responsible for the evacuation of over 2,000 airmen appear to be exaggerated.[114]

In March, 1945, for example, Donovan reported to the Joint Chiefs of Staff that the IAMM had been responsible for evacuating 800 American and British airmen.[115] These figures include a number of airmen who were initially picked up by Chetnik forces and subsequently turned over to the Partisans for evacuation. Reports from the DEPOSIT, SPIKE, and COLUMBIA missions, for example, identify twenty-two American fliers who were transferred in this matter. Undoubtedly, there were others, particularly after December, 1944, following withdrawal of the HALYARD mission.[116]

During the four-month period from May to August, 1944, when OSS had no missions with Mihailovich's forces, briefing officers in Italy advised all aircrews to make their way to Partisan units and avoid the Chetniks, who, it was alleged, were turning Allied airmen over to the Germans. Not until August 20, following the first HALYARD evacuations, did Fifteenth Air Force headquarters acknowledge that these allegations were "erroneous" and that "Allied airmen forced down in Chetnik controlled Serbia, can expect good treatment from the native population and the soldiers of General Mihailovich."[117]

Veselinovich investigated the alleged mistreatment of American airmen by the Chetniks, but found no evidence to support Partisan charges.[118] Popovich also discovered that several airmen who were reported to him by the Partisans as having been either killed or turned over to the Germans by the Chetniks later showed up in Italy, having been evacuated by OSS officers with Mihailovich.[119]

Although Popovich and Farish had continued to work primarily with aircrew evacuations until their withdrawal in June, 1944, all OSS missions attached to the Partisans assisted in the evacuation of airmen who were brought to them.[120] Upon returning to Italy, these airmen routinely underwent debriefing about their observations and experiences in Yugoslavia in the hope that some useful intelligence could be gleaned from their statements. Since the vast majority of these men did not understand the native language or have a clear understanding of political developments in the country, their information was of limited value. However, they, no less than those men who had returned from Chetnik territory, generally expressed great admiration and appreciation for the Partisans who had protected them and aided in their return to Italy.[121]

For the most part, the airmen fared as well if not better than the Partisans in terms of food and medical attention. This, of course, tended to vary from area to area since some Partisan units were better supplied than others. As a rule, the Partisans generously shared what they had with the Americans and provided medical attention for those men whose wounds precluded their immediate evacuation.[122] Unfortunately, as relations between the Allies and Partisans began to deteriorate, the treatment accorded the airmen began to reflect the breakdown. Some airmen complained that the Partisans had "a very cold attitude" toward them and were always speaking of how great the Russian people were. Others admitted that relations with the Partisans became very "strained," particularly in early 1945 when it seemed that concern over the safety and welfare of the Allied aircrews was significantly less than it had been.[123]

It was in January, 1945, that Veselinovich, whose less than hospitable treatment at the hands of the Partisans has already been noted, encountered eight American airmen in the town of Korenica where they were being housed in a room described as "beyond comprehension." According to Veselinovich, the Partisans had held the airmen for over a month and had made no effort to advise any Allied missions in the area of their presence. When Veselinovich

later learned that the airmen had had to walk to Split, despite Partisan promises to provide transportation for them, he characterized the treatment given
these men as "a disgrace to any civilized European nation."[124]

This particular incident, while unfortunate, constitutes an obvious exception to the general pattern of cooperation exhibited by the Partisans in terms
of the treatment accorded to Allied airmen. Indeed, Capt. James Goodwin,
whose FLOTSAM mission evacuated some three hundred airmen, noted that
"the Partisan Army and civilians cooperated so willingly in the case of our
flyers that I thought it only proper to give them some message of thanks."
Undoubtedly, Goodwin expressed the views of many OSS personnel and airmen when he thanked the Partisans for their contribution in locating, hous-
ing, feeding, and caring for hundreds of Allied airmen who had gone down
in their territory.[125]

By the early spring of 1945, the number of aircrew evacuations from
Yugoslavia had substantially declined, a further indication that OSS operations
of a purely military nature were coming to an end. Thayer turned over command of the IAMM to Maj. Franklin Lindsay on April 19, after having been
chosen to go to Vienna as Gen. Mark Clark's interpreter. Even before this change
of command, however, the mission had had to assume "duties which normally
would be performed by diplomatic, consular, commercial, and other legal representatives of the government." Understandably, IAMM personnel were not
at all reluctant to relinquish responsibility for these duties to Peter Constan
and Carl Norden, two Foreign Service officers who reached Belgrade in mid-
January.[126] Their arrival by no means signaled the end of OSS involvement
in Yugoslav affairs, but it did suggest that the agency would no longer be the
primary instrument of American policy in Yugoslavia. Still, Donovan sought
a role for OSS in the transition from military to political affairs in order to
demonstrate the viability and flexibility of his organization. He had no intention of seeing his brainchild survive the hazards of war only to succumb to
the perils of peace.

9. A Fait Accompli of Serious Potentialities

In Yugoslavia as in other Balkan countries, the inevitable defeat of Germany, the withdrawal of her forces from southeastern Europe, and the growing Soviet presence in the area caused Allied leaders to focus their attention more on future political problems than on immediate military ones. As a result, oss seemed destined to play a less influential role than it had previously, since the United States continued to disassociate itself from issues that were primarily political in nature.

Donovan, however, had never learned to play the role of passive observer well, and he was not inclined to do so now. For over a year he had been working to cultivate closer relations with Šubašić, perhaps to offset what he saw as unqualified British support for Tito. The "Shepherd Project," as this operation had been called, took on new importance in June, 1944, when Šubašić became prime minister.[1]

Described by Ilija Jukić as "the living embodiment of ingenuousness and vanity," Šubašić seemed ill-suited to champion the king's cause in the political arena with Tito.[2] Nevertheless, Churchill pressed ahead with efforts to broker a political agreement between Šubašić and Tito without totally abandoning Britain's commitment to the Royal Yugoslav Government. After the negotiations had gotten underway, Donovan moved the "Shepherd Project" into a new and more delicate phase. The man chosen to execute this phase of the operation was Bernard Yarrow, a New York attorney with previous ties to Radio Free Europe. Known by both King Peter and Šubašić, Yarrow carefully nurtured his relationship into that of a confidant and was soon privy to the most secret aspects of the trilateral discussions among Peter's government, Tito, and the British. From September, 1944, until February, 1945, Yarrow regularly forwarded details of these negotiations to Donovan, who in turn passed them to the president – an indication that Roosevelt knew of and had approved the operation.[3]

The major problem in all of this was that Yarrow was doing considerably more than just monitoring the Tito-Šubašić talks. That was Thayer's job. Yarrow was actually providing highly sensitive political intelligence on the British— an action that if discovered or even suspected could have produced a most detrimental effect on Anglo-American relations. Donovan assumed this risk, in part, because he felt that the bounds of legitimate intelligence operations could not be defined exclusively by immediate military and political interests. Furthermore, he wanted to weave oss into the permanent fabric of American diplomacy to insure that his organization would not be cast aside at war's end like some worn-out garment that had outlived its usefulness. To do this, oss would need to demonstrate that it could do more than supply guerrillas and blow up bridges—activities not likely to be in great demand after the war.

Yarrow's reports undoubtedly convinced Roosevelt that his decision to avoid political and military commitments in Yugoslavia was absolutely correct. To reinforce this policy, Washington sent "strict instructions" to Thayer, who was at Partisan headquarters during the Tito-Šubašić negotiations in late October, that he was "under no circumstances to get into the ring but to report the bout blow by blow." His first report, filed in early November at the conclusion of the discussions, indicated that the talks would "probably result in a forced union on Tito's terms and in a regime dominated by him."[4]

Thayer's assessment proved to be correct. In short, the Tito-Šubašić agreement provided that Yugoslavia would remain a constitutional monarchy until the people could decide on a permanent form of government through a duly elected constituent assembly. The king would not be allowed to return to Yugoslavia until after the national plebiscite had been held. In the interim, royal authority would be vested in a three-man regency appointed by the king and subject to Tito's approval. The agreement also provided for the formation of a cabinet composed of six members from Šubašić's government and twelve from Tito's National Committee. Supreme legislative power would rest with the Anti-Fascist Council.[5]

The agreement, formally approved on November 1, 1944, was far from what Churchill wanted but was perhaps the best he could get. After all, he was attempting to do nothing less than transplant an uprooted monarchy into a country that had experienced a successful Communist revolution. In the five months that had elapsed since Tito and Šubašić met on the island of Vis, Tito had skillfully avoided further political discussions while strengthening his position inside the country.[6] Not until October 23—by which time he had reached his own understanding with Stalin, Belgrade had been liberated, and he was firmly established in Serbia—had Tito agreed to continue talks with Šubašić.

Commenting on Tito's position following the agreement with Šubašić, one oss report concluded that even if those opposed to the Partisans acted under the most favorable circumstances, Tito could, with no outside help, crush them "in a matter of weeks."[7] This view confirmed what Thayer told Joyce in early

December, 1944, namely that "a handful of ex-royalist cabinet ministers from London are not capable of turning the tide that is running in Yugoslavia today." Thayer added that in his opinion the National Liberation Movement was "riding an international current which is well-nigh irresistible at least in Central and Eastern Europe."[8]

Alexander Kirk, American political adviser in the Mediterranean theater, warned that Tito's rise to power meant that the United States could not with impunity remain aloof from political events in Yugoslavia. In a candid—and gloomy—evaluation of American policy, Kirk expressed grave doubts that Yugoslavia could maintain her political independence in the postwar period and argued that "her complete absorption in the Kremlin orbit" would produce undesirable results even in western Europe. According to Kirk, the United States was

thus faced with a fait accompli of serious potentialities both for good and evil brought about not least by the moral and political bankruptcy of previous regimes and hence endowed with a considerable degree of validity in Yugoslav eyes. But we must bear in mind that our experience thus far indicates that we would be ill advised to press our military or economic aid upon a government which, at best shows many symptoms of having been unduly flattered, and even though it accepted our proffered assistance may not with any certainty be counted among our friends.[9]

Much of what Kirk said was undoubtedly true. However, like Roosevelt and Churchill, he mistakenly assumed that Tito's success was yet another victory for Moscow. Postwar accounts written by Partisan sources reveal that the leadership of the National Liberation Movement greatly resented Stalin's patronizing attitude toward their political and military efforts. Tito and his advisers came to believe that Stalin had serious misgivings about the independent nature of their movement and was quite willing to subordinate the Yugoslav revolution to Soviet interests.[10] One OSS report quoted a French intelligence source with excellent contacts among Russian officials in Turkey as saying that the Soviets were initially interested in Tito but later considered him to be "totally incapable." It was even hinted that at the right moment the Partisan leader might be liquidated.[11]

A number of OSS field reports alluded to growing tension between Partisan leaders and Moscow during the latter months of the war. However, any hint that this may have heralded a split between Tito and Stalin seemed unlikely since the two regimes had so much in common. Thayer was not alone in pointing out that "no one familiar with the Soviet Union can fail to observe the striking similarities between Belgrade and Moscow."[12]

Not enthused about political developments in Yugoslavia, Washington informed Belgrade that "provisional representation" from the United States would depend upon faithful execution of the Tito-Šubašić agreement. Further diplomatic recognition would be contingent on the holding of free elections. oss-Caserta thought such a policy to be ill-advised, noting that Tito would be "unlikely, for the sake of recognition, to jeopardize the achievement of his objectives by relaxing the control which he now exercises over the country."[13]

Caserta was obviously correct. Neither Churchill nor Roosevelt was in a position to dictate to Tito the terms by which he would exercise power in Yugoslavia. He knew, even if they did not, that the agreement with Šubašić was not the source of his political authority. That moribund document did nothing more than recognize an accomplished fact and endow his regime with a mantle of diplomatic respectability. How far was Tito willing to go to hold on to his power? Šubašić told Yarrow "as a deep secret" that at one point when relations between Churchill and Tito became quite strained, several Partisan divisions had been sent to Dalmatia with orders to resist any attempt by the British to land forces there.[14]

Given these facts one can fully appreciate the utter futility of Washington's efforts to affect – belatedly – the course of political events in Yugoslavia. Even under the most adverse circumstances, Tito had been impervious to Allied pressure. If the State Department truly believed that he would, with the reins of power in his grasp, be deterred by such an impotent threat, it was imbibing deeply from the waters of self-delusion. Short of military intervention on a scale larger than either Britain or the United States was prepared to undertake, there was little the Allies could do to alter the political situation in Yugoslavia. Accordingly, the Tito-Šubašić agreement having been approved by the Big Three at Yalta, Washington dispatched Ambassador Richard C. Patterson to Belgrade in late March, following London and Moscow in extending full diplomatic recognition to Tito's government.[15]

Recognition in this instance was a function of state that in no way implied approval. That was certainly true in Churchill's case. His heavy investments of personal influence and military capital in the Partisan movement had yielded almost nothing in the way of political return. And, as if this were not enough, there remained the haunting specter of Mihailovich and the tattered remnants of his army – a reminder that the ends of Allied policy had been achieved by less than honorable means.

The British had a strong case for supporting Tito on military grounds, but as one oss officer reported, "the case for the fact that Mihailovich was a Nazi sympathizer is woefully weak."[16] Perhaps the strongest indictment of British policy came from Julian Amery, an soe officer who was involved with British intelligence operations in the Balkans and had direct contact with many officers who served in Yugoslavia. Amery accepted the decision to support Tito, but argued that what was wrong and unworthy was to turn against the Chetnik movement as "collaborationist" because of occasional accommodations with the enemy to which we had turned a blind eye for two years and for which there were many parallels in Greece. . . .

But there is in our national character a strong urge to find a moral justification for political decisions. Instead of admitting that we had failed to get our strategy accepted and it was therefore no longer practical politics to support Mihailovitch, we made a virtue of necessity and turned the man who had been our friend into a scapegoat for our own impotence.[17]

Amery's charge that the British knew of and condoned Mihailovich's trafficking with the enemy, especially the Italians, in order to secure arms and ammunition from them, requires some elaboration. Other British officers, including Bailey, have conceded that this was the case. What is not generally acknowledged, but is well-documented, is that the British, during those times when SOE was unable to provide sufficient arms to the Chetniks, actually instructed Mihailovich "to make the best arrangement possible with the Italians and get his arms from that source if he could."[18] In other words, accommodation was an acceptable strategy so long as the British could dictate the terms by which it was implemented.

Although Churchill was the chief architect of British policy and must bear the brunt of these charges, Roosevelt was not blameless. He failed to challenge the prime minister's denunciation of Mihailovich even when a growing volume of intelligence from OSS field reports cast doubt on the validity of those allegations. Roosevelt, the State Department, and OSS all criticized the British for playing politics in the Balkans, while smugly insisting that American involvement was exclusively military in nature. However, when the British inquired in September, 1944, if the United States would assume any responsibility for the evacuation of Mihailovich should the need arise, Robert Joyce argued that the British should assume "full responsibility" for Mihailovich. The United States, he continued, should not convey the appearance of supporting Mihailovich "to the end and be left holding the bag on this one."[19]

Joyce thought it inadvisable for the United States to sacrifice whatever influence it might have in postwar Yugoslavia by assuming belatedly the consequences of a policy in which it had had so little voice. Roosevelt had consistently deferred to Churchill's judgment where the Balkans were concerned, fearing perhaps that to criticize might elicit an invitation for greater American participation. Therefore, the United States, if by nothing more than silent consent, associated itself with Britain's decision to support Tito, and ipso facto with the charges of collaboration by which that decision was in part justified.

Of course, the collaboration issue was very complicated and absorbed the attention of virtually every Allied mission that went into Yugoslavia, especially those attached to Mihailovich's forces. A fair analysis of the question requires that some distinction must be made between accommodation and collaboration. The former has long been viewed as an acceptable, even necessary, element of guerrilla warfare, characterized by temporary agreements designed for the mutual benefit of the parties involved and usually confined to relatively small geographic areas. Collaboration, on the other hand, suggests the joint pursuit of common goals – political or military – on the basis of permanent cooperation. Collaborationist activity would tend therefore to be more systematic and enduring in its execution since it would evolve from a planned strategy.[20]

In Yugoslavia the task of distinguishing between these tactical measures fell to officers who for the most part had had no prior experience working with guerrilla forces in enemy-occupied territory. They had been trained to pursue all-out war against the enemy and tended to view with suspicion any strategy that fell short of that standard. Lacking in many instances the ability to judge ultimate intentions, they frequently failed to distinguish means from ends and therefore confused accommodation with collaboration.[21]

Ideal conceptions of a united resistance on one hand pitted against Axis occupation forces on the other proved to be far removed from the grim reality of war. Heavy reprisals against the civilian population at times immobilized the resistance. Internal political differences divided it and frequently led to internecine warfare in which resistance to the external threat was subordinated to civil war. Under these circumstances Allied representatives found that the word "enemy" included all those within the country – Axis invader or native inhabitant – who opposed the political and social program of the resistance element to which they were attached.

Using the enemy to defeat the enemy was not a hollow phrase to the resistance; it was a legitimate and acceptable method of guerrilla warfare. Employing this strategy inevitably led to accommodation, and in some cases accommodation may have led to collaboration. In any case, it soon became apparent to most Allied officers that attempting to evaluate the activities of the resistance as either all white or all black was a futile practice. Gray was a far more appropriate color, and in Yugoslavia the shades of gray seemed infinite.

Recently published accounts relying on German and Italian documents clearly reveal that a pattern of accommodation and, at times, cooperation existed between Axis forces and certain Chetnik commanders over whom Mihailovich exercised varying degrees of control. This was apparent in a collection of captured Chetnik documents – fifty-three in all – that the Partisans gave to Farish when he first left Yugoslavia in October, 1943. All but one of these documents relate to Chetnik units operating within the Independent State of Croatia and most deal with forces operating under the command of Rade Radić. Research and Analysis personnel concluded that while these papers provided "concrete evidence" of cooperation between Radić's men and Croat authorities, they also revealed that the "Chetniks recognized the authority of the Croat state only formally and with mental reservations."[22]

The analysts also noted that "the slogan: 'With faith in God, for King and Fatherland!' with which communications between Chetniks are concluded shows that their primary allegiance remained unchanged." The Chetniks had undoubtedly received arms and ammunition from the Axis forces and participated with them in joint operations against the Partisans. Nevertheless, there were indications that some of these supplies were being held back for "that day of ours" at which time the Chetniks would, in conjunction with the anticipated Allied invasion, turn these arms against the Axis occupiers. R & A concluded that while these documents did not reveal a direct link between Radić and Mihailovich, it was clear that Mihailovich "knew what was going on" and "approved."[23]

The British Foreign Office regarded these documents as proof that "Mihailović's collaboration with the Axis was determined – and limited – by his conception that his first duty was to prevent a Communist control of Yugoslavia after the war."[24] It is important to keep this point in mind when considering the frequently quoted exchange that took place between Churchill and Maclean following the Teheran Conference. In the course of discussing Yugoslavia's political future, Maclean reiterated his belief that the Partisans would dominate the country after the war and impose a Communist political system very similar to that found in the Soviet Union. Thus admonished, Churchill asked Maclean if he intended to "make Jugoslavia your home after the war?" When Maclean replied that he did not, Churchill responded, "Neither do I. . . . And that being so, the less you and I worry about the form of Government they set up, the better. That is for them to decide. What interests us is, which of them is doing the most harm to the Germans."[25]

Pragmatism was a luxury Churchill could easily afford since he would never experience firsthand the political consequences that would result from his military support of Tito. Mihailovich, on the other hand, did plan to make Yugoslavia his home after the war, and he preferred that his homeland remain free from Communist control. Kenneth Greenlees, an SOE officer who served with Mihailovich's forces for approximately eighteen months, defended the general's position by pointing out that "it is not treachery to decline to accept a revolution."[26]

Mihailovich and his men did not cooperate with Axis forces in order to perpetuate Axis domination of Yugoslavia; they did so to prevent its communization by the Partisans. As Foot so eloquently points out,

Mihailović's bands were raised with the serious intention of resisting the Germans, and the Italians, and the Ustase; and the fact that their leader came to a sticky end at the hands of his rivals in the civil war should not blind us to their original aims. He failed to achieve these aims; but the failure was imposed on him by circumstance. It did not arise from any malice aforethought in his upright mind; it arose from his upbringing, his character, and the times he had to fight in. His loyalties were always to the crown and to Serbia.[27]

Maj. Scott Dickinson came to precisely the same conclusion as he and the members of his team witnessed the beginnings of the Partisan takeover in Yugoslavia. Dickinson reported: "The position Draza Mihailovich was in can now be better appreciated than it was earlier in this war. It was difficult to decide which enemy would do Yugoslavia the more harm. He believed that Tito's Partisans were more of a menace to his country than the Germans, and he was willing to fight the Partisans even if it meant temporary collaboration with the Germans. Mihailovich is continuing the fight for a free democratic Yugoslavia, which certainly does not exist today."[28]

When considering the difficult choices Mihailovich had to make, it should not be forgotten that in April, 1941, when Axis power on the continent was at its zenith, he chose to stand with Britain at a time when her allies were precious few indeed. To imagine that he would subsequently abandon the Allies and collaborate with the Germans when their armies were retreating on every major European battlefront, including the Balkans, is incomprehensible.[29]

Another problem encountered in attempting to depict Mihailovich and his men as collaborators was the pitiful existence they endured throughout the entire war. Every account given by American airmen or liaison officers who were with the Chetniks attests to this fact. Walter Mansfield found that most Chetnik soldiers had for three years endured "a hard, rugged, and miserable life" separated from their families or knowing that their families had been killed by the Germans. They had survived the bitter Serbian winters without adequate clothing, gloves, or shoes. As Mansfield put it, "They live under conditions which I would have considered it impossible for them to stand if I had not seen it with my own eyes."[30]

Medical conditions were equally appalling. During one battle, Mansfield saw men with chest and stomach wounds, who were unable to find any medical assistance in the rear lines, return to the front lines where they continued to fight until they died.[31] The HALYARD team found that many airmen in Chetnik hands had not received adequate medical attention simply because Mihailovich and his men lacked the supplies necessary to care for them. And when supplies were finally sent to Musulin and his team, they were sufficient for the needs of the Americans only, despite the fact that many of the Chetniks at Pranjani field had been wounded while rescuing American airmen from enemy hands.[32] According to Lalich, who remained with Mihailovich until the last days of 1944, this desperate lack of medical supplies persisted to the very end, leading David Martin to write that "surely no group of men 'collaborated' with the Germans for so poor a return."[33]

The pathetic existence of Mihailovich's forces guarding the airstrip at Pranjani prompted McDowell to write: "To complete our shame although the American medical personnel flown in were appalled at the almost complete lack of medical supplies and equipment available to the Nationalists, with major operations performed without anesthetics, and although the Nationalists gave the Americans the best of what they had, the only gesture of gratitude on our part was to replace the supplies expended upon the airmen at the actual point of embarkation."[34]

Evidence of heavy German reprisals in parts of Serbia where Mihailovich's forces were active belied charges that all Chetnik forces were either passive toward or collaborating with the enemy. Mansfield, Seitz, and Musulin all testified to this in their written reports. In recalling the devastation and grief he witnessed in the First Corps area during his initial mission, Musulin stated, "I talked to hundreds of widows who were dressed in black and I would ask them, 'Who did you lose?' Some had lost their husbands and others their brothers. Serbia was wrapped in black."[35] Ellsworth Kramer, who witnessed the brutality imposed by the Germans on the Serbian peasantry, sympathized "with the Serbs for their lack of complete resistance" against the Germans. "It is easy enough," he argued, "to condemn people as collaborators when your own personal family is in safety and not subject to terrorism."[36]

Kramer had seen and reported instances of German-Chetnik cooperation, but neither he nor other OSS officers who witnessed similar activities ever branded Mihailovich and his men as collaborators. Indeed, most, if not all, of the officers who were attached to Mihailovich's forces would find themselves in substantial agreement with Walter Roberts, who maintained that "the Italians and Četniks helped each other. The Germans and Četniks arranged not to hurt each other. They were and remained enemies, but they deferred reciprocal hostilities until such time as their joint main adversary, the Partisan movement might be liquidated."[37]

Hermann Neubacher, whose indirect nogotiations with Mihailovich have already been mentioned, stated during his postwar interrogation that Mihailovich never made any offers to the Germans and that he "was against Germany in sentiment throughout the war." He also said that "formally there were only local relations and agreements, purely military and not political in character between the Germans and the Chetnik leaders."[38] Both Neubacher and von Horstenau regarded such arrangements between the Germans and the Chetniks as temporary expedients reflecting strong anti-Partisan rather than pro-German sentiment on the part of Mihailovich's bands.[39]

A two-page report probably originating in Neubacher's office in Belgrade in May, 1944, confirms the postwar statements of Neubacher and von Horstenau. The document begins by pointing out that "D.M. and his organisation have been fighting the German Army since the German invasion. At the moment, he does not consider it expedient to fight us openly, but hopes that events will turn in his favour at the moment of an invasion of the Balkans." Ruling out any political agreements with Mihailovich and noting that the "military reliability" of his forces was "considered small," the Germans were convinced that their policy should be to continue support of the Nedić regime "and the furthering of its authority in Serbia." As far as cooperation with Mihailovich was concerned the report concluded:

The aims of long-term Reich policy cannot be set aside for reasons of basing momentary tactical co-operation. Thus military co-operation in the areas of anti-Communist operations does not mean an alteration of our hostile attitude to those D.M. bands with whom military co-operation is not necessary, whose leadership is found to be unreliable, or who act to the detriment either of the German Army and administration or of the Nedic authorities. We must oppose, with the available military and police means, any strengthening of D.M.'s political power in Serbia, which would mean an expansion of his organisation in the battle-free areas of the country. Sabotage raids etc, demand, of course, instant German reaction.[40]

Gen. Rudolf Lüters, a German field commander in Yugoslavia, stated in March, 1943, that "the Chetniks were never our friends . . . their aim is and remains our destruction." Consequently, during Operation Weiss, carried out in early 1943, the Germans attempted "to settle accounts with Mihailovich long before Tito's bands had been defeated."[41] This view is consistent with Walter Roberts's contention that "any direct collaboration between the Cetniks and the Germans must be excluded because the objective of the German High Command was the destruction of the Cetniks."[42]

In a postwar interview conducted in December, 1945, Dr. Wilhelm Hoettl confirmed that through the summer of 1944 there had been "no actual co-operation at all between German posts and Mihailovic." Contacts that had occurred had taken place between lower-ranking German field officers and their Chetnik counterparts, "always without sanction from higher up" and always on the basis of "military necessity." Echoing the views of von Horstenau and Neubacher, Hoettl noted that in late 1944, "the co-operation which now set in between German posts and Cetnik units of Mihailovic was anything but cordial."[43]

Testifying at Nuremberg after the war, Gen. Walter Warlimont, deputy of Gen. Alfred Jodl, chief of operations of the German High Command, stated that in the summer of 1943 both Hitler and Jodl rejected a plan proposing German cooperation with Nedić and Mihailovich against the Partisans in southern Serbia.[44] Hitler's personal view was that "Germany must determinedly resist all plans for a Greater Serbia. A Serbian Army must not be allowed to exist. It is better to have some danger from communism."[45] The subsequent deterioration of Germany's military position in the Balkans forced her to forgo the planned destruction of the Chetniks while taking on the stronger and better-armed Partisan units. Still, as an indication of ultimate intentions it does not suggest a likely basis for collaboration.

A greater Serbia was anathema to Germany, which consistently supported the various separatist movements in Yugoslavia and sought to derive political advantage from fragmenting the country. It was not Germany's desire that Serbia survive the war as a political and military entity, and Mihailovich knew this as well as anyone. Consequently, if he were guilty of being what some have charged, a chauvinistic Pan-Serb, it is difficult to find grounds on which he could have collaborated with the Germans.

For essentially the same reason, collaboration in its true sense must be ruled out between the Partisans and the Germans. These two groups shared nothing in common politically, and only common hostility toward the Chetniks prompted any sort of military cooperation between them. Tito, no less than Mihailovich, attempted to exploit the presence of the Axis forces to his own advantage in the civil conflict. Owing to Allied support, however, he was less dependent on them than was Mihailovich. For the Chetniks, accommodation became a long-term tactical necessity, while with Tito it was a temporary expedient. Walter Mansfield became convinced that if the same standard of collaboration were applied to Tito as was applied to Mihailovich, "both would have to be considered collaborators."[46] Harris Smith reached the same conclusion, arguing that "to the extent that subordinate commanders of both Chetnik and Partisan groups felt their survival required temporary accommodations with the enemy, there was indeed collaboration."[47]

Unfortunately, some OSS analysts appeared at times to be less than objective in their evaluation of similar policies initiated by the Chetniks and Partisans. There was, for example, a great deal of hand-wringing in OSS over the ties that were known to exist between Mihailovich and Nedić. On the other hand, subsequent reports from the field indicating the existence of a comparable relationship between the Partisans and the Ustasha hardly caused a stir.[48]

Eli Popovich recalls that while he and Linn Farish were working on a landing zone east of Zagreb during their last mission together, they were surprised at dinner one evening by the presence of three Ustasha officers still in uniform. Popovich did not know the two lieutenants, but he recognized the major as a "notorious Croatian Ustasha who had butchered many Serbs when the Germans first attacked Yugoslavia." According to Popovich, the major was wearing the Iron Cross he had won while fighting in the Black Legion on the Eastern Front. When he returned to Croatia and realized that Germany was losing the war, he deserted the Ustasha and was welcomed into the ranks of the Partisan movement. Popovich stated that he "raised a helluva lot of hell about this because I refused to sit at the same table with officers who were fighting the Allies and were being accepted on equal terms as I was. Needless to say this went over very badly with the Partisan commander who told me that the Partisans would welcome anyone who wanted to fight the Germans."[49]

Nick Lalich provided further confirmation of the Partisan-Ustasha connection, identifying by name many high-ranking Ustasha officers and officials, among them Pavelić's ministers of war and interior, who were permitted to join the Partisans. According to Lalich, Pavelić's representatives and high-ranking officials from the Partisan leadership also agreed to cooperate with one another in exterminating their respective internal enemies—Maček's Peasant party in Croatia and Mihailovich's followers in Serbia. The Partisans were willing to deal with the Ustasha for the sole purpose of consolidating Tito's political position within the country—a policy no less damning than anything the Chetniks did to oppose them.[50]

Before judging too harshly the sometimes questionable means by which the Chetniks and Partisans sought to achieve their military and political objectives, one should first consider certain policies pursued by the major powers both before and during the war. Acting within the larger arena of international relations, these states made decisions and followed policies that were in many respects analogous to those adopted by the resistance. How, for example, was the policy of appeasement so different from Mihailovich's decision to bide his time and husband his resources while waiting for the opportune time to strike? Churchill, imagining the English Channel filled with the corpses of British soldiers, advocated a delay in the execution of OVERLORD until decisive force could be brought to bear upon the enemy. Yet he demanded action from Mihailovich, whose caution was tempered by the blood-soaked ground of Kragujevac and the very real corpses of more than two thousand Serbs massacred there by the Germans. Did not Stalin justify his infamous pact with Hitler on the grounds that he had thus secured additional time in which his country could prepare for war with the Nazis?

OSS had little difficulty in reaching an accommodation with Gen. Reinhard Gehlen after concluding that the information his intelligence unit had collected on Soviet military capabilities might be useful.[51] Likewise, the United States found ample justification for its decision to maintain relations with the collaborationist Vichy regime—a policy defended on the grounds that it advanced American interests and did not constitute an endorsement of the Pétain government. In William Langer's words,

Vichy meant to our Department of State not only a helpless old man and a collection of unscrupulous intriguers. It meant also a large number of friends, on whom we could rely and through whose aid we could learn more about the enemy than through perhaps any source. The experience and the connections of many men in the Foreign Ministry were at our disposal, while the military intelligence service of the French army, which was clandestinely reorganized after the defeat, was freely available to us. It would have been perfectly idiotic to cut ourselves off from this vital spring of information. When the last word is said, one can hardly escape the conclusion that for intelligence purposes, if for no others, the Vichy policy was completely justified.[52]

Roosevelt justified American policy toward Vichy in a confidential remark to the press in which he quoted an old Balkan proverb: "My children, it is permitted you in time of grave danger to walk with the devil until you have crossed the bridge."[53] Unfortunately the glow provided by this bit of wisdom was sufficient only to guide American policymakers down the path of expediency that they had chosen. Neither they nor the British seemed willing to accept the maxim when applied, as it was by Mihailovich, in Yugoslavia.

These few examples serve only to illustrate that the major powers pursued expedient policies when it suited their interests to do so. Any one of these actions, if considered in isolation from other policy decisions, might appear extremely compromising. When viewed in the context of a general strategy, however, they are seen for what they are—the specific means by which larger ends are served. Applying these principles to the resistance in Yugoslavia, one would have to conclude that neither Tito nor Mihailovich was a collaborator. In pursuing their long-term political and military objectives, both engaged in deceit, treachery, and duplicity. However, success should not serve to exonerate Tito any more than failure should condemn Mihailovich to be forever labeled as a collaborator.

The final chapter of the Tito-Mihailovich drama was played out in the summer of 1946, some ten months after the untimely demise of oss itself. A number of former oss officers, some of whom had served with the Partisans, openly defended Mihailovich, but historians are left to speculate as to what official position, if any, oss would have taken in this matter.

In mid-March, 1946, a group of Tito's agents, with help from Nikola Kalabić, a former Chetnik commander in Serbia, succeeded in capturing Mihailovich, who was subsequently placed on trial for treason and war crimes. Prior to the trial, which began on June 10, the State Department made several attempts to secure the admission of evidence favorable to Mihailovich, but all efforts failed. In denying these interventions, Tito's government informed the United States chargé d'affaires on April 5 that "the crimes of the traitor Draza Mihailovich against the people of Yugoslavia are far too big and horrible that it could be or should be allowed to be discussed whether he is guilty or not."[54] The outcome of the trial was never in doubt. Mihailovich was found guilty of treason on July 15 and two days later was executed by firing squad.

On the day before Mihailovich was to be executed, eight American airmen who had been rescued by him sent a telegram to President Harry Truman urging direct intervention to prevent the general's execution.[55] But however sympathetic Truman may have been to this plea, there was nothing he could do. The Yugoslav government rejected all attempts by the United States to intervene in Mihailovich's behalf. All private efforts initiated by the airmen, former liaison officers, and other interested parties likewise ended in failure. Yet out of this failure came a renewed undertaking to remove the taint of collaboration and treason from Mihailovich's name.

On August 12, 1946, Lt. William L. Rogers, chairman of the National Committee of American Airmen to Aid General Mihailovich, and four other airmen submitted a letter supported by substantial documentation to the secretary of war, requesting that the War Department award to General Mihailovich the Medal of Freedom with Gold Palm. After reviewing the evidence accompanying the letter, the War Department passed the request on to the Department of State, where it was received rather coolly.[56]

In a letter dated September 5, 1946, the State Department acknowledged that Mihailovich's activities as an Allied commander from 1941 to 1944 "entitle him to such an award on merit" but said they thought it "inadvisable to confer the medal at this time." Apart from the deleterious effect such an action might have on American-Yugoslav relations, the department regarded a posthumous award to be a "somewhat futile gesture toward a man for whom our best efforts were insufficient to insure a fair trial and to prevent his summary execution."[57]

The War Department also agreed that "the accomplishments described merit the award," and, in fact, the Decorations Board recommended approval of the award. However, it was decided that such approval should be suspended until the State Department concurred. On January 21, 1948, three days before the deadline for the approval of awards to foreigners, the State Department was again contacted concerning release of the award. The department approved the release but suggested that it be announced in the Department of the Army Confidential Orders since it knew of no appropriate person to receive the award.[58]

Accompanying the award was a citation signed by President Truman which declared:

General Dragoljub Mihailovich distinguished himself in an outstanding manner as Commander-in-Chief of the Yugoslavian Army Forces and later as Minister of War by organizing and leading important resistance forces against the enemy which occupied Yugoslavia, from December 1941 to December 1944. Through the undaunted efforts of his troops, many United States airmen were rescued and returned safely to friendly control. General Mihailovich and his forces, although lacking adequate supplies, and fighting under extreme hardships, contributed materially to the Allied cause, and were instrumental in obtaining a final Allied Victory.[59]

The army acquiesced in State Department wishes that no publicity be given to the award and subsequently forwarded the medal and citation to the State Department until such time as arrangements for proper presentation could be made. For almost nineteen years the State Department kept all information pertaining to the award classified in order to avoid any publicity that might offend Tito. Owing to the persistent efforts of then congressman Edward J. Derwinski of Illinois, however, the department was forced to declassify its files on Mihailovich in early August, 1967. These documents revealed for the first time that the United States government had secretly accorded the highest honor possible to the man whose abandonment under the cloud of collaboration it had publicly condoned.[60]

Conclusion

Following the Teheran Conference, Winston Churchill told Fitzroy Maclean that Britain's main concern in Yugoslavia lay in assisting the resistance group that was doing most harm to the Germans. That statement was consistent with the prime minister's general view that the current status of the war, as well as operations to which the major powers had committed themselves, dictated the necessity of according primacy to military over political matters. Neither Roosevelt nor Stalin challenged Churchill's position, either in its broader context or as specifically applied to Yugoslavia where it translated into support for Tito.

Political developments inevitably followed in the wake of this initial decision, propelled along by the sweep of strategic considerations affecting the general course and direction of the war itself. After all, Churchill, Roosevelt, and Stalin were responsible for prosecuting war on a global scale. The policies they adopted toward individual countries reflected the scope of their responsibility, the limits of their power, and a sense of their priorities.

Acting within these constraints, Allied leaders framed their policy toward Yugoslavia in terms of their own interests, which they generally agreed would be better served by Tito's aggressive tactics than by Mihailovich's more cautious and calculating approach. Tito was in no small way the architect of his own success, converting a substantial Allied military investment into personal political capital. However, it must be admitted that the makeup of the Grand Alliance and its overall strategy gave him the advantage of conducting a revolution under the banner of anti-Fascism while forcing Mihailovich to resist it on the grounds of anti-Communism.

Circumstances combined to cast OSS in a supporting role in the drama of events unfolding in Yugoslavia—a role that gave the agency little, if any, influence on the course of Allied policy there. In the first place, Yugoslavia lay within a theater of operations where British interests predominated, which meant that SOE had primary responsibility for implementing policy as it related to the resistance. By the time the first American liaison officers began arriving in the country in August and September, 1943, the British had moved from a policy of exclusive support for Mihailovich to one of supporting both groups and were leaning toward exclusive support for Tito.

The first direct intelligence from American sources on the situation in Yugoslavia came from Linn Farish, whose report reached Roosevelt just before the Teheran Conference and echoed Maclean's own glowing account of the Partisan effort. Without minimizing the importance of this document, it is critical to understand its true significance. The Farish report and the circumstances surrounding its preparation said a great deal, much of it unheeded, about the intelligence-gathering process in Yugoslavia and the degree to which that process was susceptible to Partisan manipulation. On the other hand, it had little if any impact on decisions affecting American policy. Even had he not seen the Farish report, it seems unlikely that Roosevelt would have objected to Churchill's proposals at Teheran. The president's main concern with the Balkans throughout the war was how best to stay out of them. Aid to Tito's movement accomplished that end and held out the prospect at least of holding down some German units away from anticipated targets of Allied action.

Farish's report confirmed a policy position that the United States was disposed to follow in any case. The justification of that policy, insofar as it rested on the conclusions reached by Maclean and Farish, came under challenge between February and May, 1944, when Seitz, Mansfield, and Musulin delivered their reports, all of which were quite favorable to Mihailovich and his army. This body of intelligence had a significant impact within OSS, where it strengthened the hands of those who wanted the agency to pursue a more independent policy vis-à-vis the British. However, insofar as these reports implied a change in or at least a reevaluation of Allied policy, they were largely ignored.

Before the three OSS officers emerged from Yugoslavia, Churchill had decided to withdraw all British missions from Mihailovich's territory and had requested that Roosevelt do the same for American personnel. The president agreed, though at the time he had no direct intelligence from OSS sources who had been with Mihailovich's forces.

The appointment of Maclean and the subsequent decision to withdraw all Allied missions from Serbia convinced Donovan that political more than military considerations were driving British policy in Yugoslavia. Suggesting that the United States might not wish to associate itself with the pursuit of special British interests in the Balkans, Donovan persuaded Roosevelt to approve the reestablishment of intelligence missions in Serbia. When the British strenuously objected to this decision, the president beat a hasty retreat, not even bothering to defend the legitimacy of his action.

Only Donovan's persistence and the very legitimate need to evacuate American airmen from Mihailovich's territory sufficed to pry open the lid that had been clamped down on Serbia. HALYARD and the ACRU missions that operated in Partisan-held territory did outstanding work in returning hundreds of downed airmen to the war effort, an undertaking supported by both elements of the resistance. HALYARD served another purpose, however, in that it paved the way for McDowell's RANGER mission, to which Donovan and Robert Joyce, his SI chief in Bari, attached so much importance.

OSS had previously asserted the right for independent representation at Tito's headquarters, first with the Weil mission and later with the establishment of the IAMM under Huntington. That this latitude did not extend to Chetnik forces became apparent when Churchill's vigorous protests led Roosevelt to order the recall of McDowell's team. The president would later explain to Churchill that the mission was simply an oversight on his part, something it obviously was not.

With no intention of becoming directly involved in Yugoslavia, Roosevelt and his advisers never developed a coherent policy toward that country. Washington's often reiterated position that it had no political interests in Yugoslavia, did not wish to assist in promoting the special interests of any other power, and was extending support to the resistance exclusively for military purposes was as close to a statement of policy as the United States would come. These objectives may have coincided with the broad principles of American policy, but they reflected little sense of what was happening in Yugoslavia. Donovan knew that but lacked the leverage to do anything about it.

Aid to Tito's movement, particularly by the summer of 1944, was tailored to serve political more than military ends. The forbidding prospect of Soviet influence flowing into central and southern Europe cast a definite pall over Churchill's strategic thinking. Having severed all ties with Mihailovich and being unable to overcome American intransigence to sending military forces into the region, the prime minister supported Tito as the only possible means of maintaining some measure of British influence in the country. This to a great extent explains why the British never stopped the flow of supplies to the Partisans despite irrefutable evidence that the Partisans were diverting Allied assistance to operations aimed at systematically liquidating Tito's internal enemies.

Was Tito the successful revolutionary also the liberator of his country? The overwhelming preponderance of evidence from OSS field reports suggests that he definitely was not. The inexorable advance of Allied, particularly Soviet, armies toward Germany's frontiers required Hitler to withdraw forces from the extremities—the Balkans—in order to defend the vital organs of the German Reich. The key to Tito's success lay in his judicious use of the power of resistance to oppose the Germans and position himself to seize the reins of political authority within the country before the war ended. In so doing he confronted

Churchill and Stalin—both of whom found Tito to be as elusive a prey in the political arena as the Germans found him to be on the battlefield—with a fait accompli.

During the war, both London and Moscow had sought in various ways to harness Tito and his movement to the service of their own particular interests, and both failed. Allied leaders and their advisers seemed to have assumed that the concept of all-out warfare against a clearly defined enemy which guided coalition strategy could be transferred to occupied countries like Yugoslavia. In fact, neither Tito nor Mihailovich was willing to subordinate his own political or military programs to Allied interests. Tito, however, in pursuit of his internal objectives, embraced a strategy that complemented Allied military policy and was supported on that basis.

Mihailovich's fate was sealed when the Allies decided against committing substantial forces to the Balkans and chose instead to attempt to hold down as many Axis divisions as possible by sending supplies and liaison officers to the resistance. The Allied decision to avoid direct involvement in the Balkans wrecked Mihailovich's military plans and doomed Peter's political aspirations. The young king needed strong support from the Western Allies if he were to return to Yugoslavia as anything more than an ineffectual figurehead, and without a military presence in the country, the Allies could not provide that support. Undoubtedly, any attempt to reestablish the monarchy, endowed with any real authority to govern, would have encountered determined resistance from Tito and, without decisive backing from the British, would have failed.

Were Tito's rise to power and Mihailovich's abandonment the result of subversion and treachery within the British and American intelligence networks? The available evidence, at least from OSS sources, suggests not. It is one thing to contend that there were those within SOE and OSS who supported Tito for ideological reasons, an assertion which I believe is undeniable. It is quite another, however, to prove that those individuals, by all the actions attributed to them, succeeded in diverting Allied policy from the course it would have taken in any case.

The majority of OSS personnel who entered Yugoslavia did so with no predisposed ideas toward either the Chetniks or the Partisans. A few officers on both sides may have allowed personal loyalties to influence their judgment at times, but these were exceptional cases. It was possible, after all, to be pro-Partisan without being pro-Communist, though Tito's critics often failed to recognize that distinction. Likewise, those who supported Mihailovich risked having their credibility questioned on grounds that their antipathy for Communism had blinded them to the accomplishments of the Partisans.

Ideology was neither the only nor perhaps the most important factor that shaped and molded perceptions of the resistance. A comparison of field intelligence reports with analyses and policy directives circulating at the theater level reveals the great difference in perspective between the man in the field and the analyst behind the desk. The latter tended to view particular events in the broad context of general Allied strategy. Time was a factor, but not always a critical one. Casualties among the resistance were represented by figures on a piece of paper, never by human bodies lying alongside the road and mourned by grieving mothers, wives, and children. Atrocity reports were seen, but never the atrocities. In short, the resistance was regarded as yet another instrument of war to be called to action at the most propitious time in terms of overall military needs, often without due concern for casualties among the guerrillas or reprisals against innocent civilians.

To personnel in the field circumstances were far different. Time was always of the essence. Often the success or failure of a mission depended on split-second decisions made in the heat of battle. Goals were immediate, objectives were measured in terms of feet and yards, and not infrequently only a few minutes might separate an agent from a pursuing enemy. On numerous occasions only the cunning and courage of the resistance would intervene to save the field agent from capture. In a very real sense the man in the field was at the mercy of the resistance. He ate with them, slept with them, talked and drank around their campfires, shared their victories and their losses. To him the resistance was not a faceless multitude, an instrument of war, so to speak, to be manipulated by some distant force to carry out some relatively obscure phase of a prearranged master plan. The man in the field well knew that Poles, Greeks, and Yugoslavs did not die to relieve pressure on the Eastern Front, weaken Rommel's position in North Africa, or tie down German divisions away from the beaches at Normandy. They died for Poland, Greece, and Yugoslavia.

These differences never disappeared, but they did recede into the background as the certainty of military victory shifted the focus of attention to political matters and accentuated ideological divisions within OSS. Debate became sharper, reason succumbed to emotionalism, and suspicion flourished. Rooted in this fertile ground, the conspiracy theory sprang forth to explain the otherwise inexplicable—the abandonment of a loyal ally.

Their strength eroding, their supplies dwindling, and labeled by the Allies as collaborators, Mihailovich's forces found themselves locked in a losing struggle with Tito's troops, many of whom had been armed and supplied by the Allies. Even under these conditions, the Chetniks continued to expend manpower and what little they had in the way of medical supplies to aid in the rescue and evacuation of Allied, mostly American, airmen. In return for their sacrifices, the United States sent not a single planeload of medical supplies to them, not even to replace that which had been provided to the airmen. Yet all the while, as McDowell reported, Mihailovich's men sat around their campfires at night and heard Allied planes flying overhead to bring more supplies to the Partisans

—supplies they knew were being and would continue to be used against them.

Those American officials responsible for the decision to withhold medical supplies from the Chetnik forces providing protection for the ACRU operations at Pranjani stand indicted for a complete and total failure of moral courage. A modicum of humanitarian assistance would have been small payment indeed for the return of hundreds of Allied airmen to the war effort. Beyond that, it would have redeemed some measure of American honor in the eyes of the Chetniks without altering in any way the course of political or military developments in Yugoslavia.

Cut off from all access to Allied support, the Chetniks sought by varying degrees of accommodation to exploit the German presence to eliminate the Partisans. To this end they concluded agreements with local German commanders ranging from the adoption of rather benign live-and-let-live arrangements to actual cooperation in military operations against Tito's forces. OSS field reports and postwar interviews with German representatives responsible for overseeing the negotiation and implementation of these agreements clearly reveal that both parties accepted this strategy with some reluctance, with neither doubting the unyielding hostility of the other.

Mihailovich has long been condemned, not for the ends he sought, but for the means he employed—a criterion that might yield some rather interesting interpretations if rigorously applied to Tito or for that matter to the Allied powers themselves. None of the OSS officers who served with Mihailovich regarded him as a collaborator—a judgment supported by the published accounts and public remarks of a number of British officers who were attached to Chetnik forces during the war. The views of these men, as well as many OSS officers who served with the Partisans, was that Mihailovich was a faithful ally who, in spite of his abandonment, continued to render valuable service to the Allies and their cause to which he remained ultimately loyal.

More than forty-five years have passed since the conclusion of World War II. And though Mihailovich and Tito are both dead, the controversy surrounding their names remains a topic for lively debate. I do not for a moment think this book will end all of that. Mihailovich's supporters will no doubt find my treatment of Tito too lenient, while Tito's apologists will be disappointed that Mihailovich is not sufficiently vilified.

History's perception of both men may undergo significant revision as a result of recent and ongoing events in eastern Europe. That possibility notwithstanding, I believe the military contribution rendered by Tito's Partisan army is well established and should be acknowledged. Likewise, it would also seem that the United States would at last be willing to acknowledge officially its long-standing debt of gratitude to Draza Mihailovich. Surely his service to the Allies deserves more honorable recognition than that afforded by an award grudgingly granted in shameful secrecy.

APPENDIX A
Pronunciation Guide for Serbo-Croat Names

LETTER	PRONUNCIATION
c	"ts" as in ca*ts*
č	"ch" as in *ch*eck
ć	"tch" as in cru*tch* (slightly softer sound than č)
s	"s" as in *s*ound
š	"sh" as in *sh*ort
z	"z" as in *z*ebra
ž	"zh" as in Dr. *Zh*ivago
j	"y" as in *y*ellow
nj	"ny" as in ca*n*yon
g	"g" as in *g*opher
dj	"j" as in *J*ennifer
jl	"lli" as in mi*ll*ion
ai and aj	"i" as in br*i*ght

Prominent OSS Personalities

Allin, J. B., member, Field Photographic Branch

Arnoldy, Frank, chief, Y-Section, SI, OSS-Bari, Italy

Benson, Melvin O., first American liaison officer dispatched to Partisans

Benson, Nels J., American liaison officer with Partisans, ALTMARK mission

Bizic, Steven, member, SPIKE mission

Blatnik, John, American liaison officer with Partisans, ARROW mission

Buxton, Edward, assistant director, OSS

Carpenter, Walter, Fifteenth Air Force medical officer assigned to ACRU operations with Chetniks

Cheston, Charles, deputy director, OSS

Cox, Arthur, assistant chief, Y-Section, SI, OSS-Bari, under Suker; later chief, Y-Section

Deane, Rex, American liaison officer with Partisans, REDWOOD mission

Deranian, Nelson, chief of SO, OSS-Bari

Desich, Dan, American liaison officer with Partisans, ALUM mission

Devyak, Michael, radio operator, RANGER mission

Dickinson, Scott, American liaison officer with Partisans, SPIKE mission

Donovan, William J., director, COI and later OSS

Farish, Linn, senior American liaison officer with Partisans, later head of COLUMBIAN-GARGANTUAN mission

Fielding, Temple, American liaison officer with Partisans, morale operations officer for IAMM

Fisher, Charles, American liaison officer with Partisans, MAPLE mission

Galembush, Stephen, radio operator, RAKEOFF mission

Glavin, Edward, commanding officer, OSS-Caserta, Italy

Goodwin, James, American liaison officer with Partisans, FLOTSAM mission

Goodwin, John, American liaison officer with Partisans, MULBERRY mission

Grimm, Charles, American liaison officer with Partisans, WILLOW mission

Greaser, Everett, American liaison officer with Partisans, DEPOSIT mission

Green, Edward J., commanding officer, oss-Bari.

Green, Holt, American liaison officer with Partisans, RAKEOFF mission; succeeded Arnoldy as chief, Y-Section, SI, OSS-Bari

Guenther, Gustav, commanding officer, OSS-Cairo, Egypt

Hamilton, John [Hayden, Sterling], American liaison officer, Trans-Adriatic Shipping Operation and HACIENDA mission

Houlihan, Robert, OSS-Operational Group company commander

Huot, Louis, chief, SO, OSS-Bari; Trans-Adriatic Shipping Operation

Huntington, Ellery, commanding officer, Independent American Military Mission to Tito

Jibilian, Arthur, radio operator with Farish and Popovich, later with HALYARD mission

Joyce, Robert, American Foreign Service officer on loan to OSS; chief, SI, OSS-Bari

Koch, Robert, commanding officer, OSS-Bari; Immediately preceded Edward J. Green

Kraigher, George, Fifteenth Air Force, commanding officer in charge of ACRU operations

Kramer, Ellsworth, American liaison officer with Chetniks, RANGER mission

Lada-Mocarski, Valerian, chief, SI, OSS-Cairo

Lalich, Nick, American liaison officer with Chetniks, HALYARD mission; Succeeded Musulin as head of mission

Lindsay, Franklin, American liaison officer with Partisans, CUCKOLD and DURAND missions; later headed IAMM in Belgrade

Mansfield, Walter, first American liaison officer dispatched to Chetniks

Maddox, William P., chief, SI, OSS-London

Milodragovich, John, assistant chief, SI, Y-Section, OSS-Bari; member, RANGER mission

Mitrani, Jacques, Fifteenth Air Force medical officer, assigned to ACRU operations with Chetniks

Musulin, George, American liaison officer with Chetniks; REPARTEE mission, later commanding officer, HALYARD mission

McBaine, Turner, chief, SI, OSS-Cairo; established and first commanded advanced base at Bari, Italy

McDowell, Robert, American liaison officer with Chetniks; commanding officer, RANGER mission

Nowell, Robin, American liaison officer with Partisans, GEISHA mission

O'Meara, Eugene, American liaison officer with Partisans, RELATOR mission

O'Rourke, Clifford, American liaison officer with Partisans

Penrose, Stephen, chief, SI, Washington, D.C.

Pfeiffer, Timothy, American liaison officer with Partisans, DUNKLIN mission

Phillips, Robert S., American liaison officer with Partisans, TOLEDO mission

Popovich, Eli, American liaison officer with Partisans, COLOMBIAN-GARGANTUAN mission and ACRU operations

Rainer, Richard, American liaison officer with Partisans, ABBEVILLE mission

Rajacich, Michael, American liaison officer with Chetniks, HALYARD and RANGER missions

Reid, Stafford, member, IAMM; briefly succeeded Huntington as head of mission until replaced by Thayer

Rider, D. L., American liaison officer with Partisans, ASH mission

Seitz, Albert, senior American liaison officer with Chetniks

Selvig, George, American liaison officer with Partisans, RELATOR and FUNGUS missions

Shepardson, Whitney, initial chief, SI, OSS-London

Suker, Orman, chief, Y-Section, SI, OSS-Bari; succeeded Holt Green

Thayer, Charles, American Foreign Service officer on loan to OSS; succeeded Huntington as commanding officer of IAMM

Thompson, Robert, member, Trans-Adriatic Shipping Operation, Bari, Italy

Tofte, Hans, succeeded Huot as officer in charge of Trans-Adriatic Shipping Operation, Bari

Toulmin, John, commanding officer, OSS-Cairo; Succeeded Guenther

Veselinovich, Joseph, American liaison officer with Partisans, GEISHA mission

Vuchinich, Alex, member, R & A Branch, OSS-Bari

Vuchinich, Wayne, member, R & A Branch, OSS-Bari

Vujnovich, George, operations officer, OSS-Bari

Weil, Richard, American liaison officer with Partisans, CALIFORNIA mission

Weiler, Robert, American liaison officer with Partisans, WALNUT mission

West, Paul, chief, SO, OSS-Cairo

Wuchinich, George, American liaison officer with Partisans, ALUM mission

Wolff, Robert, chief, Balkan Section, R & A, Washington, D.C.

Notes

ACRU	Air Crew Rescue Unit (U.S.)
AFHQ	Allied Forces Headquarters (Algiers)
AVNOJ	Anti-Fascist Council of National Liberation of Yugoslavia (Partisan)
BAF	Balkan Air Force (Allied)
BBC	British Broadcasting Corporation
CCS	Combined Chiefs of Staff (U.S.–Britain)
COI	Coordinator of Information (U.S.)
DGFP	*Documents on German Foreign Policy, 1918–1945*
E&E	Escape and Evasion Reports
FO	Foreign Office Document
FRUS	*Foreign Relations of the United States, 1941*
IAMM	Independent American Military Mission
IMT	*Proceedings of the International Military Tribunals at Nuremberg*
JCS	Joint Chiefs of Staff (U.S.)
JIC	Joint Intelligence Committee
JICAME	Joint Intelligence Collection Agency, Middle East
MAAF	Mediterranean Allied Air Force
MEDTO	Mediterranean Theater of Operations
MID	Military Intelligence Division (U.S.)
MO	Morale Operations (OSS)
NCA	*Nazi Conspiracy and Aggression*
OG	Operational Group (OSS)
OGPU	Unified State Political Directorate (Soviet Union)
OKW	Oberkommando Der Wehrmacht (German High Command)
OSS	Office of Strategic Services (U.S.)
OWI	Office of War Information (U.S.)
PICME	Political Intelligence Committee, Middle East
PWE	Political Warfare Executive (Britain)

R & A   Research and Analysis Branch (OSS)
RG   Record Group, National Archives
SBS   Special Bari Section (OSS)
SI   Secret Intelligence Branch (OSS)
SO   Special Operations Branch (OSS)
SOE   Special Operations Executive (Britain)
WO   War Office

Chapter 1. Greetings First American

1. R. Harris Smith, *OSS: The Secret History of America's First Central Intelligence Agency*, 140. In 1950, Mansfield became a partner in the law firm of Donovan, Leisure, Newton and Irvine, an association he maintained until his appointment as Federal District Judge for the Southern District of New York in 1966. Five years later he was appointed to the Second Circuit Court of Appeals, the position he held at the time of his death in January, 1987 (*New York Times*, Jan. 8, 1987).

2. Donovan to Roosevelt, May 11, 1943, Roosevelt Papers, Franklin D. Roosevelt Library, Hyde Park, New York, President's Safe File, Donovan Reports, Box 167 (hereafter cited as PSF); Testimony of Capt. Walter R. Mansfield, May 14, 1946, before the Commission of Inquiry of the Committee for a Fair Trial for Draja Mihailovich, from "Proceedings of the Commission of Inquiry," 34–38. (hereafter cited as Commission of Inquiry). I learned that the State Department had retained a transcribed copy of the commission's hearings until 1973, when, following the publication of the 1946 Foreign Relations Papers, the document was destroyed. This decision was made despite the fact that nothing of substance derived from the hearings was incorporated into the published papers. In 1978, David Martin, who served as secretary of the Committee for a Fair Trial for Draza Mihailovich, incorporated this important document into a broader work published by the Hoover Institution under the title *Patriot or Traitor*.

3. Chedo Radovich, telephone interview with author, Feb. 26, 1988.

4. Report of Capt. Walter R. Mansfield, Mar. 1, 1944, Central Intelligence Agency, Washington, D.C. This document is one of several obtained from the CIA before it began releasing en masse the operational files of OSS to the National Archives. Documents from this collection have neither a record group nor file number and are hereafter cited as OSS/CIA.

5. Mansfield testimony, Commission of Inquiry, 38.

6. Report of Capt. Melvin O. Benson, June 22, 1944, OSS/CIA; Benson, letter to author, Oct. 13, 1970.

7. Lane to Hull, Mar. 21, 1941, U.S. Department of State, *Foreign Relations of the United States, 1941 (FRUS)*, 2:963. Lane was a career diplomat whose service with the State Department began with his appointment as secretary to the ambassador in Italy in 1916. He was appointed minister to Yugoslavia on Aug. 9, 1927, and served in that capacity until July 30, 1941. Lane resigned from the Diplomatic Corps in 1947 (U.S. Department of State, *Register of the Department of State*, 303). Gen. Lewis J. Fortier, who as American military attaché in Belgrade worked closely with Lane, described him as a "brilliant analyst and indefatigable worker" who was "not happy in and was far less prone to encourage the Yugoslavs to resist than I was" (Fortier, letter to author, July 9, 1973).

8. U.S. Department of State, *Documents on German Foreign Policy, 1918–1945,* series D, 12:364.

9. Lane to Hull, March 27, 1941, *FRUS* 2:968; *DGFP*, D, 12:412; Julian Amery, *Approach March: A Venture in Autobiography,* 227–28; Ilija Jukić, *The Fall of Yugoslavia,* 59. King Alexander Karadjeordjević had been assassinated on Oct. 9, 1934, in Marseilles, France, by members of the Ustasha, a Croatian terrorist group led by Dr. Ante Pavelić. According to Alexander's will, power passed to a three-man regency headed by his nephew, Prince Paul (U.S. Congress, Senate, Committee on the Judiciary, *Yugoslav Communism: A Critical Study,* by Charles Zalar, 87th Cong., 1st sess., 1961, 52; Robert Lee Wolff, *The Balkans in Our Time,* 123).

10. Fortier, letter to author, July 9, 1973.

11. Testimony of Hermann Goering , Mar. 15, 1946, Nuremberg Military Tribunals, *Proceedings of the International Military Tribunals at Nuremberg* (*IMT*), 9:334. Goering testified that the Simović affair was the "final and decisive factor" that led Hitler to order military action against Yugoslavia; Testimony of Alfred Jodl, June 5, 1946, *IMT* 9:386; U.S. Department of State, *Nazi Conspiracy and Aggression* (*NCA*) 4, DOC. 1756-PS, 277–79.

12. Robert St. John, *Foreign Correspondent,* 235; Robert St. John, *From the Land of Silent People,* 55; U.S. Department of the Army, *The German Campaigns in the Balkans, Spring 1941,* no. 20–260, 49. Approximately seventeen thousand people were killed in the attack on Belgrade. Twenty Yugoslav planes were shot down and forty-four destroyed on the ground. By comparison, the Germans lost two fighter planes. See also U.S. Department of the Army, *Supplementary to the Balkan Campaign,* no. MS B-525, 28–29.

13. Constantine Fotitch, *The War We Lost: Yugoslavia's Tragedy and the Failure of the West,* 140–42; Jozo Tomasevich, *War and Revolution in Yugoslavia, 1941–1945: The Chetniks,* 91–93; M. R. D. Foot, *Resistance: An Analysis of European Resistance to Nazism, 1940–1945,* 187.

14. Michael McConville, *A Small War in the Balkans: British Military Involvement in Wartime Yugoslavia, 1941–1945,* 23. Referring to Mihailovich's role in first establishing the resistance in Yugoslavia, McConville writes: "On May 11, 1941, when Pavelić was still refining his plans for genocide in Croatia, and Tito, the Comintern agent, was doing nothing to discommode the German occupiers because they were partners in the Nazi-Soviet Pact, Mihailovich reached Ravna Gora and set up his headquarters."

15. Tomasevich, *The Chetniks,* 115, 120; Allied Forces Headquarters (AFHQ), *The Četniks: A Survey of Četnik Activity in Yugoslavia, April 1941–July 1944,* 5; Zvonko (James) Vučković, letter to author, Mar. 8, 1978. Vučković was a Chetnik commander in the First Ravna Gora Corps area in Serbia (B. J. Todorovich, transcript of recording, May 29, 1973).

16. AFHQ, *Četniks,* 7–8; Jukić, *Fall of Yugoslavia,* 105; M. Joseph Milazzo, "The Chetnik Movement in Yugoslavia, 1941–1945" (Ph.D. diss., University of Michigan, 1971), 25–27. The Milazzo study was published by Johns Hopkins University Press in 1975.

17. Vučković, letter to author, Mar. 8, 1978; Todorovich transcript, May 29, 1973; "Armed Resistance in Yugoslavia," RG-226, No. 47715. This document bears neither a date nor place of origin, the latter having been excised.

18. J. G. Beevor, *SOE: Recollections and Reflections, 1940–1945,* 108. Beevor con-

tends that many rightwing or anticommunist groups took to the hills and called themselves Chetniks. Some, though not all, of them owed allegiance of some kind to Mihailovich's headquarters, "but there is little evidence that he ever exercised effective control over them, either militarily or politically" (Milazzo, "Chetnik Movement," 35).

19. Milazzo, "Chetnik Movement," 30–34; Tomasevich, *The Chetniks*, 125; Mladen Colić, "Prvi I Drugi Kosovski Četnički Korpus Draže Mihailovića," *Vojnoistorijski glasnik* 25 (1974): 161–77.

20. "Armed Resistance in Yugoslavia," RG-226, No. 47715; Walter R. Mansfield, letter to author, June 17, 1970.

21. Walter Roberts, *Tito, Mihailović, and the Allies, 1941–1945,* 34; Tomasevich, *The Chetniks,* 146–47; DGFP, D, 13:708. On December 20, 1941, Mihailovich wrote to two Chetnik leaders in Montenegro, Djordje Lasić and Pavle Djurisić, "It is important not to cause vain loss of life by our action, but to maintain our principle" (Alec Brown, *The Treason of Mihailovitch,* 2). According to James Vuckovic, Chetnik and Partisan forces cooperated with one another against the Germans until early November when reprisals against the civilian population became so severe "that the morale of the citizenry began to falter" (Vuckovic, letter to author, Feb. 5, 1978).

22. AFHQ, *Četniks,* 18; "Mihailovic and the Partisans," Nov. 1, 1942, RG-226, No. 24853; "Armed Resistance in Yugoslavia," RG-226, No. 47715.

23. Milorand Drachkovitch, "The Comintern and the Insurrectional Activity of the Communist Party in Yugoslavia, 1941–1942," in *The Comintern Historical Highlights, Essays, Recollections, Documents,* 188. Tito was born in the village of Kumrovec in Croatia. During World War I he fought against the Russians on the Carpathian Front, where in 1915 he was wounded and taken prisoner. For a time during the Russian Revolution he fought with the Bolshevik forces around Omsk. There he met his wife-to-be, with whom he returned to Zagreb, Croatia, in 1920. Broz became active in the trade union movement and in 1924 became a member of the outlawed Communist party. His opposition to the government caused him to be imprisoned several times, the longest period being from November, 1928, to March, 1934 (Phyliss Auty, *Tito,* 9, 14, 21, 27, 33, 39, 46; Roberts, *Tito, Mihailović, and the Allies,* 22–23). The charge that Tito and his forces did not begin active resistance in Yugoslavia until after Hitler invaded the Soviet Union does not go unchallenged. Louis Adamić, a leading Partisan propagandist in the United States, contends that the Communist resistance began in May, 1941, "but with Hitler's invasion of Russia it spread through the grass roots of Yugoslavia" (Louis Adamić, *My Native Land,* 44). Michael Padev dismisses the charge as "the purest nonsense" (Michael Padev, *Marshal Tito,* 67–68). Finally, a brief overview of the Partisan movement prepared by the Political Intelligence Committee, Middle East claimed that "armed resistance to the Axis forces of occupation in Yugoslavia first started on a serious scale in the Sumadija district of Old Serbia, in June 1941. . . . The signal for the rising was given by the German invasion of Russia" (Political Intelligence Committee, Middle East [PICME], *The National Liberation Movement of Yugoslavia: A Survey of the Partisan Movement, April 1941–March 1944,* 5–7.

24. Ernest Llewellyn Woodward, *British Foreign Policy in the Second World War* 3:281–82; George Musulin, interview with author, McLean, Virginia, Aug. 16, 1976; Eli Popovich, transcript of recording, Jan. 8, 1977. Popovich was an OSS-SO (Special Operations) officer who was attached to Partisan forces. Musulin was dispatched to

Mihailovich's area. Both agree, however, that radicalization of the peasantry worked to the advantage of the Partisans.

25. DGFP, D, 12:479; Steve Kosanovich, letter to author, Feb. 20, 1978. Kosanovich was originally recruited by the Partisans but on discovering the political character of their movement joined Mihailovich's forces (Tomasevich, *The Chetniks,* 154–55).

26. Tomasevich, *The Chetniks,* 147; Milazzo, "Chetnik Movement," 48, 59–62; Roberts, *Tito, Mihailović, and the Allies,* 31.

27. F. W. D. Deakin, *The Embattled Mountain,* 131–33.

28. M. R. D. Foot, SOE: *An Outline History of the Special Operations Executive, 1940–1946,* 10–13; Nigel West, *MI6: British Secret Intelligence Service Operations, 1909–1945,* 90–92. The British decided to send a mission to Yugoslavia after confirming the authenticity of signals being broadcast in the clear from Ravna Gora which had been picked up by a naval monitoring station on Malta (S. W. Bailey, "British Policy towards General Draža Mihailović," in *British Policy towards Wartime Resistance in Yugoslavia and Greece,* ed. Phyliss Auty and Richard Clogg, 59–60; Deroc, M., *British Special Operations Explored: Yugoslavia in Turmoil 1941–1943 and the British Response,* 68).

29. Woodward, *British Foreign Policy,* 3:280.

30. Deroc, *Special Operations,* 66; Bailey, "British Policy towards Mihailović," 60–61.

31. AFHQ, *Četniks,* 10–12. Hudson reported at the time that "British promise of support had the effect of worsening Cetnik-Partisan relations. When I first arrived at Ravna Gora and Uzice, at the end of October, 1941, before Cetnik-Partisan hostilities, Mihajlovic already knew by telegram that he would get British support. He felt rightly that no one outside the country knew about the Partisans or that he alone was not responsible for the revolt" (Fitzroy Maclean, *The Heretic: The Life and Times of Josip-Broz Tito,* 114; Vladimir Dedijer, *Tito Speaks, His Self-Portrait and Struggle with Stalin,* 161). Mihailovich later claimed that he had agreed to cooperate with the Partisans although he considered them "mere amateurs in military science" (*The Trial of Dragoljub-Draža Mihailović,* 110).

32. Deakin, *Embattled Mountain,* 146–49; Deroc, *Special Operations,* 89–91; Bailey, "British Policy towards Mihailović," 64–65; Mark C. Wheeler, *Britain and the War for Yugoslavia, 1940–1943,* 172. According to Wheeler, Hudson did not reestablish contact with Mihailovich until mid-May.

33. Deakin, *Embattled Mountain,* 152–54.

34. Bailey, "British Policy towards Mihailović," 73; Bailey, letter to author, Mar. 27, 1972.

35. Bailey, "British Policy towards Mihailović," 73–74; Wheeler, *War for Yugoslavia,* 174–75; Wilhelm Hoettl, *The Secret Front: The Story of Nazi Political Espionage,* 160.

36. Bailey, "British Policy towards Mihailović," 73.

37. Phyliss Auty and Richard Clogg, eds., *British Policy towards Wartime Resistance in Yugoslavia and Greece,* 234.

38. Elisabeth Barker, *British Policy in South-East Europe in the Second World War,* 149; OSS Dispatch, No. 30111, Mar. 30, 1943, Roosevelt Papers, Map Room, Box 72;

F. W. D. Deakin, "Britain and Jugoslavia, 1941–1945," paper presented at the conference on Britain and European Resistance, 1941–1945, St. Anthony's College, Oxford, Dec. 1962. I am indebted to Vane Ivanović for a copy of the Deakin paper and for Mr. Ivanović's own detailed critique of the paper. Mr. Ivanović is a Yugoslav national who served on the staff of the PWE (Political Warfare Executive) in London, Cairo, and Bari between August, 1943, and February, 1945 (Vane Ivanović, letter to author, Aug. 16, 1973).

39. Elisabeth Barker, "Fresh Sidelights on British Policy in Yugoslavia, 1942–3," *Slavonic and East European Review* 54 (Oct. 1976): 574; McConville, *Small War,* 60–62.

40. Basil Davidson, *Special Operations Europe: Scenes from the Anti-Nazi War,* 118–19; Beevor, *SOE,* 115–16. In preparing the brief advocating military support for the Partisans, Keble utilized intelligence gleaned from German intercepts to strengthen his case. Keble had been cleared to receive the intercepts in his previous post on the staff at General Headquarters, Middle East, and perhaps as an oversight, he continued to receive them in Cairo. Most likely the material to which Keble, and through him Davidson and Deakin, had access was Sicherheitsdienst intercepts, not ULTRA signals (Ralph Bennett, *Ultra and Mediterranean Strategy,* 393–96).

41. FO 371/37581/03436, Mar. 6, 1943.

42. F. H. Hinsley et al., *British Intelligence in the Second World War, Its Influence on Strategy and Operations,* vol. 3 pt. 1, 143–44.

43. Deakin, *Embattled Mountain,* 1–7. Similar reports were also being sent by Maj. William Jones, who had parachuted into Croatia on May 18 and had subsequently moved into Slovenia. Details of his mission may be found in Jones's postwar account entitled *Twelve Months with Tito's Partisans.*

44. Deakin, *Embattled Mountain,* 14; Jukić, *Fall of Yugoslavia,* 208.

45. F. W. D. Deakin, "Great Britain and European Resistance," in *European Resistance Movements, 1939–1945,* 111–12.

46. Bailey, "British Policy towards Mihailović," 81.

47. Roberts, *Tito, Mihailović, and the Allies,* 120; Hinsley, Thomas, et al., *British Intelligence,* vol. 3, pt. 1, 150.

48. Maclean, *Heretic,* 193.

49. Bailey, "British Policy towards Mihailović," 73.

Chapter 2. A British Show

1. John G. Winant to Hull, U.S. Department of State, *FRUS, 1943,* 2:1007–1009.

2. Memorandum by Cavendish W. Cannon, Division of European Affairs, May 17, 1943, *FRUS, 1943,* 2:1010.

3. Donovan to Roosevelt, Apr. 13, 1942, Roosevelt Papers, PSF, Donovan Reports, Box 165.

4. Smith, *OSS,* 34; Anthony Cave Brown, ed., *The Secret War Report of the OSS,* 102.

5. Bickham Sweet-Escott, *Baker Street Irregular,* 145.

6. Roberts, *Tito, Mihailović, and the Allies,* 98; Corey Ford, *Donovan of OSS,* 165; George Selvig, transcript of recording, Feb. 26, 1973; George Musulin, inter-

view with author, Aug. 16, 1976; Norman Kogan, "American Policies towards European Resistance," in *European Resistance Movements, 1939–1945,* 72–73; David Martin, interview with author, Aug. 16, 1976.

7. "OSS/SOE Collaboration in Middle East," Aug. 20, 1943, Roosevelt Papers, PSF/OSS, Box 167.

8. Roberts, *Tito, Mihailović, and the Allies,* 98; Turner H. McBaine, telephone interview with author, May 18, 1988.

9. Testimony of George Musulin, Commission of Inquiry, 122.

10. Guenther to Bailey, July 7, 1943, Selvig Papers, in author's files.

11. Melvin O. Benson, letter to author, Oct. 30, 1971; Benson Report, June 22, 1944, OSS/CIA.

12. Mansfield Report, Mar. 1, 1944, OSS/CIA.

13. PICME, *Survey of Partisan Movement,* 12. An OSS report dated Oct. 21, 1943, identified two Mihailovich men who claimed that as early as September 5, the general had sent them to Susak to enter into negotiations with the Italians there, but on September 9, the Germans arrived and both men evacuated the area by boat for Brindisi, Italy (RG-226, OSS File No. 47310, Oct. 21, 1943).

14. Benson Report, June 22, 1941, OSS/CIA.

15. Ibid.

16. Ibid. According to Benson, when an Allied convoy arrived to evacuate the Italians from Split, "General Becuzzi and staff were the first to get aboard." Deakin's version of the negotiations at Split, which varies in some points from Benson's, may be found in Deakin, *Embattled Mountain,* 231–39.

17. Benson Report, June 22, 1944, OSS/CIA.

18. Mansfield Report, Mar. 1, 1944, OSS/CIA.

19. Ibid.

20. Ibid. Additional information on the Berane incident may be found in David Martin, *The Web of Disinformation: Churchill's Yugoslav Blunder,* 152–54, and Michael Lees, *The Rape of Serbia: The British Role in Tito's Grab for Power 1943–1944,* 99–103. Both of these works are critical of British policy in Yugoslavia, especially the role played by SOE-Cairo. Lees even suggests that SOE-Cairo ordered Bailey to have Italian forces brought under Allied command in order to ensure that their arms would ultimately go to the Partisans rather than the Chetniks.

21. Mansfield Report, Mar. 1, 1944, OSS/CIA; Testimony of Walter Mansfield, Commission of Inquiry, 72.

22. PICME, *Survey of Partisan Movement,* 13 (the figures cited in the PICME publication were taken from a speech delivered by Tito at Jajce in November, 1943, a copy of which was sent to me by Eli Popovich); David Martin, interview with author, Aug. 16, 1976; RG-226, OSS File No. 47715, Sept.–Oct., 1943.

23. Barker, *British Policy in South-East Europe,* 165.

24. Michael Howard, *Grand Strategy* 4:483; Winston S. Churchill, *Closing the Ring,* vol. 5 of *History of the Second World War,* 465; Auty and Clogg, *Wartime Resistance,* 39, 226. Deakin claims that Maclean's arrival "marked implicitly the *de facto* recognition of the Yugoslav National Liberation Army as a military force fulfilling a significant role in South-Eastern Europe" (Deakin, *Embattled Mountain,* 242).

25. Brig. Charles Douglas Armstrong, transcript of recording, Apr. 23, 1973.

26. Report of Col. Albert B. Seitz, "Mission to Mihailovich," n.d., OSS/CIA; report of Maj. Linn Farish, Oct. 29, 1943, OSS/CIA (this report is reproduced in U.S. Department of State, *FRUS, The Conferences at Cairo, and Teheran, 1943* 606–15; Farish's third report, which was a more critical appraisal of the Partisan movement and of American policy in general, was not declassified until 1974), Fitzroy Maclean, *Eastern Approaches,* 304.

27. Smith, *OSS,* 135–36; Seitz Report, n.d., OSS/CIA.

28. Seitz Report, n.d., OSS/CIA.

29. Ibid.

30. "Report Received from Wix (Armstrong), British Head of Allied Military Mission at Mihailovitch HQ.," Nov. 7, 1943, OSS/CIA. This report was attached as Appendix C to Donovan's Memorandum to the Joint Chiefs of Staff of Nov. 26, 1943.

31. Mansfield, letter to author, June 17, 1970; Mansfield report, Mar. 1, 1944, OSS/CIA.

32. Seitz Report, n.d., OSS/CIA. At his initial conference with Mihailovich, Armstrong produced a number of letters, one of which was from Gen. Henry Maitland Wilson, Allied commander in the Mediterranean theater. Mihailovich later showed Wilson's letter to Seitz, who described it as a "blunt, forthright, almost arrogant letter demanding that Mihailovich intensify sabotage and guerilla [sic] activities immediately."

33. Ibid.

34. Armstrong transcript, Apr. 24, 1973.

35. Seitz Report, n.d., OSS/CIA; "Basic Estimate of Position of American Officers with British Missions Attached to General Mihailovich," Oct. 25, 1943, OSS/CIA.

36. Mansfield, letter to author, June 17, 1970.

37. Mansfield Report, Mar. 1, 1944, OSS/CIA. Mansfield reported that at the end of his first month in the country he had sent ninety-six signals to Cairo and received four replies. One congratulated him on his arrival; he could not decode the second; the third advised him to keep his messages under three hundred letters and to stay at Mihailovich's headquarters rather than accompany Bailey to Priboj; and the fourth provided information on theater command.

38. Armstrong transcript, Apr. 24, 1973.

39. Ibid.; Seitz Report, n.d., OSS/CIA.

40. Mansfield Report, Mar. 1, 1944, OSS/CIA.

41. Excerpts from Operational Logs: Yugoslavia – Nov. 1943. Armstrong (Wix) to Cairo, Nov. 13, 1943, RG-226, E. 144, B. 97, F. 1017.

42. David Martin, *Ally Betrayed: The Uncensored Story of Tito and Mihailovich,* 222.

43. George Musulin, "Field Report of Marko, Member of British-American Mission to General Draza Mihailovich's HQ from 19 October, 1943 to 28 May, 1944," n.d., OSS/CIA.

44. Armstrong and Bailey to Lord Glenconner, SOE-Cairo, Nov. 18, 1943, FO 371/37167/03425. I am indebted to David Martin for a copy of this document.

45. Benson Report, June 22, 1944, OSS/CIA.

46. Turner McBaine, telephone interview with author, May 18, 1988.

47. Roberts, *Tito, Mihailović, and the Allies,* 201–202. SOE also established a base at Bari—Advanced Headquarters, Force 266.

48. "Final Report on Operation AUDREY," May 16, 1944, RG-226, E. 99, B. 28, F. 137.

49. Ibid.; Louis Huot to Strategic Services Officer, Middle East, "Reconnaissance of Dalmation [*sic*] Coast," Oct. 18, 1943, OSS/CIA.

50. Huot to Strategic Services Officer, Middle East, "Reconnaissance of Dalmation [*sic*] Coast," Oct. 18, 1943, OSS/CIA.

51. Ibid.; "Final Report on Operation AUDREY," May 16, 1944, RG-226, E. 99, B. 28, F. 137.

52. "Trip to Tito's HQ in Jajce, 20–27 October, 1943," Maj. Louis Huot, n.d., RG-226, E. 116, B. 6, F. 45.

53. Benson Report, June 22, 1944, OSS/CIA.

54. "Final Report on Operation AUDREY," May 16, 1944, RG-226, E. 99, B. 28, F. 137.

55. Louis Huot, *Guns for Tito,* 229. Huot's portrayal of Tito written shortly after his return from Partisan headquarters was no less laudatory. Huot found Tito to be "friendly and informal," a man who exhibited "none of the traits and characteristics of a Dictator, and quite obviously does not think of himself as one." Huot continued: "Of modest stature and sturdy build, he wears a simple tunic of heavy grey material, grey breeches, and black riding boots with clinking spurs. His short, square head looks Slavic and there is a suggestion of Semitic blood about the curl of his hair, his blue eyes and the articulation of his features. The face is that of a sensitive resolute person, not that of an intellectual; a man of action rather than polemics, a man with no self-imposed discipline beyond that which his current purpose exacts of him" (Huot, "Trip to Tito's HQ," n.d., RG-226, E. 116, B. 6, F. 45).

56. Huot, "Trip to Tito's HQ"; Huot, *Guns for Tito,* 257.

57. Toulmin to Donovan, Nov. 3, 1944, OSS/CIA.

58. Conyers Read to Donovan, Mar. 5, 1945, RG-226, E. 99, B. 40, F. 99b. This document contains a critique of Huot's book by Maj. Carleton Coon, as well as additional details concerning Huot's dismissal from OSS.

59. Capt. Hans V. Tofte, "Operation AUDREY," Apr. 1, 1944, RG-226, E. 116, B. 6, F. 6.

60. "Final Report on Operation AUDREY," May 16, 1944, RG-226, E. 99, B. 28, F. 137.

61. Benson Report, June 22, 1944, OSS/CIA; Tofte, "Operation AUDREY," Apr. 1, 1944, RG-226, E. 116, B. 6, F. 6.

62. Tofte, "Operation AUDREY." Additional details on various aspects of Operation AUDREY may be found in a report filed by Major Huot on Nov. 8, 1943, RG-226, E. 144, B. 99, F. 1039, and in a handwritten logbook, apparently maintained by Huot, Thompson, and Tofte, covering the period Nov. 2, through Dec. 16, RG-226, E. 190, B. 116, F. 404.

63. McBaine, letter to author, Mar. 26, 1991; McBaine to Toulmin, Dec. 28, 1943, RG-226, E. 190, B. 120, F. 458. The officers involved were Tofte, Thompson, and Hamilton.

64. Read to Donovan, Mar. 5, 1945, RG-226, E. 99, B. 40, F. 99b.

65. "Final Report on Operation AUDREY," May 16, 1944, RG-226, E. 99, B. 28, F. 137.

66. Read to Donovan, Mar. 5, 1945, RG-226, E. 99, B. 40, F. 99b; Benson Report, June 22, 1944, OSS/CIA. In a letter dated Oct. 13, 1971, Benson wrote that he gave Huot about two hundred photographs, captured documents, and some of his own notes during Huot's visit to Tito's headquarters. Much of this information was used in Huot's book. Benson later asked Donovan to intervene in an attempt to recover the photographs, but Huot claimed that they had been lost.

67. Donovan to Joint Chiefs of Staff, Nov. 26, 1943, OSS/CIA.

68. History, Cairo Office, n.d., RG-226, E. 99, B. 43, F. 214.

69. Musulin Testimony, Commission of Inquiry, 118.

70. Musulin, interview with author, Aug. 16, 1976.

71. Ibid.

72. Musulin Report, n.d., OSS/CIA; Musulin Testimony, Commission of Inquiry, 127–28, 146–47.

73. Vucković, letter to author, Feb. 5, 1978.

74. Seitz, "American Officers with Mihailovich," Oct. 25, 1943, OSS/CIA; Mansfield Report, Mar. 1, 1944, OSS/CIA; Todorovich transcript, May 29, 1973. See also Boris Todorovich, *Last Words: A Memoir of World War II and the Yugoslav Tragedy*, 265–98.

75. Armstrong and Bailey to Glenconner, SOE-Cairo, Nov. 18, 1943, FO 371/37167/03425.

76. *Times* (London), June 18, 1943, 3.

77. Bogdan Raditsa, "Tito's Partisans," *The Nation*, Oct. 2, 1943, 381. Raditsa described the Partisans as a "popular front composed of Slovenes, Croats, Serbs, Moslems, Catholics, Jews, and anti-Fascists from all Southeastern Europe. It is trying to build a new Yugoslavia and a new Balkan order based on a commonwealth of free nations" ("Charges and Chetniks," *Newsweek*, Mar. 1, 1943, 52; "War within a War," *Time*, Feb. 8, 1943, 29).

78. Donovan to Roosevelt, Oct. 28, 1943, Franklin D. Roosevelt Papers, OSS/PSF, Box 167, Franklin D. Roosevelt Library, Hyde Park, N.Y. An OSS report dated Dec. 29, 1942, included the following statement: "It can be safely stated that the Partisan movement in Yugoslavia is not inspired to any great extent by Communist ideology. The myth that the Partisans are communists has been created by Axis propaganda" (RG-226, No. 26257, Dec. 29, 1942).

79. McBaine, interview with author, May 18, 1988.

80. Foot, *Resistance*, 192.

81. Maclean, *Eastern Approaches*, 347.

82. Report by Brigadier F. H. R. Maclean, Commanding Allied Military Mission to the Partisan Forces in Yugoslavia, Nov. 6, 1943, FO 371/37615, R 11589/2/G. I am indebted to Prof. Stevan K. Pavlowitch of the University of Southampton for a copy of this report.

83. Ibid.

84. Ivanović, letter to author, Oct. 15, 1973. From Sept., 1941 to Aug., 1943, Ivanović served as the Yugoslav member of the Inter-Allied Information Center, an organization that provided the American public background information on the

Allied war effort. While with the PWE (Political Warfare Executive) in London, he was responsible for preparing the weekly political appreciations that went to the War Cabinet. Ivanović had personal contact with a number of OSS and SOE agents in Bari and had direct access to pertinent intelligence data that had a bearing on Allied policy decisions affecting Yugoslavia.

85. Donovan to Joint Chiefs of Staff, Nov. 26, 1943, OSS/CIA.

86. Farish Report, Oct. 29, 1943, OSS/CIA.

87. Ibid.; Louis Adamić, *Dinner at the White House*, 150.

88. Farish Report, Oct. 29, 1943, OSS/CIA.

89. Ibid.

90. Ibid.

91. Popovich transcript, Jan. 8, 1977; Benson Report, June 22, 1944, OSS/CIA; Robert H. McDowell, letter to author, Feb. 25, 1970. Colonel McDowell, who served on the Joint Intelligence Collection Agency, Middle East (JICAME) and later headed the last American military mission to Mihailovich, had the opportunity to interview numerous American and British officers who had been attached to the resistance. He claims that Farish had to operate under the same restrictions encountered by other liaison officers with the Partisans and was not able to confirm intelligence on a firsthand basis.

92. Benson Report, June 22, 1944, OSS/CIA.

93. While most of Roosevelt's top military advisers opposed sending American forces into the Balkans, Gen. Mark Clark, commander of American forces in Italy, came to a different conclusion. In July, 1977, I sent a series of questions to General Clark, one of which touched upon the feasibility of a Balkan invasion. Clark replied, "I felt we should do it, we could have done it, and we would have been into Vienna, Budapest, and other countries now under Communist domination, before the Communists ever got there" (Gen. Mark W. Clark, letter to author, July 27, 1977).

94. Peter Karadjeordjević, *A King's Heritage*, 178–79, 197.

95. Carl Norden, transcript of recording, May 12, 1977.

96. Harold Macmillan, who served as British political adviser to the Supreme Allied Commander, Mediterranean Theater, wrote that by Dec. 1943, "the most informed British opinion was that the Partisans would rule and that the monarchy had little future and had ceased to be a unifying element" (Harold Macmillan, *The Blast of War, 1939–1945*, vol. 2 of *The Memoirs of Harold Macmillan*, 436–37. In late December, Ralph Stevenson, British ambassador of the Yugoslav government, sent the following message to Churchill: "Our policy must be based on three new factors: The Partisans will be the rulers of Yugoslavia. They are of such value to us militarily that we must back them to the full, subordinating political considerations to military. It is extremely doubtful whether we can any longer regard the Monarchy as a unifying element in Yugoslavia" (Churchill, *Closing the Ring*, 401).

97. RG-226, OSS File No. 52519, Dec. 14, 1943.

98. Robert Murphy, letter to author, Aug. 1, 1977.

99. Deakin, "Great Britain and European Resistance," 107; Deakin, *Embattled Mountain*, 88.

Chapter 3. A Hostile Brief

1. Deakin, *Embattled Mountain*, 262–63.

2. Amery, *Approach March*, 271. Brigadier C. M. Woodhouse, who commanded

as SOE mission in Greece, has suggested that no one fully thought out the implications of what was being done in Greece and Yugoslavia. In his opinion "the two countries might have been on Mars and Venus for all connection that was seen between them" (Auty and Clogg, *Wartime Resistance,* 274; "Inside Greece," Nov. 26, 1943, OSS/CIA).

3. FO 371-37617-X/M00655, Dec. 1, 1943.

4. FO 371-37167/03425/, Dec. 3, 1943.

5. Hinsley et al., *British Intelligence,* vol. 3 pt. 1, 160; Woodward, *British Foreign Policy* 3:300.

6. McCONVILLE, *Small War,* 75; Armstrong transcript, Apr. 24, 1973. Michael Lees sheds new light on the December 29 ultimatum from recently declassified British documents (Lees, *Rape of Serbia,* 253–62). See also Martin, *Web of Disinformation,* 201–208.

7. Martin, *Web of Disinformation,* 201–208.

8. Deakin, "Britain and Jugoslavia," 13; Macveagh to Hull, Feb. 21, 1944, *FRUS, 1944,* 4:1348; Cairo to AGWAR, Feb. 19, 1944, Roosevelt Papers, MR-300 "The Balkans," Folders 1 and 2, Box 79; Armstrong transcript, Apr. 24, 1973.

9. Michael Lees, *Special Operations Executed in Serbia and Italy,* 136–37.

10. Mansfield Report, Mar. 1, 1944, OSS/CIA.

11. Musulin Report, n.d., OSS/CIA; Jasper Rootham, *Miss Fire: The Chronicle of a British Mission to Mihailovich, 1943–1944,* 176–77.

12. WO 201-1599 X/M891, Dec. 28, 1943.

13. George Rendel, *The Sword and the Olive: Recollections of Diplomacy and the Foreign Service, 1913–1943,* 215. Rendel, who was the British minister and later ambassador to the Yugoslav government-in-exile, wrote that the government's loss of prestige, both among the Allied governments and the Yugoslav peoples, coupled with persistent internal power struggles among various elements of the officer corps, made it possible for Britain "to abandon them with hardly a qualm and to acquiesce in Tito's anti-monarchial revolution."

14. History, Cairo Office, n.d., RG-226, E. 99, B. 43, F. 214. An OSS report dated July 8, 1944, concluded that "with aid going to Mihailovic in the East, reinforcement or replacement of perhaps five, maybe ten [German] divisions would be necessary to maintain objectives" (RG-226, E. 146, B. 64, F. 876; unfortunately, this document contains no cover page by which to determine its origin or authorship).

15. OSS report, July 8, 1944, RG-226, E. 146, B. 64, F. 876.

16. West to Donovan, Nov. 9, 1943, RG-226, E. 99, B. 34, F. 170.

17. Macveagh to Hull, Feb. 2, 1944, *FRUS, 1944,* 4:1349.

18. Donovan to Roosevelt, Mar. 2, 1944, Roosevelt Papers, PSF/OSS, Donovan Papers.

19. Hull to Roosevelt, Mar. 21, 1944, Roosevelt Papers, PSF/OSS, Donovan Reports; Roosevelt to Donovan, Mar. 22, 1944, Roosevelt Papers, PSF/OSS, Donovan Reports.

20. Roosevelt to Donovan, Mar. 22, 1944, Roosevelt Papers, PSF/OSS, Donovan Reports.

21. History, Cairo Office, n.d., RG-226, E. 99, B. 43, F. 214.

22. Francis L. Lowenheim, Harold D. Langley, and Manfred Jonas, eds., *Roosevelt and Churchill: Their Secret Wartime Correspondence,* 482–83.

23. Ibid.

24. History, Cairo Office, n.d., RG-226, E. 99, B. 43, F. 214.

25. Ibid. Decisions like this led Constantine Fotitch to lament that while the United States did not fully endorse the "unremitting exertions" of the British policy, "Roosevelt . . . allowed the Prime Minister to press his unfortunate experiment to its tragic end" (Fotitch, *War We Lost*, 287). The SI Branch had prepared three teams for infiltration to Mihailovich's forces. MINNESOTA under Lt. Charles Grimm was to go to Mihailovich's headquarters; TEXAS under Capt. Robert S. Phillips was to go to the Homolje area; and MICHIGAN under Lt. Robert J. Weiler had no specific destination cited (History, Cairo Office, n.d., RG-226, E. 99, B. 43, F. 214).

26. From 106 to Glavin, Apr. 11, 1944, RG-226, E. 154, B. 58, F. "Daily Ops. Reports, Bari."

27. Woodward, *British Foreign Policy* 3:313.

28. RG-226, OSS File No. 45022-5, Sept. 10, 1943; Henry M. Christman, ed., *The Essential Tito*, 10; Vladimir Dedijer, *The Battle Stalin Lost: Memoirs of Yugoslavia, 1948–1953*, 49–50.

29. Mosha Pijade, *About the Legend That the Yugoslav Uprising Owed Its Existence to Soviet Assistance*, 23.

30. PICME, *Survey of Partisan Movement*, 34–35; Anthony Eden, *The Reckoning*, 500.

31. Deakin, "Britain and Jugoslavia," 121.

32. Mansfield Report, Mar. 1, 1944, OSS/CIA; Seitz Report, n.d., OSS/CIA; Mansfield, Field Diary, 54, in author's files.

33. Mansfield Report, Mar. 1, 1944, OSS/CIA.

34. Ibid.; Mansfield, Field Diary, 20–21. Mansfield begins the diary entry that describes his encounter with the Germans with the phrase "Biggest and most hair-raising day in this country."

35. Mansfield, Field Diary, 20–21.

36. Ibid.

37. Seitz Report, n.d., OSS/CIA.

38. Ibid.

39. Ibid.

40. Ibid.

41. Ibid.

42. Mansfield Report, Mar. 1, 1944, OSS/CIA.

43. Ibid.

44. Ibid.

45. Ibid.; Testimony of Walter Mansfield, Commission of Inquiry, 55, 110, 112. Mansfield testified that he never found evidence to support allegations that Mihailovich personally collaborated with the Germans. He did see posters in several railroad stations on which the names of hostages killed by the Germans as reprisals for acts of sabotage by Mihailovich were signed by the local German commandant. He also saw a Croat newspaper containing an announcement that the Germans were offering 100,000 Reichmarks for both Tito and Mihailovich, dead or alive. As for the questionable activities of Captain Kalabić, neither Seitz nor Mansfield labeled the controversial Chetnik commander as a collaborator. Mansfield testified that he saw 150

homes in Stragari which had been burned down by the Germans as the result of an attack by Kalabić. Seitz also learned that Kalabić's father had been killed by the Gestapo by being dragged over broken glass until he bled to death. Seitz was certain that Kalabić had no love whatsoever for the Germans (Seitz Report, n.d., oss/cia).

46. Mansfield Report, Mar. 1, 1944, oss/cia.

47. Martin, *Ally Betrayed,* 122, 127.

48. rg-226, oss File No. 65109, Mar. 28, 1944. In a report filed on June 13, 1944, R. H. Markham wrote that "no one in Serbia is fighting Germans . . . there is open and extensive collaboration between the Nedich men and the Chetniks" (Macveagh to Hull, June 13, 1944, Department of State, Unpublished State Department Papers, no file number, National Archives).

49. rg-226, oss File No. 65109, Mar. 28, 1944.

50. Edward J. Green to Langer, "An Appraisal of the Position of General Mihailovich," Apr. 1944, rg-226, E. 83, B. 2, F. Miscellaneous Reports–Yugoslavia.

51. Ibid.

52. rg-226, oss File No. 64730, Mar. 8, 1944.

53. Report of Lt. George Musulin to Headquarters, Special Balkan Service, Research and Analysis, June 7, 1944. George Musulin provided me with a copy of this report from his personal files. According to David Martin, the Communist party was also invited to attend this Congress but declined to do so (Martin, interview with author, Aug. 16, 1976).

54. Musulin Report, June 7, 1944.

55. Ibid.

56. Martin, interview with author, Aug. 16, 1976.

57. Vane Ivanović, *LX: Memoirs of a Jugoslav,* 220–21.

58. fo 371/44262, "Conversation with Dr. Topalovic," July 28, 1944. Vane Ivanović was the officer who interviewed Dr. Topalović, and I am indebted to him for a copy of this report. In an earlier report prepared for Political Warfare Executive, Ivanović pointed out the critical dilemma in which Mihailovich found himself at the beginning of the year. He argued that the Chetniks had lost "to Nedic the leadership in the preservation of the Serbs and to Tito the leadership in the active warfare against the Germans and Quislings" (Ivanović to J. D. Stewart, Feb. 8, 1944, fo 371/44250).

59. Musulin Report, n.d., oss/cia; Musulin Testimony, Commission of Inquiry, 159–61.

60. The cynicism with which the British viewed the Ba proposals is evident in the following excerpt from the afhq handbook *The Četniks:* "That this meeting was mainly a piece of window dressing, lacking in real popular character, and primarily designed to go one better than the Partisan success in announcing the formation of avnoj is suggested by blo and other reports. The main object of Mihailovich and his group remained as ever the suppression of their Partisan rivals." Just how the authors of this publication reached such a conclusion is not at all clear. The British had no liaison officers to attend the conference, and the one American officer who did attend reported favorably on the proceedings.

61. Musulin Report, n.d., oss/cia.

62. Ibid.

63. Musulin, interview with author, Aug. 16, 1976.

64. Musulin, interview with author, Aug. 16, 1976; Nelson Deranian, interview with author, Jan. 26, 1988.

65. Musulin Report, n.d., oss/cia.

66. Ibid.

67. Ibid.

68. Ibid.

69. Ibid.; Musulin, interview with author, Aug. 16, 1976; Musulin Testimony, Commission of Inquiry, 135.

70. Lawrence Edward Modisett, "The Four-Cornered Triangle: British and American Policy Toward Yugoslavia, 1939–1945." (Ph.D. diss., Georgetown University, 1981), 429.

71. Seitz to Cairo, Dec. 13, 1943, RG-226, E. 146, B. 64, F. 876.

72. Hinsley et al., *British Intelligence*, vol. 3 pt. I, 146–47.

73. Ibid.

74. *Intelligence from Enemy Radio Communications, 1939–1945*, DEFE 3 (New York: Clearwater Publishing Company, 1979), Dec. 9, 1943, VL 1526, Reel 10; Feb. 8, 1944, VL 5775, Reel 10. These Ultra documents were available on microfilm from Florida State University. This collection will be cited hereafter as DEFE 3.

75. DEFE 3, Dec. 3, 1943, VL 1059, Reel 3. His attitude was revealed in numerous transmissions: DEFE 3, Feb. 11, 1944, VL 6015, Reel 10; DEFE 3, Mar. 23, 1944 VL 9202, Reel 14; DEFE 3, Mar. 25, 1944, VL 9405, Reel 14; DEFE 3, Apr. 17, 1944, KV 1237, Reel 16.

76. DEFE 3, Dec. 29, 1943, VL 2830, Reel 6.

77. DEFE 3, May 5, 1944, KV 2645, Reel 18.

78. Hinsley et al., *British Intelligence*, vol. 3 pt. I, 159.

79. DEFE 3, Apr. 3, 1944, KV 111, Reel 15.

80. John Ehrman, *Grand Strategy*, vol. 5, *August 1943 – September 1944,* 270.

81. David Martin, *Patriot or Traitor: The Case of General Mihailovich,* 70–82; Mansfield Report, Mar. 1, 1944, oss/cia.

82. Davidson, *Special Operations Europe,* 282.

83. Ibid., 103.

84. Hoettl, Situation Report: Yugoslavia, Dec. 21, 1945, RG-226, E. 109, B. 52, F. 294.

85. Lees, *Special Operations Executed,* 105–106, 114–15, 128–29, 130–31, 143–44.

86. Michael Lees, letter to author, May 30, 1988. Manić confirmed Lees's point: Bora Manić, letter to author, Feb. 10, 1985.

87. DEFE 3, Nov. 25, 1943, VL 517, Reel 2; DEFE 3, Dec. 21, 1943, VL 2320, Reel 5. At times these operations involved units of significant size as indicated by this report, which refers to a clash between Partisan and German forces around Karlovac. The Germans found themselves confronted by a Partisan unit of between a thousand and twelve hundred men, from which they were not able to disengage until nightfall (See also DEFE 3, Dec. 21, 1943, VL 2347 LM SB OO, Reel 5; DEFE 3, Dec. 23, 1943, VL 2512 LM SB CO, Reel 6; DEFE 3, Jan. 17, VL 4155, 1944, Reel 7; DEFE 3, Feb. 10, 1944, VL 5981, Reel 9; DEFE 3, Mar. 16, 1944, VL 8615, Reel 13). This

signal refers to significant guerrilla activity in the areas of Karlovac, Plaski, Bihać, and Banjaluka. Approximately four hundred guerrillas armed with automatic weapons attacked a German train, leaving twenty-two Germans dead and several others wounded.

88. DEFE 3, Nov. 20, 1943, VL 138, Reel 1; DEFE 3, Nov. 30, 1943, VL 833, Reel 2; DEFE 3, VL 1342, Dec. 7, 1943, Reel 3; DEFE 3, Dec. 3, 1943, VL 1059, Reel 3.

89. DEFE 3, Dec. 3, 1943, VL 1093, Reel 3; DEFE 3, Dec. 13, 1943, VL 1797, Reel 5; DEFE 3, Mar. 12, 1944, VL 8269, Reel 13; DEFE 3, Apr. 13, 1944, KV 871, Reel 16. This signal refers to a Partisan attack that was repulsed by Chetnik forces at Golubić. However, Partisan units forced the Chetniks to retreat from the Ivanjica area toward the north bank of the Morava River (DEFE 3, Apr. 17, 1944, KV 1235, Reel 16). This report indicates that a Chetnik unit defeated a rather sizable Partisan force of about fifteen hundred men roughly twenty-six kilometers north of Rogatica (DEFE 3, Apr. 22, 1944, KV 1669, Reel 17).

90. Robert Lee Wolff, letter to author, July 1, 1970.

Chapter 4. Uninformed and Misinformed

1. "Brief Survey of the Partisan Movement," Mar. 15, 1944, RG-226, E. 154, B. 18, F. 245. This report credited the Partisans with holding down as many divisions as Allied forces in Italy.

2. Foot, *Resistance*, 193.

3. PICME, *Survey of Partisan Movement*, 9–12; Milovan Djilas, *Wartime*, 245. The seven offensives initiated by German forces against the Partisans were conducted between November, 1941, and May, 1944. The Second Offensive began in January, 1942, the Third in September, 1942, the Fourth in January, 1943, the Fifth in May, 1943, the Sixth in September, 1943, and the Seventh in May, 1944. Djilas provides an excellent and rather detailed account of these operations from the Partisan perspective. The German view of these operations may be found in the Department of the Army publication entitled *German Antiguerrilla Operations in the Balkans, 1941–1944*.

4. Donovan to Joint Chiefs of Staff, Nov. 26, 1943, OSS/CIA; Brown, *Secret War Report*, 276–77. By way of comparison, the British had thirteen missions with Mihailovich's forces in December, 1943, and as many as eighteen with the Partisans in November, 1944 (communication from the British Foreign and Commonwealth Office, July 22, 1971).

5. "History of the Cairo Office," n.d., RG-226, E. 99, B. 43, F. 214.

6. Ibid.; Musulin interview, Aug. 16, 1976; Popovich transcript, Jan. 8, 1977. The cover sheet of Wuchinich's field report dated Nov. 28, 1944, contains the following notation: "In reading this report it is well to bear in mind that Captain Wuchinich is a very energetic, intense and sincere officer who admits his devotion to the Partisan's cause in Yugoslavia. Captain Wuchinich proudly takes sides after what he considers adequate proof of the justice and virtue of Tito's struggle. In such a role it is quite impossible for the author objectively to view the complex Yugoslav scene" (RG-226, E. 146, B. 205, F. 2870).

7. Recommendation of the Award of Legion of Merit to Captain George Selvig, 27 September, 1945, by Hans V. Tofte, Selvig Papers; "Report on Field Conditions,"

Dec. 4, 1944, Selvig Papers; "Report on Activity in Yugoslavia," n.d., RG-226, E. 190, B. 660, F. 985; RG-226, E. 154, B. 23, F. COLUMBIA-GARGANTUAN, n.d.; Popovich transcript, Jan. 8, 1977.

8. Report on Field Conditions, Dec. 4, 1944, Selvig Papers; Selvig transcript, Nov. 6, 1973.

9. Benson Report, June 22, 1944, OSS/CIA.

10. Ibid.

11. Ibid.

12. Report on Field Conditions, Dec. 4, 1944, Selvig Papers.

13. Churchill, *Closing the Ring*, 403. Shortly after Churchill sent his letter, a reliable Yugoslav source indicated that the British Embassy had suggested unofficially to the Yugoslav government-in-exile that King Peter should "recognize Tito and his Partisans as the only representatives of the King and people of Yugoslavia and denounce General Mihailovich" (RG-226, OSS File No. 54512, Jan. 3, 1943; U.S.S.R. Ministry of Foreign Affairs, *Correspondence Between the Chairman of the Council of Ministers of the U.S.S.R. and the Presidents of the U.S.A. and the Prime Ministers of Great Britain During the Great Patriotic War of 1941–1945*, 1:184).

14. Eden, *The Reckoning*, 502.

15. Memorandum by Carl F. Norden, Jan. 19, 1944, *FRUS, 1944*, 4:1339.

16. Memorandum by Assistant Secretary of State Adolf Berle, *FRUS, 1944*, 4:1339–40.

17. "History of Cairo Office", n.d., RG-226, E. 99, B. 43, F. 214; McBaine, interview with author, May 18, 1988.

18. Robin W. Winks, *Cloak and Gown: Scholars in the Secret War, 1939–1961*, 220; SMITH, OSS, 148; George Vujnovich, interview with author, Mar. 6–8, 1987; John R. Milodragovich, interview with author, July 10, 1989; Nick Lalich, interview with author, Jan. 6, 1988.

19. Maj. Richard Weil, "CALIFORNIA, Chronological Account," n.d., RG-226, E. 146, B. 64, F. 875.

20. Ibid.

21. Ibid.

22. Ibid.

23. Ibid.; Capt. James Goodwin, "Final Report of FLOTSAM Mission," n.d., RG-226, E. 154, B. 25, F. Bari-SI; James Goodwin, interview with author, Garden City, N.Y., Mar. 7, 1987. Goodwin recalls that it took roughly a month to make the trip to Slovenia, by which time Jones had been relieved. Goodwin later sent a message to Farish requesting reassignment because of the very minor role American personnel were playing in that area. He told Farish in his final report that he considered this a matter of national prestige and insisted that his "loyal instincts for the U.S. does [sic] not permit me to play a willing part in it."

24. Goodwin to Farish, Mar. 14, 1944, RG-226, E. 154, B. 4, F. Bari-OSS-OP-13.

25. Weil, "CALIFORNIA, Chronological Account," n.d., RG-226, E. 146, B. 64, F. 875.

26. Ibid.

27. Ibid.; "History of Cairo Office," n.d., RG-226, E. 99, B. 43, F. 214.

28. Weil to Whitney Shephardson, Chief-SI, May 22, 1944, RG-226, E. 110, B. 13,

F. 3. After his return to Bari, Weil was interviewed by Lt. Col. Robert H. McDowell, who was then attached to the Joint Intelligence Collection Agency, Middle East. During the course of their conversation Weil admitted that he had personally observed only a small fraction of the two hundred thousand to three hundred thousand men the Partisans claimed to have under arms and personally doubted the accuracy of those figures. Maclean had given roughly the same numbers in his report, although according to McDowell he later admitted privately in Cairo to having seen only about thirty thousand troops. Weil confessed that during his trip to Washington he realized his mistake in not attempting to verify these figures and hoped upon returning to Yugoslavia "to somewhat remedy this situation." A copy of the report of McDowell's interview with Weil, dated June 12, 1944, was forwarded to me by McDowell on Nov. 22, 1971.

29. Clifford O'Rourke to Commanding Officer, SBS, June 16, 1944, RG-226, E. 165, B. 6, F. 53. O'Rourke advised Bari that in his view the Partisans "were willing to sacrifice any help that this SI operation could furnish in order to gain the mission with Tito."

30. Report of Maj. Richard Weil, Jr., Feb. 29–Mar. 20, 1944, Roosevelt Papers, PSF, Box 6.

31. Memorandum for Cavendish Cannon, May 9, 1944, Unpublished State Department Papers, National Archives (NA), File No. 860H.00/1626 1/2.

32. Daniel Desich, transcript of recording, Jan. 19, 1973.

33. Weil Report, Mar. 20, 1944, Roosevelt Papers, PSF, Box 6.

34. Goodwin, "Final Report of FLOTSAM Mission," n.d., RG-226, E. 154, B. 25. B. Bari-SI.

35. Weil Report, Mar. 20, 1944, Roosevelt Papers, PSF, Box 6.

36. Ibid.

37. Memorandum for Cavendish Cannon, May 9, 1944, Unpublished State Department Papers, NA, File No. 860H.00/1626 1/2.

38. Joint Intelligence Committee, (JIC), Weekly Summary, Nov. 24, 1943, Roosevelt Papers, MR, Vol. 229, 6–7; RG-226, OSS File No. 35419, Feb. 26, 1943; JIC, Weekly Summary, Oct. 20, 1943, Roosevelt Papers, MR, Vol. 229, 8.

39. RG-226, OSS File No. 47715, Oct., 1943. This report put Partisan strength at 200,000 and Chetnik strength at 30,000. A later report dated Feb. 4, 1944, put Partisan strength at 220,000 maximum but claimed that only 80,000 of these were armed combat troops (RG-226, OSS File No. 60209, Feb. 4, 1944). David Martin correctly asserts that the true measure of the value of the resistance in Yugoslavia was more in terms of the number of enemy troops that were tied down than in the relatively small number of men actually killed by either side of the resistance. He also maintains that there was always a higher concentration of German troops in Mihailovich's area than in Tito's (Martin, interview with author, Aug. 16, 1978. See also JIC, Weekly Summary, May 18, 1944, Roosevelt Papers, MR, Vol. 232, 3).

40. Lt. Col. Robert H. McDowell, "Disintegration of Yugoslav Partisan Organization," Aug. 4, 1944, McDowell Papers, Hoover Institution Archives, Box 2.

41. Robert H. McDowell, unpublished manuscript in author's files.

42. Macveagh to Hull, June 13, 1944, Unpublished State Department Papers, NA, no file number; Ivanović, LX, 247. Ivanović says of Reuben Markham that he was the only man on the British or American side to be "constantly concerned about

the appalling sacrifices that my people – more than most in occupied Europe – were being asked to make in the war" (Ivanović, letter to author, Oct. 15, 1973). John Keegan concludes that "strategically, estimates of Tito's diversion of force from Hitler's main centres of operation are now seen to be exaggerated" (John Keegan, *The Second World War*, 494).

43. Milazzo, "Chetnik Movement," 354.

44. Tomasevich, *The Chetniks*, 248, 253.

45. F. W. Deakin, "The Germans and Allied Plans for A Balkan Landing," in *The Third Reich and Yugoslavia, 1933–1945*, ed. Pero Moraca, 482.

46. Milazzo, "Chetnik Movement," 344–45.

47. Roberts, *Tito, Mihailović, and the Allies*, 108; Hoettl, *Secret Front*, 165.

48. Djilas, *Wartime*, 231.

49. Roberts, *Tito, Mihailović, and the Allies*, 108–109.

50. Hoettl, *Secret Front*, 165–66. Hoettl indicates that Velebit suggested that the Partisans would fight with the Germans to oppose an Allied invasion of the Balkans. See also Hoettl, "Situation Report: Yugoslavia," Dec. 21, 1945, RG-226, E. 109, B. 52, F. 294.

51. Tomasevich, *The Chetniks*, 264.

52. Glaise von Horstenau Interrogation, Aug. 9, 1945, RG-226, OSS File No. XL-13599.

53. RG-226, OSS File No. OB-7702, Dec. 28, 1943; Report of Capt. Richard F. Rainer, Nov. 14, 1944, OSS/CIA.

54. Djilas, *Wartime*, 244; Adamić, *My Native Land*, 86.

55. Adamić, *My Native Land*, 86.

56. Nora Beloff, *Tito's Flawed Legacy: Yugoslavia and the West Since 1939*, 81–82; *Times* (London) *Literary Supplement*, Nov. 27, 1970.

57. Wheeler, *Britain and the War for Yugoslavia*, 226–27.

58. Von Horstenau Interrogation, RG-226, OSS File No. XL-13599, Aug. 9, 1945.

Chapter 5. The Shape of Things to Come

1. Popovich transcript, Jan. 8, 1977; Testimony of Eli Popovich, Commission of Inquiry, 420–42; Goodwin, "Final Report of FLOTSAM Mission," RG-226, E. 154, B. 25, F. Bari-51; Philip Hart, "Heroes of the OSS: Eli Popovich," *Serb World USA* 4, no. 2 (Nov.–Dec., 1987), 8–9.

2. Popovich transcript, Jan. 8, 1977.

3. Ibid.

4. Ibid.

5. Ibid.

6. Ibid.

7. Farish to Green, May 9, 1944, RG-226, E. 136, B. 35, F. X-82.

8. Farish to Green, May 22, 1944, RG-226, E. 136, B. 35, F. X-82.

9. Popovich transcript, Jan. 8, 1977.

10. Farish to Green, May 8, 1944, RG-226, E. 136, B. 35, F. X-82.

11. Farish to Green, May 23, 1944, RG-226, E. 136, B. 35, F. X-82.

12. Farish to Green, May 16, 1944, RG-226, E. 136, B. 35, F. X-82.

13. Popovich transcript, Jan. 8, 1977.

14. Ibid.

15. Cyrus L. Sulzberger, *A Long Row of Candles: Memoirs and Diaries, 1945–1954,* 244; Report of Maj. Linn Farish, June 16, 1944, OSS/CIA.

16. Report of Maj. Linn Farish, June 16, 1944, OSS/CIA.

17. Ibid.

18. Ibid.

19. Ibid.

20. Ibid.

21. Ibid.

22. Popovich transcript, Jan. 8, 1977. In 1941, Linn Farish wrote for private publication a brief pamphlet entitled *The True Strength of America.* In the second paragraph of the work, Farish wrote to his friends outside the United States: "In all probability we shall never meet again, because it seems impossible for those who are supposed to guide our destinies to gather in friendly conference and discuss their mutual problems as did you and I. This is all that I can do to repay you; to exert the little influence that I can to place the strength of my country behind a policy which will eventually aid in the creation of a better world for all us." Those who knew Linn Farish would no doubt agree that he gave his life attempting to fulfill this pledge.

23. Farish to Green, May 9, 1944, RG-226, E. 136, B. 35, F. X-82.

24. Bari to Farish, June 2, 1944, RG-226, E. 136, B. 35, F. X-82; Farish to Bari, June 1, 1944, RG-226, E. 136, B. 35, F. X-82; Farish to Bari, May 31, 1944, RG-226, E. 136, B. 35, F. X-82.

25. Farish to West, Mar. 9, 1944, RG-226, E. 144, B. 96, F. 1015.

26. Joyce to Donovan, Aug. 8, 1944, RG-226, E. 154, B. 1, F. "Top Secret File."

27. Ibid.

28. Rex K. Deane, "Final Report of REDWOOD Mission," June 15, 1944, RG-226, E. 154, B. 25, F. 354.

29. Green to West, Feb. 1, 1944, RG-226, E. 190, B. 116, F. 392; Green to West Feb. 20, 1944, RG-226, E. 190, B. 116, F. 392.

30. Stephen Galembush, "Candidate for OSS and the RAKEOFF Mission," an unpublished manuscript in the author's files. Rex Deane, who headed the REDWOOD mission and knew both Hunter and Green, confirmed that the attitudes of both officers underwent rather drastic change during the course of their work in Yugoslavia. According to Deane, Hunter had entered the country "full of ideals and a terrific admiration for the Partisan resistance movement, and now felt that it was useless staying on further as his judgement and feelings had become so warped" (Deane, "REDWOOD Mission," Jan. 31, 1945, RG-226, E. 154, B. 25, F. Bari-SI-PRO 55).

31. Galembush, "Candidate for OSS."

32. Algiers to Cheston, Sept. 5, 1944, RG-226, E. 134, B. 232, F. Algiers-IN.

33. Report of Lt. Dan Desich, Apr. 15, 1945, Desich Papers, in author's files; Desich transcript, Jan. 19, 1973.

34. RG-226, OSS File No. L-43790, Aug. 17, 1944.

35. Hull to Chapin, Counselor of Missions at Algiers, July 8, 1944, *FRUS, 1944,* 4:1387.

36. Merrill to Murphy, July 2, 1944, RG-226, E. 136, B. 35, F. Bari Cables, 12/43-09/44.

37. RG-226, OSS File No. 84611, July 14, 1944.

38. Martin, *Ally Betrayed,* 234–35.

39. Donovan to Hull, Apr. 7, 1944, File No. 860H.20/130, OSS/CIA.

40. Berle to Hull, Apr. 29, 1944, Unpublished State Department Papers, 860H.20/130.

41. Hull to Donovan, May 18, 1944, Unpublished State Department Papers, NA, 860H, 20/130.

42. Koch to Toulmin, Feb. 3, 1944, RG-226, E. 190, B. 128, F. 690.

43. Milton Carsen, Report from Y-Section, SI, Bari, Mar. 13, 1944, RG-226, E. 165, B. 6, F. 51. This document includes a report from Palm mission which had been approved by Velebit. The HEMLOCK mission had also been approved by Velebit (RG-226, E. 165, B. 6, F. 51).

44. Henry Maitland Wilson, *Eight Years Overseas, 1939–1947,* 213.

45. Franklin A. Lindsay, interview with author, Lexington, Massachusetts, Aug. 13, 1976.

46. Popovich transcript, Jan. 8, 1977; Desich transcript, Jan. 19, 1973; Musulin, interview with author, Maclean, Virginia, Aug. 16, 1976.

47. History, Cairo Office, n.d., RG-226, E. 99, B. 43, F. 214.

48. Ibid.

49. Maj. F. N. Arnoldy, "Activities, Yugoslav Section, S.I., Bari, Italy, Oct. 30, 1943 to July 12, 1944," RG-226, E. 99. B. 40, F. 199-g. According to Arnoldy, Maj. Carleton Coon was in charge of the base at Bari when he arrived (McBaine, interview with author, May 18, 1988).

50. Arnoldy, "Activities, Yugoslav Section," RG-226, E. 99, B. 40, F. 199-g.

51. Organization Chart, Y-Section, Bari, RG-226, E. 165, B. 8, F. 80; Milodragovich, telephone interview with author, July 10, 1989.

52. Martin, *Ally Betrayed,* 91–92; Milodragovich, telephone interview with author, July 10, 1989.

53. Milodragovich, telephone interview with author, July 10, 1989; Veselinovich to Chief, Y-Section, Feb. 17, 1945, RG-226, E. 154, B. 4, F. Bari-SI-INT, 5.

54. Holt Green to Commanding Officer, SBS, July 29, 1944, RG-226, E. 190, B. 114, F. 379.

55. Final Report of DURAND Team, n.d., RG-226, E. 99, B. 35, F. 175.

56. Arnoldy, "Activities, Y-Section," RG-226, E. 99, B. 40, F. 199-g.

57. Ibid.

58. McBaine, interview with author, May 18, 1988; Deranian, interview with author, Jan. 26, 1988; Vujnovich, interview with author, New York City, Mar. 6–8, 1987.

59. Vujnovich, interview with author, Mar. 6–8, 1987; Arnoldy to C. O. SBS Advanced Base, BARI, Nov. 24, 1943, RG-226, E. 165, B. 6, F. 47.

60. Arnoldy to Lieutenant Colonel Lada-Mocarski, Dec. 29, 1943, RG-226, E. 165, B. 8, F. 80. Vujnovich, who was a medical student at the time the Germans attacked Yugoslavia, barely managed to escape the country. He and his wife, Mirjana, traveled through Hungary, Istanbul, and ultimately into Palestine, where they worked for almost a year with a British intelligence unit. Vujnovich later went to work for Pan American Airways and was transferred to Lagos, where OSS recruiters approached him. The officer who first interviewed Vujnovich was a Colonel Kristofferson, father of the famous pop singer Kris Kristofferson (Vujnovich, interview with author, Mar. 6–8, 1987).

61. Roberts, *Tito, Mihailović, and the Allies,* 202; Milodragovich, interview with author, July 10, 1989. Milodragovich had previously complained to Joyce about Arnoldy and some members of the major's staff, including Irene Parent.

62. Algiers to Donovan, Sept. 5, 1944, RG-226, E. 134, B. 189, F. Bari-si. This is a repeat of a cable sent on Aug. 31.

63. Eugene W. de Moore to Executive Officer, si, Aug. 8, 1944, RG-226, E. 99, B. 28, F. 140a.

64. Ibid.

65. Popovich transcript, Jan. 8, 1977.

66. Thomas G. Early, Executive Officer, to E. J. Green, SBS, June 16, 1944, RG-226, E. 190, B. 114, F. 379.

67. Green to CO/OSS, Italy, May 30, 1944, RG-226, E. 190, B. 120, F. 474.

68. Lt. John Hamilton, "Script for Photographic Unit," n.d., RG-226, E. 190, B. 120, F. 474.

69. Wayne S. Vuchinich to Stuart Hughes and Robert Wolff, June 14, 1944, RG-226, E. 83, B. 1, F. Bari-Balkan Correspondence.

70. Hughes to Wolff, Dec. 1, 1943, RG-226, E. 83, B. 2, F. Washington Correspondence. Hughes was in Algiers at the time this cable was sent. Wolff was chief of the Balkan Section of R & A in Washington.

71. Vuchinich to Hughes and Wolff, June 14, 1944, RG-226, E. 83, B. 1, F. Bari-Balkan Correspondence.

72. Popovich transcript, Jan. 8, 1977; Musulin, interview with author, Aug. 16, 1976; Vujnovich, interview with author, Mar. 6–8, 1987.

73. Alexander Vuchinich, "The Mihailovich Myth," RG-226, E. 154, B. 40, F. 609; Dušan Biber, "Neuspeh neke misije: Ameriški podpolkovnik OOS Robert Mc-Dowell v štabu Draže Mihailovića leta 1944," *Revija Borec* 41 (Oct.–Nov., 1989): 1067. Ironically, Vuchinich prepared this report at about the same time the Partisan leadership opened high-level discussions with German representatives in Zagreb in response to Operation Weiss—an Axis military offensive aimed at liquidating both the Partisan and Chetnik movements.

74. McDowell report, dated June 12, 1944, forwarded to me by Colonel Mc-Dowell on November 22, 1971.

75. Martin, *Patriot or Traitor,* 117.

76. Biber, "Neuspeh neke misije," 1090; McDowell, letter to author, Nov. 8, 1975. McDowell's description of his political views as given in this letter was actually an excerpt taken from a written response submitted to the Commission of Inquiry.

77. Report of Lt. Joseph Veselinovich, Feb. 19, 1945. A copy of this report was given to me by David Martin.

78. Different interpretations of the role Ultra played in the Drvar operation may be found in Ralph Bennett, "Knight's Move at Drvar: Ultra and the Attempt on Tito's Life, 25 May 1944," *Journal of Contemporary History* 22 (1987): 195–208. See also Hinsley, Thomas, et al., *British Intelligence*, vol. 3 pt. 1, 164–65.

79. Hinsley, *British Intelligence*, vol. 3 pt. 1, 164–65.

80. Wilson, *Eight Years Overseas*, 213; Hinsley, et al., *British Intelligence*, Vol. 3 pt. 1, 164–65; Brown, Anthony Cave, *The Last Hero: Wild Bill Donovan*, 458.

81. Report of Capt. Cecil Drew, CALIFORNIA Meteorological Team, June 15, 1944, RG-226, E. 165, B. 6, F. 49.

82. Hoettl, *Secret Front*, 167; Maj. Harris G. Warren, *Special Operations: AAF Aid to European Resistance Movements, 1943–1945.*

83. Beevor, *SOE*, 120–121.

84. Wilson to Chiefs of Staff, May 29, 1944, Roosevelt Papers, MR, "The Balkans," Section 1 and 2, Box 79.

85. Deakin, "Britain and Jugoslavia," 4.

86. Warren, *Special Operations*, 125.

87. Robert Houlihan, interview with author, Lexington, Kentucky, July 14, 1987.

88. Report on Operation FLOUNCED, June 13, 1944, R-226, E. 99, B. 40, F. 199a. This report, prepared by Capt. A. W. Kerr and forwarded to Headquarters, SBS, is one of several included as part of a general history of OG operations in Yugoslavia.

89. Warren, *Special Operations*, 125.

90. Ibid., 125–26; Beevor, *SOE*, 120–21.

91. Chiefs of Staff to Middle East, June 12, 1944, Roosevelt Papers, MR, "The Balkans," Section 1 and 2, Box 80.

92. Joint Staff Mission to British Chiefs of Staff, June 12, 1944, Roosevelt Papers, MR, "The Balkans," Section 1 and 2, Box 80.

93. Brown, *Last Hero*, 456–65. According to Brown, Lt. Col. Živan Knezević, the Royal Yugoslav Government's military attaché, and Boris Todorović were the embassy personnel considered most likely to have had access to the information that was supposedly passed to Cairo and ultimately to the Germans. Todorović, it should be recalled, had served as General Mihailovich's liaison with the Seitz-Mansfield mission until its withdrawal in early 1944.

94. DEFE 3, Dec. 21, 1943, VL 2431, Reel 5; DEFE 3, Dec. 28, 1943, VL 2794, Reel 6; DEFE 3, Dec. 27, 1943, VL 2732, Reel 6; DEFE 3, Dec. 14, 1943, VL 1899, Reel 6.

95. Macmillan, *Blast of War*, 438.

96. Karadjeordjević, *King's Heritage*, 224–29; Maclean, *Eastern Approaches*, 481–82. Roosevelt wrote to Churchill just before Šubašić assumed power on June 1 to remind the prime minister of an earlier American proposal to establish three governments in Yugoslavia with Peter at the head of a "reconstituted Serbia." The president indicated that while he would "rather have a Yugoslavia . . . three separate states with separate governments in a Balkan Confederation might solve many problems." Lastly, Roosevelt suggested to Churchill that "you and I should bear some possibility in mind in case the new government does not work out" (Roosevelt to Churchill, May 18, 1944, *F.D.R., His Personal Letters, 1928–1945*, ed. Elliot Roosevelt, 2:1509.

97. Hull to Chapin, Counselor of Missions at Algiers, July 8, 1944, *FRUS, 1944,* 4:1387.

98. Karadjeordjević, *King's Heritage,* 234–35; Winston Churchill, *Triumph and Tragedy,* vol. 7 of *History of the Second World War,* 93; Maclean, *Eastern Approaches,* 478–79.

99. Eden, *The Reckoning,* 546–47.

100. Ivanović to Deakin, Jan. 23, 1963; I am indebted to Mr. Ivanović for a copy of this letter.

101. Roberts, *Tito, Mihailović, and the Allies,* 245; Smith, *OSS,* 88. According to Smith, Huntington was a former Wall Street attorney and previously had been commander of the OSS detachment at Gen. Mark Clark's headquarters.

102. Winks, *Cloak and Gown* 208–209; Brown, *Last Hero,* 286; Smith, *OSS,* 88–89.

103. Donovan to Huntington, Aug. 11, 1944, RG-226, E. 99, B. 34, F. 170.

104. Huntington to C.O., 2677th Rgt., Sept. 1, 1944, RG-226, E. 190, B. 114, F. 372.

105. Joyce to Donovan, Aug. 8, 1944, RG-225, E. 154, B. 1, F. "Top Secret File."

106. Green to Donovan, May 21, 1944, RG-226, E. 190, B. 114, F. 372.

107. Joyce to Donovan, Aug. 8, 1944, RG-226, E. 154, B. 1, F. "Top Secret File."

108. Donovan to Huntington, Aug. 10, 1944, RG-226, E. 99, B. 22, F. 112.

109. Lt. Timothy Pfeiffer, Final Report of DUNKLIN Mission, n.d., RG-226, E. 154, B. 25, F. Bari-SI, PRO-35. Following Huntington's arrival on Vis, Pfeiffer was sent to Dubrovnik as head of the DUNKLIN team.

Chapter 6. Their Return Overrides All Objections

1. Gus T. Brown, letter to author, Nov. 1, 1971; National Committee of American Airmen to Aid General Mihailovich and the Serbian People, *Press Clippings* 3:9 (cited hereafter as Committee, *Press Clippings*); testimony of Gus T. Brown, May 15, 1946, Commission of Inquiry, 194–98.

2. Committee, *Press Clippings* 3:9; Brown Testimony, Commission of Inquiry, 199–200.

3. James M. Inks, "Eight Against the Enemy," *Blue Book Magazine* 97 (Sept. 1953): 103; Escape Statement of Thomas E. Howard, 2nd Lt., 414th Bomb Sq., 97th Bomb Gp., May 11, 1944, Escape and Evasion Reports (E&E), Jan.–Aug., 1944, 670.6141; Escape statements of William R. Harris, 2nd Lt., Denzil Radabaugh, S/Sgt., and Robert H. Knowlton, S/Sgt., all of the 724th Sq., 451st Bomb Gp., Aug. 13, 1944, E&E; Escape Statement of Lee McAlister, 2nd Lt., 414th Sq., 97th Bomb Gp., Aug. 13, 1944, E&E. All of these E&E documents were found in the Fifteenth Air Force Records, "Escape and Evasion Reports, 1943–1945," Albert F. Simpson Historical Research Center, Maxwell Air Force Base, Montgomery, Alabama.

4. Richard Felman, "Fate Was Merciless," *¡Ole!* May 16, 1970, 13.

5. Ibid., 10; Richard Felman, "Mihailovic and I," *Serbian Democratic Forum,* Oct. 1972, 16–17. I am indebted to Major Felman for a typewritten copy of his manuscript for "Mihailovic and I," which is some fifty pages in length.

6. Felman, "Mihailovic and I," 18. Major Felman currently serves as president of the National Committee of American Airmen Rescued by General Mihailovich.

7. Farish to Bari, May 28, 1944, RG-226, E. 136, B. 35, F. X-82.

8. Merrill to Murphy, June 20, 1944, RG-226, OSS File No. 86812.

9. The conference was also attended by Deranian, Edward J. Green, Eli Popovich, and two airmen who had been evacuated from Partisan territory (Deranian, to Chief, SO-Washington, Sept. 26, 1944). This document was included in papers furnished to me by George Musulin. See also Deranian interview, Jan. 26, 1988.

10. Eaker to Wilson, July 3, 1944, and Col. George Kraigher to Commander-MAAF, Aug. 15, 1944, both in Fifteenth Air Force Crew Rescue Documents (ACRU), Air Force Archives, File No. 670.614-1, 1944–1945; Bari to Donovan, July 16, 1944, RG-226, E. 154, B. 56, F. Caserta SO-OP-23.

11. Joyce to Chief, SI-OSS/ME, Aug. 18, 1944, RG-226, E. 154, B. 3, F. 68.

12. Deranian to C.O., 2677th Rgt., OSS-Bari, Aug. 15, 1944, RG-226, E. 190, B. 115. F. 389.

13. Donovan to Toulmin and Green, July 19, 1944, RG-226, E. 143, B. 7, F. 108.

14. Memorandum by B. Nelson Deranian, Chief, SO-Bari, July 1, 1944. This document was provided by George Musulin.

15. Jibilian transcript, Jan. 20, 1977.

16. Deranian, Chief, SO-Bari to Chief, SO-Washington, Sept. 26, 1944, Musulin Papers, in author's files; Green to Musulin, Rajacich, and Jibilian, July 8, 1944, Musulin Papers.

17. Mihailovic to Force 399, July 11, 1944. A series of the Villa Resta messages dated July 11 to July 22, 1944, was included in the Musulin Papers.

18. Deranian to Chief, SO-Washington, September 26, 1944, Musulin Papers.

19. Musulin, interview with author, Aug. 16, 1976; Martin, *Patriot or Traitor*, 89.

20. T. K. Oliver, letter to author, Apr. 14, 1972. A copy of this message as received in Italy may be found in ACRU Documents, July, 1944–June, 1945, 670.614-1.

21. Oliver, letter to author, Apr. 14, 1972.

22. ACRU Documents, July 1944–June 1945, 670.614-1.

23. Report of 1st Lt. George S. Musulin on HALYARD, Sept. 20, 1944, RG-226, E. 99, B. 34, F. 170.

24. Richard M. Kelly, "The Halyard Mission," *Blue Book Magazine* 83 (Aug. 1946): 57.

25. Musulin Report, Sept. 20, 1944, RG-226, E. 99, B. 34, F. 170.

26. HALYARD to Colonel Gallahan, Aug. 8, 1944, ACRU Documents, July 1944–June 1945, 670.614-1.

27. Gallahan to HALYARD, Aug. 8, 1944, ACRU Documents, July 1944–June 1945, 670.614-1.

28. John E. Scroggs, letter to author, May 5, 1972. George Hurd, who suffered a broken leg when his plane went down about ninety miles west of Belgrade, was cared for by a Serbian family that "practically adopted" him. Hurd would later write that "under the circumstances, I couldn't have been better had I been with my own people" (Hurd, letter to author, Feb. 10, 1971). Anthony Orsini wrote, "Some of the rec-

ollections are vague, but the memory of the selfless sacrifices that the followers of General Mihailovich made on my behalf and on behalf of all rescued airmen is indelibly etched on my mind" (Orsini, letter to author, Jan. 3, 1977). Other airmen who responded favorably to letters of inquiry concerning the treatment they received by Mihailovich's forces included Preston Angleberger, Mar. 7, 1972; Hal Souter, Apr. 26, 1972; Paul Mato, Mar. 20, 1977; David La Bissoniere, Jan. 16, 1972; Charles Davis, Sept. 13, 1976; Mike McKool, Apr. 13, 1971; Clell Card, Jan. 30, 1971; George Salapa, Apr. 13, 1971; and Leland Porter, Feb. 2, 1972.

29. Escape Statement of 2nd Lt. Raymond F. Smith, 340th Sq. 97th Bomb Gp., Nov. 16, 1944, E&E Reports, "C," Nov., 1944, 670.614-1.

30. Escape Statement of 1st Lt. Lewis M. Perkins, 776th Sq., 464th Bomb Gp., Sept. 24, E&E Reports, Sept., 1944, 670.614-1.

31. Testimony of Robert N. Vlachos, Commission of Inquiry, 485–86.

32. Merrill Walker, letter to author, June 2, 1971; *Los Angeles Times,* Dec. 13, 1970, 16.

33. Walker, letter to author, June 2, 1971. Kacarević and Walker met one another again after the war in Los Angeles. The *Los Angeles Times* did a special on them and they also appeared together on television.

34. Escape Statement of S/Sgt. Karl Clive Smith, 726th Sq., 451st Bomb Gp., Dec. 30, 1944, E&E Reports, "D," December, 1944, 670.614-1; Escape Statement of S/Sgt. Leon W. Hoadley, 830th Sq., 485th Bomb Gp., Sept. 22, 1944, E&E Reports, Sept., 1944, 670.614-1; Escape Statement of 2d Lt. Robert L. Eagan, 758th Sq., 459th Bomb Gp., Oct. 13, 1944, E&E Reports, "B," Oct., 1944, 670.614-1. Eagan witnessed Chetnik forces take the Partisan-held town of Poljice while simultaneously conducting a holding action against a German force of about three thousand men.

35. Thomas C. Richards, letter to author, Feb. 23, 1986.

36. Escape Statement of F/O Robert D. Fulks, 5th Sq., 52nd FTR. Fp., Nov. 7, 1944, E&E Reports, "C," Nov., 1944, 670.614-1; Fulks to author, Jan. 8, 1977.

37. Felman, "Fate Was Merciless," 12.

38. William K. Callam, letter to author, Mar. 7, 1986.

39. William B. Harrell, Jr., letter to author, Feb. 28, 1986.

40. Inks, "Eight Against the Enemy," 100. Inks confided to his diary: "We are in the middle of a queer situation, which we have not yet got clear. The Chetniks are allied with the Germans, but claim they do not like them. Until recently, they say we were supporting them, and they were fighting the Nazis. But then we shifted our support to the Partisans, who are led by a man named Tito. The Chetniks claim Tito is a Communist. The Chetniks are Royalist, supporting their king who is in exile, but they insist that they are at the same time democratic, like the English."

41. Ibid., 107. Ray Weber also told about being clothed in native dress and traveling with a group of Chetniks when a German column passed them on the road (Weber, letter to author, Sept. 10, 1986). Arthur Hoodecheck was actually driven through the streets of Belgrade in a jeep while carrying papers that identified him as a deaf mute (Hoodecheck, letter to author, Feb. 8, 1986).

42. Inks, "Eight Against the Enemy," 109, 111.

43. Ibid., 108.

44. John E. Scroggs, letter to author, May 5, 1972. I am indebted to Mr. Scroggs for copies of documents which clearly reveal that Mihailovich had contact with

Fotitch in Washington and that Fotitch was notifying the parents of American airmen who had been rescued by Chetnik forces. In many cases Fotitch got this information to the parents before the news could travel through official military channels (Testimony of William T. Emmett, Commission of Inquiry, 491–96). Emmett was in Air Force intelligence and was responsible for interviewing more than two hundred airmen who were evacuated from Chetnik-held territory. In all these debriefings, he testified, he never found a single instance of airmen being either maltreated or turned over to the Germans, though the Germans continually posted rewards for the capture of Allied airmen.

45. Kelly, "Halyard Mission," 60.

46. Ibid., 61.

47. Musulin Report, HALYARD Mission, Sept. 20, 1944, RG-226, E. 99, B. 34, F. 170; Musulin, Rajacich, and Jibby to Green, Aug. 10, 1944, RG-226, E. 190, B. 113, F. 368.

48. Nick Lalich, Report on ACRU-HALYARD, Dec. 31, 1944, RG-226, E. 99, B. 22, F. 112. Other than the Americans, there were six British, twelve Russian, and four French personnel included in this second evacuation. In addition there were the eight Yugoslavs from Mihailovich's headquarters and seven Italians (Philip Hart, "Heroes of the OSS: Nick Lalich," *Serb World USA* 5 (Sept.–Oct., 1988): 6–12; Lalich, interview with author, Jan. 6, 1988).

49. Green to Rajacich, Aug. 10, 1944, RG-226, E. 190, B. 113, F. 368. In a separate message to Musulin, Green indicated that he and Joyce felt that the request for arms was "most reasonable" and that they would do everything possible to carry it out.

50. Joyce to C.O., 2677th Rgt., Aug. 14, 1944, RG-226, E. 190, B. 113, F. 360.

51. Joyce to Toulmin, Aug. 15, 1944, RG-226, E. 99, B. 34, F. 170.

52. Kraigher and Green to Musulin, Aug. 12, 1944, and Musulin to Green and Joyce, Aug. 12, 1944, both in ACRU Documents, July, 1944–June, 1945, 670.614-1. One of the Yugoslav delegates sent to Bari was Zvonimir Vučković, whose forces had been providing security for the airmen at Pranjani and who had been sent by Mihailovich to work in liaison with the Fifteenth Air Force (Vučković letter to author, Feb. 5, 1978).

53. Rajacich to Deranian, Aug. 14, 1944, RG-226, E. 190, B. 115, F. 385.

54. Musulin to Kraigher, Aug. 20, 1944, ACRU Documents, July, 1944–June, 1945, 670.614-1.

55. Musulin to Kraigher, Aug. 26, 1944, ACRU Documents, July, 1944–June, 1945, 670614-1; "Report on HALYARD Mission," Jan. 10, 1945, RG-226, OSS File No. XL-5727.

56. Lalich, interview with author, Jan. 6, 1988.

57. Vujnovich, interview with author, Mar. 6–8, 1987.

58. Musulin, interview with author, Aug. 16, 1976.

59. Deranian, Chief-SO, to Adjutant, Co. B., Aug. 26, 1944, RG-226, E. 99, B. 20, F. 106.

60. Musulin, interview with author, Aug. 16, 1976. I last saw George Musulin in the summer of 1985 when he appeared before a Congressional committee that was hearing testimony from the National Committee of American Airmen concerning its effort to erect a monument to General Mihailovich's memory in Washington. Having suffered a stroke and the loss of one leg due to diabetes, Musulin had to be pushed

into the hearing room in a wheelchair. The man who was pushing the chair was Charles Davis, one of the airmen who had been evacuated from Pranjani by the HALYARD team almost forty years earlier. Some eighteen months after the hearing, Musulin finally succumbed to the ravages of diabetes. During his last days in the Bethesda Naval Hospital, however, he received many cards, letters, phone calls, and visits from the airmen he had helped to save in one of the most daring rescue operations of the war. George Musulin died on Feb. 21, 1987, and was buried four days later in Arlington National Cemetery with full military honors (Philip D. Hart, "Heroes of the OSS: George 'Gov' Musulin," *Serb World USA* 4, no. 3 (Jan.–Feb., 1988): 14–19.

61. Testimony of Michael Rajacich, Commission of Inquiry, 527.

Chapter 7. No Excuses or Apologies to Tito

1. Donovan to Roosevelt, July 4, 1944, Roosevelt Papers, MR/Naval Aide's Files, Box 164.

2. Donovan to Joint Chiefs of Staff, Aug. 3, 1944, Roosevelt Papers, MR/Naval Aide's Files, Box 164.

3. Joyce to Donovan, Aug. 8, 1944, RG-226, E. 154, B. 1, F. "Top Secret File;" Joyce to Holt Green, July 8, 1944, RG-226, E. 154, B. 14, F. 34. In a separate message to Cairo, Joyce referred to the McDowell mission as the "big show," which constituted a "most important political act" and a defiance of British policy (History, Cairo Office, n.d., RG-226, E. 99, B. 43, F. 214). Biber suggests that one of McDowell's objectives was to work through Mihailovich to establish contact with other nationalist groups in surrounding countries (Biber, "Neuspeh neke misije," 1076). John Milodragovich, McDowell's executive officer, insists, however, that "McDowell had one mission—intelligence in the Mihailovich controlled areas of Yugoslavia. This was amended to include evacuation of Allied airmen" (Milodragovich to author, July 24, 1991).

4. History, Cairo Office, n.d., RG-226, E. 99, B. 43, F. 214.

5. Stephen Penrose, Chief, SI to Joyce, RG-226, E. 99, B. 43, F. 214.

6. Joyce to Commanding Officer, SBS, Aug. 16, 1944, RG-226, E. 99, B. 20, F. 105.

7. Joyce to Donovan, Aug. 8, 1944, RG-226, E. 154, B. 1, F. "Top Secret File."

8. Donovan to Joint Chiefs of Staff, Aug. 3, 1944, Roosevelt Papers, MR/Naval Aide's Files, Box 164; Toulmin to Edward H. Dodd, Jr., Aug. 15, 1944, RG-226, E. 110, B. 15, F. 15.

9. McDowell, letter to author, Dec. 30, 1969.

10. Statement of Col. Robert H. McDowell to Commission of Inquiry into Case of Draja Mihailovich, typed copy prepared by Colonel McDowell and forwarded to author, July 1, 1971. McDowell's statement and his responses to a series of interrogatories were incorporated into the final report of the Commission of Inquiry.

11. McDowell, unpublished manuscript in possession of the author; McDowell to C.O., JICA, USAFIME, June 6, 1944, McDowell Papers, Hoover Institution Archives, Stanford, California, Box 2.

12. Donovan to Toulmin and Green, Aug. 2, 1944, RG-226, E. 190, B. 114, F. 372.

13. Milodragovich, letter to author, June 22, 1972; Ellsworth Kramer, "Factual and Chronological Report," Oct. 31, 1944, RG-226, E. 99, B. 28, F. 140b, MEDTO Field Reports, Book II.

14. Milodragovich, interview with author, July 10, 1989.

15. Maclean, *Eastern Approaches,* 487.

16. Testimony of Michael Rajacich, Commission of Inquiry, 527; DEFE 3, XL 8679, Aug. 31, 1944, Reel 39.

17. DEFE 3, HP 1199, Sept. 25, 1944, Reel 42; DEFE 3, HP 1759, Oct. 1, 1944, Reel 44; DEFE 3 2481, Oct. 7, 1944, Reel 44.

18. DEFE 3, HP 1204, Sept. 25, 1944, Reel 42; DEFE 3, SL 9159, Sept. 5, 1944, Reel 40; DEFE 3, HP 1018, Sept. 24, 1944, Reel 42.

19. Robert H. McDowell, "Report on Mission to Yugoslavia, Ranger Unit," Nov. 23, 1944, OSS/CIA; Kramer Report, Oct. 31, 1944, RG-226, E. 99, B. 28, F. 140b, MEDTO Field Reports, Book II; 2d Lt. Michael Rajacich, "Field Reports from Serbia," Nov. 22, 1944, McDowell Papers, Hoover Institution Archives, Box 2. Rajacich's permanent rank was Master Sergeant.

20. McDowell Report, Nov. 23, 1944, OSS/CIA.

21. McDowell to Joyce, Sept. 4, 1944, RG-226, E. 136, B. 30, F. US-64.

22. Milodragovich Report, Nov. 22, 1944, McDowell Papers, Hoover Institution Archives, Box 2.

23. McDowell Report, Nov. 23, 1944, OSS/CIA; Testimony of Michael Rajacich, Commission of Inquiry, 543–44.

24. Milodragovich Report, Nov. 22, 1944, McDowell Papers, Hoover Institution Archives, Box 2.

25. McDowell to Joyce, Sept. 13, 1944; McDowell to Joyce, Sept. 15, 1944; McDowell to Joyce, Oct. 6, 1944; McDowell to Joyce, Oct. 7, 1944. All of these messages appear in a compilation of communications that passed between McDowell and Bari in RG-226, E. 154, B. 24, F. IAMM to Marshal Tito, #5.

26. Carpenter to C.O., 2677th Rgt., OSS, Sept. 19, 1944, RG-226, E. 99, B. 20, F. 106.

27. McDowell Report, Nov. 23, 1944, OSS/CIA.

28. Wilson, *Eight Years Overseas,* 238.

29. Kramer Report, Oct. 31, 1944, RG-226, E. 99, B. 28, F. 140b, MEDTO Field Reports, Book II; Testimony of Ellsworth Kramer, Commission of Inquiry, 445–47. Kramer testified that in one instance the Chetnik forces he was with were engaged against a Partisan force but were forced to break off the attack when they ran out of ammunition. That evening Allied planes made a supply drop to the Partisans, who carried out a successful counterattack the following day.

30. McDowell Report, Nov. 23, 1944, OSS/CIA.

31. Ibid.

32. Ibid.

33. Ibid.

34. Huntington to Reid, Nov. 14, 1944, RG-226, E. 154, B. 24, F. IAMM to Marshal Tito, #5.

35. RG-226, OSS File No. XL-2151, Nov. 4, 1944.

36. Lowenheim, Langley, and Jonas, *Roosevelt and Churchill,* 571.

37. XDET Algiers to Donovan, Sept. 8, 1944, RG-226, E. 134, B. 288, F. Algiers Outgoing.

38. Lowenheim, Langley, and Jonas, *Roosevelt and Churchill,* 571.

39. Donovan to Glavin (Caserta), Sept. 19, 1944, RG-226, E. 136, B. 21, F. 1.

40. Donovan to Roosevelt, Sept. 24, 1944, Roosevelt Papers, MR/Naval Aide's Files, Box 164. Wilson's message to Tito, dated Sept. 16, is paraphrased in Donovan's memorandum to the president.

41. Maclean to Wilson, Oct. 30, 1944, RG-226, E. 154, B. 25, F. McDowell Unit; Wilson to Maclean, Oct. 31, 1944, RG-226, E. 154, B. 25, F. McDowell Unit.

42. Cheston to Roosevelt, Sept. 8, 1944, Roosevelt Papers, PSF/OSS, Donovan Reports, Box 167. Referring to McDowell, Glavin said, "Valuable intelligence reports have already been received from him and it is much to be regretted we are to lose this source of military, political, and economic intelligence at this time" (Glavin to Donovan, Sept. 18, 1944, RG-226, E. 134, B. 288, F. Algiers Outgoing).

43. Memorandum by Robert Murphy, Sept. 5, 1944, Roosevelt Papers, MR/Naval Aide's Files, Box 164.

44. Green to McDowell, Sept. 14, 1944, RG-226, E. 110, B. 13, F. 1; Green to Glavin, Sept. 14, 1944, RG-226, E. 110, B. 13, F. 1.

45. Kraigher to Commanding General, MAAF, Nov. 3, 1944, ACRU Documents, July 1944–June 1945, 670.614-1G; Lalich, interview with author, Jan. 6, 1988.

46. Donovan to Glavin, Sept. 19, 1944, RG-226, E. 136, B. 21, F. 1.

47. Lalich, interview with author, Jan. 6, 1988.

48. Kraigher to Commanding General, MAAF, Nov. 3, 1944, ACRU Documents, July 1944–June 1945, 670.614-1.

49. McDowell, unpublished manuscript in possession of the author.

50. Huntington to Glavin, Oct. 16, 1944, RG-226, E. 110, B. 13, F. 1.

51. Deane to Suker, Oct. 13, 1944, RG-226, E. 136, B. 20, F. US-12.

52. Glavin and Joyce to Huntington, Oct. 19, 1944, RG-226, E. 110, B. 13, F. 1.

53. Glavin and Joyce to Donovan, Oct. 25, 1944, RG-226, E. 110, B. 13, F. 1.

54. Kramer Report, Oct. 31, 1944, RG-226, E. 99, B. 28, F. 140b, MEDTO Field Reports, Book II.

55. Ibid.

56. Ibid.

57. Ibid.

58. Ibid.

59. Ibid.

60. Ibid. According to Nick Lalich's field diary, Allin had been evacuated from Yugoslavia on Sept. 17 (*American Serb Life,* May, 1948, 18). According to Kramer, Keserović was subsequently executed by the Partisans after confessing to charges that he collaborated with the Germans (Testimony of Ellsworth Kramer, Commission of Inquiry, 459).

61. Kramer testimony, Commission of Inquiry, 459.

62. Joyce to Ross, Oct. 20, 1944, RG-226, E. 99, B. 34, F. 170; Ross to McDowell, Oct. 18, 1944, RG-226, E. 154, B. 24, F. IAMM to Marshal Tito, #5; McDowell to

Green and Joyce, Oct. 18, 1944, RG-226, E. 154, B. 24, F. IAMM to Marshal Tito, #5.

63. Joyce and Glavin to McDowell, Oct. 21, 1944, RG-226, E. 99, B. 34, F. 170. According to Hoettl, the Germans maintained a very efficient radio security service that allowed them routinely to "listen in" on a great volume of Partisan and Chetnik radio communications (Hoettl, "Situation Report: Yugoslavia," Dec. 21, 1945, RG-226, E. 109, B. 52, F. 294).

64. McDowell to Joyce, Oct. 23, 1944, RG-226, E. 99, B. 34, F. 170.

65. Glavin and Joyce to McDowell, Oct. 21, 1944, RG-226, E. 99, B. 34, F. 170. See also Biber, "Neuspeh neke misije," 1085–86.

66. Joyce to Glavin, Oct. 19, 1944, RG-226, E. 110, B. 13, F. 1.

67. McDowell later claimed that pro-Communist elements in Washington tried to have him court-martialed for refusing this order, but the attempt was quashed by the War Department (McDowell, unpublished manuscript in possession of the author). Those inclined to accept the conspiracy thesis to explain Churchill's support of Tito have recently focused much attention on James Klugmann, claiming that he was most influential in slanting intelligence in favor of Tito and against Mihailovich. The most recent works of David Martin and Michael Lees cited in this study are the best examples. Others have dismissed these charges, pointing out that Klugmann's rank hardly put him in a position to exercise as much influence as has been attributed to him. On the other hand, a recent work by Christopher Andrew and Oleg Gordievsky suggests that Klugmann's influence exceeded his rank considerably (*KGB: The Inside Story of Its Foreign Operations from Lenin to Gorbachev*, 295). Unfortunately, speculation about Klugmann's role must suffice until British and Soviet wartime records are made more accessible to researchers.

68. Joyce to Thayer, Nov. 7, 1944, RG-226, E. 110, B. 13, F. 3.

69. Joyce to Thayer, Dec. 6, 1944, RG-226, E. 121, B. 49, F. J-4.

70. Maddox to Joyce, Sept. 20, 1944, RG-226, E. 110, B. 13, F. 1. Joyce subsequently advised both McDowell and Lalich that without "explicit instructions" neither of them should "take any action in this matter since any question concerning the evacuation of Mihailovich is related to high policy" (Joyce to McDowell and Lalich, Oct. 29, 1944, RG-226, E. 136, B. 30, F. US-64).

71. McDowell, unpublished manuscript in possession of the author.

72. McDowell to Communications Officer, OSS/Bari, Nov. 23, 1944, RG-226, E. 99, B. 34, F. 170.

73. Joyce to Donovan, Dec. 10, 1944, RG-226, E. 154, B. 19, F. Chronological Balkan File.

74. Harold Macmillan, *War Diaries: Politics and War in the Mediterranean, January 1943–May 1945*, 576.

75. Glavin and Joyce to 109, Dec. 1, 1944, RG-226, E. 110, B. 13, F. 3.

76. McDowell, unpublished manuscript in possession of the author.

77. Ibid.

78. Ibid.

79. Ibid.

80. Ibid.; Rajacich Report, Nov. 22, 1944, McDowell Papers, Hoover Institution Archives, Box 2.

81. McDowell Report, Nov. 23, 1944, OSS/CIA.

82. Green to McDowell, Aug. 15, 1944, RG-226, E. 99, B. 22, F. 112; McDowell, unpublished manuscript in possession of the author; Martin, *Patriot or Traitor*, 472–73. The Germans apparently thought they would have the opportunity to meet with Mihailovich directly. An intercept dated Sept. 16 stated in part: "Discussions with Mihailovich RPT DM are now to take place. They are conducted by Neubacher. Neubacher has reserved for himself personally this type of meeting" (CX/MSS/C, Sept. 16, 1944).

83. McDowell to Joyce, Sept. 4, 1944, RG-226, E. 136, B. 30, F. US-64.

84. Joyce to McDowell, Sept. 5, 1944, RG-226, E. 136, B. 30, F. US-64.

85. "Interrogation of Dr. Hermann Neubacher," Oct. 15, 1945, RG-226, OSS File No. XL-22947. Additional details on the McDowell-Stärker talks may be found in Biber, "Neuspeh neke misije," 1080–81.

86. *The Trial of Mihailović*, 307–308, 310; Glavin and Joyce to Donovan, Nov. 1, 1944, RG-226, E. 110, B. 13, F. 3.

87. Martin, *Patriot or Traitor*, 475.

88. Milodragovich, interview with author, July 10, 1989.

89. McDowell, unpublished manuscript in possession of the author.

90. Kraigher to Lalich, Nov. 25, 1944, ACRU Documents, July 1944–June 1945, 670.614-1.

91. Kraigher to Lalich, Dec. 6, 1944, ACRU Documents, July 1944–June 1945, 670.614-1.

92. Lalich, interview with author, Jan. 8, 1988.

93. Lalich to Kraigher, Dec. 8, 1944, ACRU Documents, July 1944–June 1945, 670.614-1.

94. Lalich, interview with author, Jan. 8, 1988.

95. Ibid.

96. Report of ACRU Unit, "HALYARD," Dec. 31, 1944, ACRU Documents, July 1944–June 1945, 670.614-1.

97. Ibid.

98. Lalich Report, Jan. 10, 1945, RG-226, OSS File No. XL-5727.

99. Ibid.; Lalich, interview with author, Jan. 8, 1988.

100. McDowell Report, Nov. 23, 1944, OSS/CIA.

Chapter 8. Kicking against the Pricks

1. Memorandum of Conversation with Brigadier Maclean and Marshal Tito, Aug. 10, 1944, RG-226, E. 99, B. 20, F. 105. Although designated as the Independent American Military Mission, Huntington's independence, as such, extended only to SI and MO. The British remained responsible for all SO functions, particularly the control of supplies (Memorandum of Information, Donovan to Joint Chiefs of Staff, Mar. 20, 1944, RG-226, E. 190, B. 956, F. 972; Green to Chief, SO/Washington, June 30, 1944, RG-226, E. 154, B. 58, F. Daily Ops. Reports, Bari, Apr.–Aug., 1944).

2. Holt Green, Chief, Y-Section, SI to Huntington, Aug. 19, 1944, RG-226, E. 190, B. 113, F. 368. The officers in charge of these missions were Capt. Eugene

O'Meara, RELATOR; Capt. George Selvig, FUNGUS; Lt. Nels J. Benson, ALTMARK; Maj. Franklin Lindsay, CUCKOLD; Capt. Jim Goodwin, FLOTSAM; Lt. Dan Desich, ALUM; Lt. Harry S. Plowman, DARIEN; Maj. Scott Dickinson, SPIKE; Capt. Richard Ranier, ABBEVILLE; Lt. Everett Greaser, DEPOSIT. Even after Huntington assumed command of the IAMM, some OSS personnel remained with the joint American-British missions to which they had been previously assigned until SOE could relieve them. Indeed, American officers were in some cases in command of these missions (Franklin A. Lindsay, letter to author, June 30, 1990).

3. Green to C.O., BAF, Aug. 18, 1944, RG-226, E. 99, B. 34, F. 170.

4. Donovan to Roosevelt, Sept. 1, 1944, Roosevelt Papers, MR/Naval Aide's Files, Balkan Countries #5, Box 164.

5. Lindsay, interview with author, Aug. 13, 1976; RG-226, OSS File No. XL-53588. Franklin Lindsay later reported that "the examples of non-cooperation, and bad faith and obstructionism became so numerous that it is impossible to explain them as carelessness or ignorance on the part of individual staff officers." German sources confirmed that restrictions imposed on Allied missions attached to Partisan forces came directly from Tito's headquarters. One directive admonished Partisan commanders against providing any information to the English and American missions concerning "strength, equipment and rations of the troops. Nor might queries about the morale of combat units be answered" (Hoettl, "Situation Report: Yugoslavia," Dec. 21, 1945, RG-226, E. 109, B. 52, F. 294).

6. Holt Green to Paul West, Feb. 1, 1944, RG-226, E. 190, B. 116, F. 392.

7. Tomasevich, *The Chetniks*, 412.

8. Huntington and Joyce to Donovan, Sept. 23, 1944, RG-226, E. 110, B. 13, F. 1.

9. Donovan to Roosevelt, Sept. 24, 1944, Roosevelt Papers, MR/Naval Aide's Files, Box 164.

10. Report of Capt. Charles B. Grimm, Willow Team, n.d., RG-226, E. 154, B. 23, F. 339.

11. Lindsay to Maclean, Oct. 19, 1944, RG-226, E. 154, B. 23, F. CUCKOLD Mission.

12. Capt. James M. Goodwin, "Report of FLOTSAM Mission," n.d., RG-226, E. 154, B. 25, F. Bari-SI-PRO-44.

13. Report of Capt. Charles O. Fisher, Dec. 4, 1944, RG-226, E. 190, B. 168, F. Caserta-SI.

14. SPIKE Mission, Final Report, n.d., RG-226, E. 154, B. 25, F. 338.

15. Rear Echelon IAMM to Tito, Oct. 5, 1944, RG-226, E. 154, B. 24, F. IAMM to Tito.

16. Desich to Huntington, Oct. 11, 1944, RG-226, E. 136, B. 31, F. ALUM-IN.

17. HQ, IAMM to Tito, Oct. 16, 1944, RG-226, E. 154, B. 24, F. IAMM to Tito.

18. Supplementary Report of Lieutenant Desich, ALUM Team, Apr. 15, 1945. A copy of this report was forwarded to me by Dan Desich on Oct. 5, 1973.

19. Deranian to C.O., Co. B, 2677th Rgt., Oct. 11, 1944, RG-226, E. 154, B. 24, F. IAMM to Tito.

20. Suker, Chief Y-Section, SI to IAMM, n.d., RG-226, E. 154, B. 23, F. FUNGUS Mission.

21. Ibid.

22. Capt. Conrad G. Selvig, Report on Activity in Jugoslavia, n.d., RG-226, E. 190, B. 660, F. 985; Recommendation of the Award of Legion of Merit to Capt. George Selvig, by Maj. Hans V. Tofte, Sept. 27, 1945, Selvig Papers, in possession of the author; Selvig transcript, Nov. 6, 1973.

23. Nels J. Benson to Force 266, July 16, 1944, RG-226, E. 190, B. 113, F. 368; Selvig Report, n.d., RG-226, E. 190, B. 660, F. 985.

24. Selvig Report, n.d., RG-226, E. 190, B. 660, F. 985.

25. Ibid.

26. Lindsay, interview with author, Aug. 13, 1976.

27. Veselinovich Report, Feb. 14, 1945, RG-226, E. 154, B. 4, F. Bari-SI-INT-5.

28. Ibid.

29. Ibid.

30. Capt. Robert S. Nowell, "Final Report of GEISHA Mission," n.d., RG-226, E. 154, B. 23, F. GEISHA Mission. Although there is no specific date on Nowell's report, copies of it were forwarded to Joyce by Y-Section on Oct. 26, 1944.

31. Capt. Robert Weiler, "Report of WALNUT Mission," n.d., RG-226, E. 154, B. 25, F. 346, WALNUT Mission. This document, which was not declassified until July 26, 1988, was obtained through the Freedom of Information Act (FOIA).

32. Veselinovich Report, Feb. 14, 1945, RG-226, B. 4, F. Bari-SI-INT-5.

33. Lindsay, interview with author, Aug. 13, 1976. At the time I interviewed Mr. Lindsay he indicated that the OSS Labor Desk might have been responsible for dispatch of the two agents into Croatia. He is now preparing his own account of his work in OSS, which, with the recent declassification of voluminous OSS records, may shed new light on this interesting episode.

34. "Account of experiences of Capt. Fielding on mission to Split," Fielding to Huntington, Nov. 24, 1944, RG-226, E. 154, B. 25, F. Bari-SI-PRO-48.

35. Ibid.

36. Ibid.

37. Ibid.

38. Ibid.

39. Ibid.

40. Ibid.

41. Ibid.

42. Ibid.

43. Ibid.

44. Ibid.

45. Ibid.

46. Ibid.; Statement of Sgt. Bernard H. Bridges, Nov. 24, 1944; Statement of Maj. John Irvine, R.A.M.C., Nov. 23, 1944. The statements of Bridges and Irvine (Irvine's is improperly dated) are attached to and are part of the report filed by Fielding. I contacted Temple Fielding in the mid-seventies, asking that he respond to a number of written questions relating to his experiences in Yugoslavia. This he diplomatically declined to do, citing prohibitions under the British Secrets Act that he thought might still be applicable. Fielding was a prolific writer and for a while after World War II pursued a career as a foreign correspondent. He founded Fielding Publica-

tions, Inc. and served as its president from 1966 to 1983, during which time he and his wife collaborated to produce the popular Fielding Travel Guides. Fielding was living in New York City at the time of his death, May 18, 1983.

47. In addition to those reports previously cited, the following contain information relating to the adverse effect on American intelligence operations resulting from the severe restrictions imposed by the Partisans: Blatnik, ARROW Mission, Mar. 28, 1945, RG-226, E. 154, B. 25, F. Bari-SI-PRO-49; John G. Goodwin, "Final Report of Mulberry Team," n.d., RG-226, E. 154, B. 25, F. 357; Rider, ASH Team, Oct. 28, 1944, and Supplemental Report, Nov. 24, 1944, RG-226, E. 154, B. 23, F. Bari-SI-PRO-27; O'Meara, "Report of RELATOR Mission," n.d., E. 154, B. 25, F. 342; Capt. Rex Deane, "Report of the DURAND Team," n.d., RG-226, E. 99, B. 35, F. 175.

48. Deane, REDWOOD Mission, Jan. 31, 1945, RG-226, E. 154, B. 25, F. 354; Dickinson, SPIKE Mission, n.d., RG-226, E. 154, B. 25, F. 338.

49. O'Meara, RELATOR Mission, n.d., RG-226, E. 154, B. 25, F. 342.

50. Roberts, *Tito, Mihailović, and the Allies,* 203; Buxton to Hull, Feb. 15, 1944, RG-226, E. 146, B. 64, F. 876. Col. Charles Thayer describes General Korneyev as "a highly educated old gentleman with a thinly veiled contempt for his uncouth Slav brethren of the Balkans" (Charles W. Thayer, *Hands across the Caviar,* 19–20).

51. Popovich transcript, Jan. 8, 1977.

52. Ibid.

53. Rider, ASH Team, n.d., RG-226, Oct. 28, 1944, E. 154, B. 23, F. 345; Don Rider, telephone interview with author, Apr. 8, 1990; John Blatnik, ARROW Mission, Mar. 28, 1945, RG-226, E. 154, B. 25, F. 332.

54. Selvig transcript, Feb. 26, 1973; Rex Deane, REDWOOD Mission, Jan. 31, 1945, RG-226, E. 154, B. 25, F. 354; John Blatnik, ARROW Mission, Mar. 28, 1945, RG-226, E. 154, B. 25, F. 332.

55. Desich transcript, Jan. 19, 1973.

56. Ellery C. Huntington, Independent American Military Mission to Marshal Tito, Final Report, Dec. 27, 1944, RG-226, E. 154, B. 25, F. Bari-SI-PRO-51. Huntington reported that relations with the Russian mission, headed by General Melnikov, were largely of a "social order." There was no routine exchange of information with the Soviets as there was with the British, although the former did make supplies and facilities available to the Americans when called upon to do so (John Blatnik, ARROW Mission, Mar. 28, 1945, RG-226, E. 154, B. 25, F. 332).

57. Desich transcript, Jan. 19, 1973; Report of Lt. Dan Desich, Apr. 15, 1945, Desich Papers; Scott Dickinson, SPIKE Mission, n.d., RG-226, E. 154, B. 25, F. 338; Charles Grimm, WILLOW Team, n.d., RG-226, E. 154, B. 23, F. 339.

58. Rex Deane, REDWOOD Mission, Jan. 31, 1945, RG-226, E. 154, B. 25, F. 354; Scott Dickinson, SPIKE Mission, n.d., RG-226, E. 154, B. 25, F. 338.

59. Rear Echelon-IAMM to Donovan, Oct. 6, 1944, RG-226, E. 154, B. 24, F. IAMM to Tito; Eugene O'Meara, RELATOR Mission, n.d., RG-226, E. 154, B. 25, F. 342.

60. Robert Weiler, WALNUT Mission, n.d., RG-226, E. 154, B. 25, F. 346.

61. Ellery Huntington, IAMM, Final Report, Dec. 27, 1944, RG-226, E. 154, B. 25, F. Bari-SI-PRO-51.

62. Dan Desich, Political Report, ALUM Team, Apr. 15, 1945, Desich Papers.

63. Popovich transcript, Jan. 8, 1977.

64. OSS Dispatch, Caserta, Jan. 9, 1945, RG-226, E. 190, B. 565, F. 293.

65. Charles Grimm, WILLOW Team, n.d., E. 154, B. 23, F. 339.

66. Robin S. Nowell, GEISHA Mission, n.d., RG-226, E. 154, B. 23, F. Bari-SI-PRO-26; Robert Weiler, WALNUT Mission, n.d., RG-226, E. 154, B. 25, F. 346.

67. Rex Deane, REDWOOD Mission, June 15, 1944, RG-226, E. 154, B. 25, F. 354.

68. Ellery Huntington, "The Jugoslav Army of National Liberation: Its Potentialities for Allied Use," Nov. 8, 1944, RG-226, E. 154, B. 24, F. IAMM to Marshal Tito. #5, Nov. 1–15, 1944.

69. Ernst Schramm, ed., *Kriegstagebuch des Oberkommandos der Wehrmacht*, vol. 4, 640, 706. At this point the Germans regarded the Chetniks as "almost devoid of military importance without strong partner" (DEFE 3, HP 7071, Nov. 19, 1944, Reel 50). Specific Ultra references to Partisan actions include DEFE 3, HP 529, Sept. 18, 1944, Reel 42; DEFE 3, HP 5448, Nov. 3, 1944, Reel 48; DEFE 3, HP 4739, Oct. 27, 1944, Reel 47; DEFE 3, HP 5668, Nov. 5, 1944, Reel 48.

70. DEFE 3, HP 5800, Nov. 6, 1944, Reel 49; DEFE 3, BT 184, Dec. 23, 1944, Reel 43; DEFE 3, HP 3180, Oct. 13, 1944, Reel 45.

71. DEFE 3, HP 9127, Dec. 12, 1944, Reel 53.

72. DEFE 3, HP 5991, Nov. 8, 1944, Reel 49.

73. D. L. Rider, ASH Team, n.d., RG-226, E. 154, B. 23, F. 345, ASH Team; Rider, telephone interview with author, Apr. 8, 1990.

74. Dickinson, SPIKE Mission, n.d., RG-226, E. 154, B. 25, F. 338.

75. DEFE 3, XL 9304, Sept. 6, 1944, Reel 40; Schramm, *Kriegstagebuch*, vol. 4, 707–708.

76. Schramm, *Kriegstagebuch*, vol. 4, 708; DEFE 3 CX/MSS/C.334, Sept. 16, 1944.

77. DEFE 3, HP 7071, Sept. 19, 1944, Reel 50.

78. Schramm, *Kriegstagebuch* vol. 3, part 2, 1304. The War Diary also makes reference to a cease-fire agreement between German and Chetnik forces in the border area between Serbia and Montenegro, but emphasizes that "Mihailovic was not involved" (vol. 3, part 2, 1296).

79. *Kriegstagebuch*, vol. 4, 636–37, 640–41, 708. A more critical interpretation of the German-Chetnik agreements may be found in Jovan Marjanović, "The Neubacher Plan and Practical Schemes for the Establishment of a Greater Serbian Federation, 1943–1944," in *The Third Reich and Yugoslavia, 1933–1945*, 486–501.

80. Lindsay, Military Mission to IV Operational Zone, Jan. 13, 1945, RG-226, E. 99, B. 23, F. 115.

81. Deane, REDWOOD Mission, Jan. 31, 1945, RG-226, E. 154, B. 25, F. 354.

82. Ibid.

83. Desich, Political Report, ALUM Team, Apr. 15, 1945, Desich Papers.

84. Joyce to C.O., Sept. 1, 1944, RG-226, E. 99, B. 20, F. 105.

85. Jukić, *Fall of Yugoslavia*, 251.

86. Donovan to Roosevelt, Oct. 2, 1944, Roosevelt Papers, PSF/Donovan Reports.

87. Col. Charles Thayer, "Activities of the American Military Mission, Oct. 9,

1944–Apr. 15, 1945," OSS/CIA; Thayer to Joyce, Nov. 26, 1944, RG-226, E. 134, B. 9, F. J-4.

88. Donovan to Roosevelt, Nov. 21, 1944, Roosevelt Papers, PSF/Donovan Reports.

89. Rider, ASH Team, Nov. 24, 1944, RG-226, E. 154, B. 23, F. 345.

90. Grimm, WILLOW Team, n.d., RG-226, E. 154, B. 23, F. 339.

91. Churchill, *Triumph and Tragedy*, 227–28; Auty and Clogg, *British Policy towards Wartime Resistance*, 247–48.

92. Dedijer, *The Battle Stalin Lost*, 59–66.

93. Pijade, *About the Legend*, 1, 23–24.

94. Blatnik, ARROW Mission, Mar. 28, 1945, RG-226, E. 154, B. 25, F. 332.

95. Goodwin, FLOTSAM Mission, n.d., RG-226, E. 154, B. 25, F. Bari-SI-PRO-44; Wuchinich, ALUM Mission, Aug. 22, 1944, E. 108, B. 74, F. GB-Balkans.

96. Deane, REDWOOD Mission, Jan. 31, 1945, RG-226, E. 154, B. 25, F. 354; Grimm, WILLOW Team, n.d., RG-226, E. 154, B. 23, F. 339.

97. O'Meara, RELATOR Mission, n.d., RG-226, E. 154, B. 25, F. 337.

98. IAMM to IV Operational Zone, Jan. 13, 1945, RG-226, E. 99, B. 23, F. 115; Wuchinich, ALUM Mission, Aug. 22, 1944, RG-226, E. 108, B. 74, F. GB-Balkans.

99. Desich, ALUM Mission, Apr. 15, 1945, Desich Papers, in author's files.

100. British Intelligence Document, GB-600, June 9, 1944, E. 108, B. 72, F. Balkans, GB-600; IAMM to IV Operational Zone, Jan. 13, 1945, RG-226, E. 99, B. 23, F. 115; Sabotage Activities, Sept. 14, 1944, Desich Papers, in author's files. Keegan claims that "the liberation of Yugoslavia was the direct result of the arrival of Russian troops in the country in September 1944" (Keegan, *The Second World War*, 494). A far more favorable assessment of the liberation issue from the Partisan perspective may be found in "Information on the People's Liberation War in Yugoslavia," in *Les Systèmes d'Occupation en Yougoslavie, 1941–1945*, ed. Petar Brajović, Jovan Marjanović, and Franjo Tudman, 9–45.

101. Report of 2d Lt. John Hamilton, HACIENDA Mission, Sept. 28, 1944, RG-226, E. 144, B. 69, F. 615/A. After completing his work with Operation AUDREY in Dec. 1943, Hamilton conducted a number of hazardous missions to Greece and Albania, infiltrating OSS personnel into those countries and supplying them. When these operations concluded in March, 1944, he returned to Bari and accepted a series of assignments that kept him in contact with events in Yugoslavia, though he did not reenter the country until the HACIENDA Mission was infiltrated on Aug. 20.

102. Foot, *Resistance*, 193.

103. Deane, REDWOOD Team, Jan. 31, 1945, RG-226, E. 154, B. 25, F. 354.

104. Report of Lt. Col. Charles Thayer, n.d., OSS/CIA. According to Don Rider, the Partisans did fight aggressively in the campaign to liberate Belgrade. Russian forces provided artillery and armored support, but most of the infantry fighting was carried out by Partisan units.

105. MEDTO Daily Report, June 16, 1944, RG-226, E. 110, B. 13, F. 4; Smith, *OSS*, 152.

106. Thayer to Joyce, Nov. 18, 1944, RG-226, E. 154, B. 24, F. IAMM to Marshal Tito.

107. Thayer Report, n.d., OSS/CIA.

108. Lada-Mocarski to Toulmin and McBaine, Mar. 21, 1944, RG-226, E. 165, B. 8, F. 80; Memorandum, June 8, 1944, RG-226, E. 190, B. 113, F. 360; Donovan to Bruce and Armour, Aug. 12, 1944, RG-226, E. 121, B. 77, F. Caserta-SO.

109. Edward A. Mosk, Labor Desk-SI to C.O., Co. B, 2677th Rgt., Feb. 1, 1945, RG-226, E. 190, B. 114, F. 377.

110. Ibid.

111. Devers to Marshal, Sept. 27, 1944, RG-226, E. 136, B. 35, F. Reports Office – Incoming.

112. Memorandum by Joint Staff Planners, Dec. 4, 1944, RG-226, E. 190, B. 129, F. 692.

113. O'Meara, RELATOR Mission, n.d., RG-226, E. 154, B. 25, F. 337; Nowell, GEISHA Mission, n.d., RG-226, E. 154, B. 23, F. Bari SI-PRO-26; John G. Goodwin, MULBERRY Mission, n.d., RG-226, E. 154, B. 25, F. 357.

114. Warren, *Special Operations*, 134.

115. Donovan to Joint Chiefs of Staff, Mar. 1945, RG-226, E. 99, B. 22, F. 112.

116. Greaser, DEPOSIT Mission, n.d., RG-226, E. 154, B. 25, F. 344; Dickinson, SPIKE Mission, n.d., RG-226, E. 154, B. 25, F. 338; Deane, REDWOOD Mission, Jan. 31, 1945, RG-226, E. 154, B. 25, F. 354; Field Diary of 2nd Lt. Eli Popovich, Apr. 15, 1944 to June 16, 1944, RG-226, E. 99, B. 19, F. 103; Martin, *Patriot or Traitor*, 172–73, 77.

117. Memorandum, Headquarters, Fifteenth Air Force, Aug. 20, 1944, RG-226, E. 154, B. Escape Information Series, A-15.

118. Testimony of Joseph Veselinovich, Commission of Inquiry, 318. Nick Lalich also found evidence refuting Partisan claims that the Chetniks had been responsible for the deaths of ten American airmen who had been identified by name. Lalich found that all ten had returned safely to Italy (Lalich to AFHQ, G-2, June 13, 1945, RG-226, E. 154, B. 5, F. Bari-SI-INT-17). In fact, one of the ten, Joseph Harmuth, was killed in an automobile accident in Greenwich, Connecticut, in 1976. (Joseph Harmuth, Sr., letter to author, Feb. 5, 1986).

119. Popovich transcript, Jan. 8, 1977.

120. Pfeiffer, DUNKLIN Mission, n.d., RG-226, E. 154, B. 25, F. 334. Pfeiffer reported that between December 23, 1944, and January 24, 1945, his mission evacuated sixty-five American airmen (Deane, REDWOOD Mission, Jan. 31, 1945, RG-226, E. 154, B. 25, F. 354). Deane's mission claimed credit for eighty-six evacuees between May, 1944, and January, 1945. In a subsequent assignment with the DURAND mission, Deane's team evacuated 152 airmen between Feb. 20 and May 20. A number of American airmen also crossed into Yugoslavia from Austria and were subsequently evacuated by the Partisans (Report from Military Mission to IV Operational Zone, Jan. 13, 1945, RG-226, E. 99, B. 23, F. 115). Capt. John Blatnik's ARROW Mission was dispatched to Croatia on Aug. 20, 1944, primarily as an ACRU mission, but no figures were cited in the report as to the number of evacuees handled by his team (Blatnik, ARROW Mission, Mar. 28, 1945, RG-226, E. 154, B. 25, F. 332). According to John Goodwin, MULBERRY Team evacuated approximately two hundred and fifty airmen between Mar., 1944, and Mar., 1945 (Goodwin, MULBERRY Team, n.d., RG-226, E. 154, B. 25, F. 357).

121. Statement of Stanley J. Skowronski, S/Sgt., Harold H. Inekenga, Sgt., and Elmer T. Brettens, 777th Bomb Sq., 464th Bomb Gp., Dec. 16, 1944, E&E Reports,

"D," Dec., 1944; Escape Statement of Theodore C. Schaetzle, Sgt., 727th Sq., 451st Bomb Gp., Dec. 18, 1944, E&E Reports, "C," Nov., 1944, 670.614-1; Escape Statement of Arthur E. Dunsire, Sgt., 826th Sq., 484th Bomb Gp., Nov. 24, 1944, E&E Reports, "C," Nov., 1944, 670.614-1.

122. Escape Statement of Gene C. Nalley, Sgt., and Thaddeus J. Wenzke, Sgt., 722nd Sq., 450th G Bomb Group, Nov. 16, 1944, E&E Reports, "C," Nov., 1944, 670.614-1. Both of these men indicated that the treatment given to them by the Partisans was "nice" and that they were given the best food the Partisans had to offer (Escape Statement of Seymour L. Rosenthal, 2d Lt., 817th Sq., 483rd Bomb Gp., Jan. 7, 1945, E&E Reports, Jan. 1–15, 1945, 670.614-1; Escape Statement of Harold Corwin Adams, 2d Lt., 725th Sq., 451st Bomb Gp., Sept. 3, 1944, E&E Reports, Sept., 1944, 670.614-1). Adams was treated in a Partisan hospital for five months and three weeks before his evacuation (Escape Statement of Philip Barber, S/Sgt., 414th Sq., 97th Bomb Gp., June 11, 1944, E&E Reports, Jan.–Aug., 1944, 670.614-1). Barber was also cared for in a Partisan hospital before his evacuation. These statements are generally indicative of the treatment accorded American airmen by the Partisans through the latter days of 1944.

123. Escape Statement of Donald Bell, 2d Lt., John M. Negra, S/Sgt., Daniel M. Babin, S/Sgt., and James B. Mulling, T/Sgt., Jan. 9, 1945; Escape Statement of Dale C. Haertel, 1st Lt., 318th Sq., 325th Fighter Gp.; and Statement of Morton W. Malkin, S/Sgt., 726th Sq., 451st Bomb Gp., Jan. 14, 1945, all in E&E Reports, Jan. 1–15, 1945, 670.614-1.

124. Veselinovich to Chief, Y-Section, Feb. 17, 1945, RG-226, E. 154, B. 4, F. Bari, SI-INT-5.

125. Research Institute of Ljubljana, *Allied Airmen and Prisoners of War Rescued by the Slovene Partisans.*

126. Thayer Report, Apr. 15, 1945, OSS/CIA.

Chapter 9. A Fait Accompli of Serious Potentialities

1. Churchill, *Closing the Ring*, 476–78.

2. Jukić, *Fall of Yugoslavia*, 235.

3. Brown, *The Last Hero*, 663–64; the reports Donovan sent to Roosevelt are found in the Roosevelt Papers, PSF, boxes 169–170.

4. Thayer, *Hands Across the Caviar*, 101; Joyce to Donovan and O'Gara, Nov. 1, 1944, RG-226, E. 110, B. 13, F. 3.

5. Donovan to Roosevelt, Nov. 3, 1944, and Donovan to Roosevelt, Nov. 17, 1944, both in Roosevelt Papers, PSF, box 169.

6. Jukić, *Fall of Yugoslavia*, 251.

7. Cheston to Roosevelt, Jan. 1, 1945, Roosevelt Papers, MR, box 73. Šubašić had earlier confided to Yarrow that the possibility of Peter retaining his throne was "absolutely nil" (Donovan to Roosevelt, Dec. 23, 1944, Roosevelt Papers, PSF, box 169. See also RG-226, OSS File No. XL-2711, Nov. 18, 1944).

8. Thayer to Joyce, "The Future of Yugoslavia as Revealed by Present Trends," Dec. 4, 1944, RG-226, E. 154, B. 24, F. IAMM to Marshal Tito.

9. Kirk to Hull, Dec. 11, 1944, *FRUS, 1944*, 4:1429–32; Rendel, *Sword and Olive*, 230.

10. Pijade, *About the Legend*, 23–24; Dedijer, *The Battle Stalin Lost*, 49, 54; Djilas, *Conversations with Stalin*, 8; Edvard Kardelj, *Reminiscences, the Struggle for Recognition and Independence: The New Yugoslavia, 1944–1957*, 64.

11. RG-226, OSS File No. 63278, Jan. 17, 1944.

12. Thayer to Joyce, Nov. 22, 1944, RG-226, E. 154, B. 24, F. IAMM to Marshal Tito; Lindsay to IV Operational Zone, Jan. 13, 1945, RG-226, E. 99, B. 23, F. 115; Dickinson, SPIKE Mission, n.d., RG-226, E. 154, B. 25, F. 338; Grimm, WILLOW Team, n.d., RG-226, E. 154, B. 23, F. 339; Blatnik, ARROW Mission, Mar. 28, 1945, RG-226, E. 154, B. 25, F. 332; Goodwin, FLOTSAM Mission, n.d., RG-226, E. 154, B. 25, F. Bari, SI-PRO-44.

13. Cheston to Roosevelt, Jan. 31, 1945, Roosevelt Papers, PSF, box 170. Almost three months earlier, Carl Norden had recommended to Huntington, who agreed with the proposal, that the United States might withhold full diplomatic recognition from the new Yugoslav government until such time as it was convinced that the regime would be democratic in nature (Huntington to Donovan, Nov. 7, 1944, RG-226, E. 190, B. 129, F. 692).

14. Donovan to Roosevelt, Dec. 23, 1944, Roosevelt Papers, PSF, box 170. When Stalin asked Tito in October, 1944, what he would do if British troops attempted to land in Yugoslavia, Tito responded that he would resist, Apparently, he was prepared to do just that.

15. Roberts, *Tito, Mihailović, and the Allies*, 317.

16. Carpenter to C.O., 2677 Rgt., OSS-Bari, Sept. 19, 1944, RG-226, E. 99, B. 20, F. 106. Walter Carpenter was a medical officer who was sent to Mihailovich's headquarters to provide care for wounded American airmen who were awaiting evacuation.

17. Amery, *Approach March*, 271–72.

18. Modisett, "Four-Cornered Triangle," 462.

19. Joyce to Glavin and Maddox, Sept. 16, 1944, RG-226, E. 110, B. 13, F. 1.

20. Todorovich transcript, May 30, 1973. Todorovich, who, as previously noted, experienced guerrilla warfare firsthand with Mihailovich's forces, makes the following statement about the issue of collaboration: "It is indeed silly to talk about collaboration in the guerrilla warfare conducted in occupied country. The nature of guerrilla warfare requires many actions which may seem strange and sometimes completely unnecessary during the conduct of normal military operations."

21. An OSS report originating in Cairo, dated Sept. 14, 1944, noted that the British had publicly based their support of Tito on military expedience, but concluded that "Britain's attitude toward Mihailovich has been formulated largely upon information forwarded to Mr. Churchill and the Foreign Office by officers whose opinions were neither unbiased nor unprejudiced and whose experience in both military affairs and intelligence work was limited" (RG-226, OSS File No. L-45847, Sept. 14, 1944).

22. "Captured Chetnik Documents," RG-226, R&A No. 1662, June 15, 1944.

23. Ibid.

24. Woodward, *British Foreign Policy*, 3, 315n.1.

25. Maclean, *Eastern Approaches*, 412–13.

26. Kenneth Greenlees, "The Record of Mihailović: A Personal Testimony," (London) *Tablet* 188 (July 6, 1946): 4.

27. Foot, *Resistance*, 190.

28. Dickinson, SPIKE mission, n.d., RG-226, E. 154, F. 25, F. 338.

29. Greenlees argued that "it seems extraordinary that a man who threw in his lot with the British when they were at their lowest ebb and his own country had been overrun by the enemy should now be accused of collaborating with the same enemy at a time, when beaten they were preparing to withdraw from his country and the Allies were heading for certain victory" (Greenlees, "The Record of Mihailović," 4).

30. Mansfield Report, Mar. 1, 1944, OSS/CIA.

31. Ibid.

32. Musulin, interview with author, Aug. 16, 1976.

33. Lalich, interview with author, Jan. 6, 1988; Martin, *Ally Betrayed*, 265.

34. McDowell, unpublished manuscript in possession of the author.

35. Musulin, interview with author, Aug. 16, 1976.

36. Kramer to Joyce, Oct. 23, 1944, RG-226, E. 110, B. 13, F. 1.

37. Roberts, *Tito, Mihailović, and the Allies*, 226. A perfect example of the kind of arrangement to which Roberts refers is found in a weekly summary report of the Joint Intelligence Committee. The document states in part that "authoritative confirmation has been received of the Partisan claims that Mihailovich received arms from the Italians and had at least an implicit understanding with the Germans whereby Chetnik and German military units left each other strictly alone" (JIC, Weekly Summary, Nov. 3, 1943, Vol. 229, Roosevelt Papers).

38. RG-226, OSS File No. XL-22947, Oct. 15, 1945.

39. RG-226, OSS File No. XL-13599, Aug. 9, 1945.

40. "The Germans and Mihailović," n.d., RG-226, OSS File No. L-49640.

41. Tomasevich, *The Chetniks*, 111, 155, 196; Milazzo, "Chetnik Movement," 363, 308.

42. Roberts, *Tito, Mihailović, and the Allies*, 101.

43. Dr. Wilhelm Hoettl, "Situation Report," Dec. 21, 1945, RG-226, E. 109, B. 52, F. 294. Hoettl added that as far as the Germans and Chetniks were concerned, "One partner mistrusted the other; various information intimated that the Cetniks were only awaiting the moment to turn – in common with the English and American troops, landings by whom were at that time definitely expected – against the Germans." Hoettl further noted that in Mar., 1945, Stärker, whose meetings with McDowell have been discussed previously, paid a visit to Mihailovich, who "revealed his deep dissatisfaction with German assistance; he was utterly despairing because his troops were in a downright desolate condition."

44. Testimony of Walter Warlimont, Oct. 16, 1945, *NCA*, Supplement B, 1638–39. According to Warlimont, Hitler was convinced that "Mihailovich's assistance to the Germans was only a temporary expedient."

45. Walter Warlimont *Inside Hitler's Headquarters, 1939–1945*, 469.

46. Mansfield, letter to author, Mar. 13, 1972.

47. Smith, *OSS*, 133; Hoettl, "Situation Report," Dec. 21, 1945, RG-226, E. 109, B. 52, F. 294.

48. Goodwin, MULBERRY team, Mar., 1945, RG-226, E. 154, B. 25, F. 357; Dean, DURAND team, n.d., RG-226, E. 99, B. 35, F. 175.

49. Popovich transcript, Jan. 8, 1977. Before leaving the area on Sept. 24, Popovich saw four more Ustasha officers who had deserted to the Partisans.

50. Lalich to AFHQ, G-2, June 14, 1945, RG-226, E. 154, B. 5, F. Bari-SI-INT-17. Ultra also provided useful information on the disintegration of the Ustasha movement, revealing defections of brigade- and battalion-size units to the Partisans. One battalion of the 369th division also defected to the Chetniks. Furthermore, a report from southern Dalmatia indicated that "for first time Cetniks had united in one area with Ustachas and Partisans," to oppose the Germans (DEFE 3, XL 9975, Sept. 13, 1944, Reel 43; DEFE 3, HP 1949, Oct. 2, 1944, Reel 43; DEFE 3, HP 4006, Oct. 20, 1944, Reel 46; DEFE 3, HP 6148, Nov. 10, 1944, Reel 48).

51. Smith, OSS, 239–40; Brown, *Last Hero*, 753; Winks, *Cloak and Gown*, 454–55.

52. William L. Langer, *Our Vichy Gamble*, 387–88.

53. Lowenheim, Langley, and Jonas, *Roosevelt and Churchill*, 282.

54. Commission of Inquiry, 10.

55. Telegram from the National Committee of American Airmen to Aid Draja Mihailovich to President Harry S. Truman, July 16, 1946. This telegram was signed by Alex Chester, Melvin Surrey, Robert N. Vlachos, Alan Friedberg, Richard L. Felman, Oscar Menaker, Marvin Stoloff, and John F. O'Grady. A copy of this message is in the author's personal files.

56. William L. Rogers, Chairman, National Committee of American Airmen to Aid General Mihailovich and the Serbian People, to the Secretary of War, Aug. 12, 1946, MA, RG-407, Records of the Adjutant General's Office, File No. 091.713. Accompanying this letter were affidavits signed by Lt. Rogers, T/Sgt. Rudolph Charles Schmidt, Lt. Fred L. Irwin, Capt. Temple O. Looney, and S/Sgt. Thomas F. Paul.

57. R. D. Muir, Acting Chief, Division of Protocol, Department of State, to Lt. Col. H. E. Lyman, Recorder, War Department Decorations Board, Sept. 5, 1946, RG-407, AG File No. 091.713.

58. Maj. Gen. W. S. Paul, Division of Personnel and Administration, War Department, to the Chief of Staff of the Army, Sept. 12, 1946, and War Department Summary Sheet, March 30, 1948, both in RG-407, AG File No. 091.713.

59. The citation signed by Truman was pursuant to the following order signed by Secretary of the Army Dwight D. Eisenhower. It was based on a citation published in the Army General Orders, which read: "Legion of Merit. By direction of the President, under the provisions of the act of Congress approved 20 July 1942 (sec. III, WD Bul. 40, 1942) and Executive order 9260, 29 Oct. 1942 (sec. I, WD Bul. 54, 1942) the Legion of Merit, in the Degree of Commander-in-Chief for exceptionally meritorious conduct in the performance of outstanding service during the period indicated is posthumously awarded to the following named officer: General Dragoljub Mihailovich, Yugoslavian Army, December 1941 to December 1944" (Citation for Publication in General Orders, Jan. 23, 1948, RG-407, AG File No. 091.713).

60. Secretary of State to the Secretary of the Army, Apr. 21, 1948, RG-407, AG File No. 091.713; News Release from the office of Congressman Edward J. Derwinski, Aug. 4, 1967. A copy of this release is in the author's personal files.

Bibliography

NOTE ON SOURCES

Indispensable to any study of OSS wartime operations is the massive collection of documents held by the Military Records Division of the National Archives and designated as Record Group 226. Included in this collection are almost one thousand cubic feet of records from the Research and Analysis Branch that devolved to the Department of State following the dissolution of the OSS in 1945. The department subsequently made the papers available to the Archives in 1946. After declassifications, the R&A records were opened for research in 1976. A second and much larger collection, which may ultimately encompass more than four thousand cubic feet of material, contains the operational records of the OSS, the first installments of which were opened by the National Archives in 1984–85 after being declassified by the Central Intelligence Agency. Included in these files are reports prepared by heads of missions upon returning from the field, message files, correspondence, field office histories, branch histories, diaries, messages to and from Donovan concerning planned and ongoing operations, and a great deal of the routine paperwork one would expect to be generated by any government agency.

This material is further divided into entries, most of which have finding aids developed by the staff of the Military Records Division. The aids show the field station office from which the records came and the general nature of the documents, whether administrative (ADM), radio and cable communications (R&C), or operational (OP)—the latter being designated as either secret intelligence (SI), special operations (SO), or morale operations (MO). Usually, the finding aids will show the number of boxes in each entry, the number of folders in each box, and a general description of the contents therein.

As far as Yugoslavia is concerned, records from the Cairo, Caserta, and Bari field stations proved most useful. There is a certain amount of duplication among the holdings of these offices, as well as those of Algiers and Washington. This proves useful to the researcher, who will on occasion find a cover letter referring to an attached report that cannot be found in the documents under review. As a rule the nature of the missing report – or an accompanying distribution sheet, when one exists – will indicate which other offices would have received copies of the report.

Although RG-226 consists overwhelmingly of textual records, some photographs or negatives remain in the collection. In many cases these items were simply placed in an envelope or small packet and stapled to the report they were to accompany. Some of the photos were properly captioned, apparently by the OSS personnel who took them; others, unfortunately, were not. Indeed, I found a number of small collections that offered no means of identifying either the persons or scenes in the photographs. Perhaps I should point out that while OSS had its own Field Photographic Branch, the pictures to which I am referring were located in material from the SI and SO branches.

While many of the entries contained valuable nuggets of information, those mined most heavily for this work were 99, 110, 146, 154, and 190. Assuming that the content of these entries provides an adequate sampling of the entire collection, researchers will find that only a small percentage of documents remain classified. Efforts to secure this material through the Freedom of Information Act (FOIA), even when successful, is time-consuming and frequently disappointing.

Apart from holdings in the National Archives, a substantial body of OSS documentation exists in the Roosevelt Papers deposited in the Presidential Library at Hyde Park, New York. The Air Force Archives, held in the Albert F. Simpson Historical Research Center at Maxwell Air Force Base in Montgomery, Alabama, contain records pertinent to the work of Air Crew Rescue Units (ACRU) in Yugoslavia. These units represented a joint effort between OSS and the Fifteenth Air Force. The Escape and Evasion Reports of airmen returned to Italy from Yugoslavia and documents relating to supply operations conducted in support of the Yugoslav resistance may also be found in the records at Maxwell. Lastly, there are the Donovan Papers located in the United States Army Military History Institute at Carlisle Barracks, Pennsylvania. I was not able to consult this collection, which was not completely opened to researchers until June 1, 1990. However, Anthony Cave Brown, who had exclusive access to the Donovan Papers while preparing his biography of Donovan, provides an excellent description of this valuable source. It is my understanding that a copy of the microfilm portion of the Donovan collection will ultimately be available to researchers in the National Archives.

ARCHIVAL AND MANUSCRIPT SOURCES

Adjutant General. Record Group 407. National Archives, General Archives Division, Washington, D.C.

Central Intelligence Agency. Operational Records of the OSS in Yugoslavia, 1943–1945. National Archives, Washington, D.C.

Committee for a Fair Trial for Draja Mihailovich. "Proceedings of the Commission of Inquiry." New York, 1946. Typescript in possession of author.

Deakin, F. W. "Britain and Jugoslavia, 1941–1945." Paper presented at the conference on Britain and European Resistance, 1941–1945, at St. Anthony's College, Oxford, December, 1962.

Felman, Richard L. "Mihailovich and I." Typescript in possession of author.

Galembush, Stephen. "Candidate for O.S.S. and the Rakeoff Mission." Typescript, in possession of author.

Lindsay, Franklin A. Papers. Hoover Institution, Stanford, Calif.

McDowell, Robert H. "The Key Role in Southeastern Europe during World War Two of the Serbs and Their Commander General Draza Mihailovich despite Their Abandonment by Churchill and Roosevelt." Typescript, in possession of author.

———. Papers. Hoover Institution, Stanford, Calif.

Mansfield, Walter R. Field Diary of Captain Walter R. Mansfield. Typescript, from handwritten notes, in possession of author.

Milazzo, Joseph Matteo. "The Chetnik Movement in Yugoslavia, 1941–1945." Ph.D. diss., University of Michigan, 1977.

Modisett, Lawrence Edward. "The Four-Cornered Triangle: British and American Policy toward Yugoslavia, 1939–1945." Ph.D. diss., Georgetown University, 1981.

Office of Strategic Services. Record Group 226. National Archives, Military Archives Division, Washington, D.C.

Roosevelt, Franklin D. Papers. Franklin D. Roosevelt Library, Hyde Park, New York.

U.S. Air Force. Archives. Fifteenth Air Force Records. "Escape and Evasion Reports, 1943–1945." Albert F. Simpson Historical Research Center, Montgomery, Ala.

U.S. Department of State. Unpublished Papers of the Department of State, 1941–1944. National Archives, Civil Archives Division, Washington, D.C.

PUBLISHED SOURCES

Adamić, Louis. *Dinner at the White House.* New York: Harper & Brothers, 1946.

———. *My Native Land.* New York: Harper & Brothers, 1943.

Alcorn, Robert Hayden. *No Bugles for Spies.* New York: David McKay Co., 1962.

Allied Forces Headquarters. *The Četniks: A Survey of Četnik Activity in Yugoslavia, April 1941–July 1944.* Bari, Italy: Allied Forces Headquarters, 1944.

Amery, Julian. *Approach March: A Venture in Autobiography.* London: Hutchinson & Co., 1973.

Andrew, Christopher, and Oleg Gordievsky. *KGB: The Inside Story of Its Foreign Operations from Lenin to Gorbachev.* New York: Harper Collins, 1990.

Atanaković, Zarko, Ahmet Donhagić, and Dušan Plenca. *Yugoslavia in the Second World War.* Belgrade: Medunarodna Stampa Interpress, 1967.

Auty, Phyliss. *Tito.* New York: Ballantine Books, 1972.

———, and Richard Clogg, eds. *British Policy towards Wartime Resistance in Yugoslavia and Greece.* New York: Macmillan, 1975.

Bailey, S. W. "British Policy towards General Draža Mihailović." In Phyllis Auty and Richard Clogg, eds. *British Policy toward Wartime Resistance in Yugoslavia and Greece.* New York: Macmillan, 1975.

Barker, Elisabeth. *British Policy in South-East Europe in the Second World War.* London: Victor Gollancz, 1980.

──────. "Fresh Sidelights on British Policy in Yugoslavia, 1942–3." *Slavonic and East European Review* 54 (October, 1976): 572–85.

Beevor, J. G. *SOE: Recollections and Reflections, 1940–1945.* London: Bodley Head, 1981.

Beloff, Nora. *Tito's Flawed Legacy: Yugoslavia and the West since 1939.* Boulder, Colo.: Westview, 1985.

Bennett, Ralph. "Knight's Move at Drvar: Ultra and the Attempt on Tito's Life, 25 May 1944." *Journal of Contemporary History* 22 (1987): 195–208.

──────. *Ultra and Mediterranean Strategy.* New York: William Morrow and Company, 1989.

Biber, Dušan. "Neuspeh neke misije: Ameriški podpolkovnik OOS Robert McDowell v štabu Draže Mihailovića leta 1944." *Revija Borec* 41 (October–November, 1989): 1065–91.

Brajović, Petar; Jovan Marjanović; and Franjo Tudman. *Les Systèmes d'Occupation en Yougoslavie, 1941–1945.* Belgrade: L'Institut pour l'Étude du Mouvement Ouvrier, 1963.

Brown, Alec, ed. *The Treason of Mihailovitch.* London: Yugoslav Embassy Information Office, n.d.

Brown, Anthony Cave. *The Last Hero: Wild Bill Donovan.* New York: Times Books, 1982.

──────, ed. *The Secret War Report of the OSS.* New York: Berkley Publishing Corporation, 1976.

"Charges and Chetniks," *Newsweek,* March 1, 1943, 52.

Christman, Henry M., ed. *The Essential Tito.* New York: St. Martin's Press, 1970.

Churchill, Winston S. *Closing the Ring.* Vol. 5 of *History of the Second World War.* Boston: Houghton Mifflin Company, 1953.

──────. *The Grand Alliance.* Vol. 3 of *History of the Second World War.* Boston: Houghton Mifflin Company, 1950.

──────. *Triumph and Tragedy.* Vol. 6 of *History of the Second World War.* Boston: Houghton Mifflin Company, 1953.

Clark, Mark W. *Calculated Risk.* New York: Harper & Brothers, 1950.

Clissold, Stephen. *Whirlwind: An Account of Marshal Tito's Rise to Power.* New York: Philosophical Library, 1949.

Colić, Mladen. "Prvi I Drugi Kosovski Četnićki Korpus Draže Mihailovića." *Vojnoistorijski glasnik* 25 (1974): 161–77.

Congressional Record. Vols. 88–89. Washington, D.C.

Cookridge, E. H. *Inside SOE: The Story of Special Operations in Western Europe, 1940–1945.* London: Arthur Baker, 1966.

Davidson, Basil. *Special Operations Europe: Scenes from the Anti-Nazi War.* London: Victor Gollancz, 1980.

Deakin, F. W. "Great Britain and European Resistance." In *European Resistance Movements, 1939–1945,* 98–119. Oxford: Pergamon Press, 1964.

──────. *The Embattled Mountain.* New York: Oxford University Press, 1971.

Deakin, William, Elisabeth Barker, and Jonathan Chadwick. *British Political and Military Strategy in Central, Eastern and Southern Europe in 1944.* New York: St. Martin's Press, 1988.

Dedijer, Vladimir. *The Battle Stalin Lost: Memoirs of Yugoslavia, 1948–1953.* New York: Viking Press, 1971.

———. *Tito Speaks: His Self-Portrait and Struggle with Stalin.* London: Weidenfield and Nicolson, 1953.

Deroc, M. *British Special Operations Explored: Yugoslavia in Turmoil 1941–1943 and the British Response.* Boulder, Colo.: East European Monographs, 1988.

De Santis, Hugh. "In Search of Yugoslavia: Anglo-American Policy and Policy-Making, 1943–45." *Journal of Contemporary History* 16 (1981): 541–63.

Djilas, Milovan. *Conversations with Stalin.* Translated by Michael B. Petrovich. New York: Harcourt, Brace and World, 1962.

———. *Wartime.* New York: Harcourt, Brace, Jovanovich, 1977.

Drachkovitch, Milorand. "The Comintern and the Insurrectional Activity of the Communist Party in Yugoslavia, 1941–1942." In *The Comintern Historical Highlights, Essays, Recollections, Documents.* Edited by Milorand Drachkovitch and Branko Lazitch. New York: Frederick A. Praeger, 1966.

Eden, Anthony. *The Reckoning.* Boston: Houghton Mifflin Company, 1965.

Ehrman, John. *Grand Strategy.* Vol. 5, *August 1943–September 1944.* London: H.M.S.O., 1956.

———. *Grand Strategy.* Vol. 6, *October 1944–August 1945.* London: H.M.S.O., 1956.

Farish, Linn M. *The True Strength of America.* Bismarck, N. Dak.: Privately printed, 1941.

Feis, Herbert. *Churchill, Roosevelt, Stalin: The War They Waged, the Peace They Sought.* Princeton, N.J.: Princeton University Press, 1957.

Felman, Richard. "Fate Was Merciless." *¡Ole!* May 16, 1970, 10–13.

———. "Mihailovic and I" *Serbian Democratic Forum,* Oct., 1972, 15–23.

Foot, M. R. D. *Resistance: An Analysis of European Resistance to Nazism, 1940–1945.* London: Eyre-Methuen, 1976.

———. *SOE: An Outline History of the Special Operations Executive, 1940–1946.* Rev. ed. Frederick, Md.: University Publications of America, 1986.

Ford, Corey. *Donovan of OSS.* Boston: Little, Brown and Company, 1970.

Fotitch, Constantine. *The War We Lost: Yugoslavia's Tragedy and the Failure of the West.* New York: Viking Press, 1948.

"Grand Strategy." *Time,* April 7, 1941, 23.

Greenlees, Kenneth. "The Record of Mihailovic: A Personal Testimony." (London) *Tablet* 188 (July 6, 1946), 4–5.

Hart, Philip. "Heroes of the OSS: Eli Popovich." *Serb World USA* 4, no. 2 (November–December, 1987): 6–13.

———. "Heroes of the OSS: George Musulin." *Serb World USA* 4, no. 3 (January–February, 1988): 14–19.

———. "Heroes of the OSS: Nick Lalich." *Serb World USA* 5, no. 1 (September–October, 1988): 6–12.

————. "Heroes of the OSS: Steve Bizic." *Serb World USA* 7, no. 3 (January–February, 1991): 48–55.

Hayden, Sterling [John Hamilton]. *Wanderer.* New York: Alfred A. Knopf, 1963.

Hehn, Paul. *The German Struggle Against Yugoslav Guerrillas in World War II: German Counter-Insurgency in Yugoslavia, 1941–1943.* Boulder, Colo.: East European Monographs, 1979.

Hinsley, F. H., E. E. Thomas, et al. *British Intelligence in the Second World War: Its Influence on Strategy and Operations.* 3 vols. in 4 parts. London: H.M.S.O., 1979 (vol. 1) and 1981 (vol. 2). New York: Cambridge University Press for H.M.S.O., 1984 (vol. 3, pt. 1).

"Hitler's New Gamble." *New Republic,* April 21, 1941, 487.

Hoettl, Wilhelm. *The Secret Front: The Story of Nazi Political Espionage.* New York: Frederick A. Praeger, 1954.

Howard, Michael. *Grand Strategy.* Vol. 4, *August 1942–September 1943.* London: H.M.S.O., 1972.

————. *The Mediterranean Strategy in the Second World War.* New York: Frederick A. Praeger, 1968.

Hull, Cordell. *The Memoirs of Cordell Hull.* 2 vols. New York: Macmillan Company, 1948.

Huot, Louis. *Guns for Tito.* New York: L. B. Fischer, 1945.

Inks, James M. "Eight Against the Enemy." *Blue Book Magazine* 97 (September, 1953): 93–128.

Ivanović, Vane. *LX: Memoirs of a Jugoslav.* London: Harcourt, Brace, Jovanovich, 1977.

Jones, William. *Twelve Months with Tito's Partisans.* London: Bedford Books, 1946.

Jukić, Ilija. *The Fall of Yugoslavia.* Translated by Dorian Cooke. New York: Harcourt, Brace, Jovanovich, 1974.

Karadjeordjevich, Peter. *A King's Heritage.* New York: G. P. Putnam's Sons, 1954.

Kardelj, Edvard. *Reminiscences, the Struggle for Recognition and Independence: The New Yugoslavia, 1944–1957.* London: Blond & Briggs, 1982.

Katz, Barry M. *Foreign Intelligence: Research and Analysis in the Office of Strategic Services, 1942–1945.* Cambridge, Mass.: Harvard University Press, 1989.

Keegan, John. *The Second World War.* New York: Viking, 1989.

Kelly, Richard M. "The Halyard Mission." *Blue Book Magazine* 83 (August, 1946): 52–62.

Kesselring, Albert. *A Soldier's Record.* New York: William Morrow and Company, 1954.

Knezevich, Živan L. *General Mihailovich and U.S.S.R., with Official Memoranda and Documents.* Washington, D.C.: Central National Committee of Yugoslavia, 1945.

Kogan, Norman. "American Policies towards European Resistance." In *European Resistance Movements, 1939–1945.* Oxford: Pergamon Press, 1964.

Langer, William. *Our Vichy Gamble.* Hamden, Conn.: Archon Books, 1965.

Lasić-Vasojević, Milija M. *Enemies on All Sides: The Fall of Yugoslavia.* Washington, D.C.: North American International, 1976.

Lazic, Branco M. *La Tragédie du général Draja Mihailovitch: le conflit Mihailovitch-Tito et la politique des Alliés.* Paris: Editions du Haute-Pays, 1946.

Lees, Michael. *The Rape of Serbia: The British Role in Tito's Grab for Power, 1943–1944.* New York: Harcourt, Brace, Jovanovich, 1990.

———. *Special Operations Executed in Serbia and Italy.* London: William Kimber & Company, 1986.

Leighton, Richard M. "Overlord Revisited." *American Historical Review* 68, no. 4 (July, 1963): 919–39.

———, and Robert W. Coakley, *U.S. Army in World War II: Global Logistics and Strategy, 1940–1943.* Washington, D.C.: Office of the Chief of Military History, 1953.

Lowenheim, Francis L.; Harold D. Langley; and Manfred Jonas, eds. *Roosevelt and Churchill: Their Secret Wartime Correspondence.* New York: Saturday Review Press, 1975.

McConville, Michael. *A Small War in the Balkans: British Military Involvement in Wartime Yugoslavia, 1941–1945.* London: Macmillan, 1987.

Maček, Vladvo. *In the Struggle for Freedom.* Translated by Elizabeth and Stephan Gazi. University Park, Pa.: Pennsylvania State University Press, 1957.

Maclean, Fitzroy. *Eastern Approaches.* London: Jonathan Cape, 1950. Reprint. New York: Time, 1964.

———. *The Heretic: The Life and Times of Josip-Broz Tito.* New York: Harper & Brothers, 1957.

Macmillan, Harold. *The Blast of War, 1939–1945.* Vol. 2 of *The Memoirs of Harold Macmillan.* New York: Harper & Row Publishers, 1968.

———. *War Diaries: Politics and War in the Mediterranean, January 1943–May 1945.* New York: St. Martin's Press, 1984.

Marjanović, Jovan. "Draža Mihailović izmedu Britanaca i Nemaca-Nemacki partner." *Jugoslovenski istorijski casopis* 20 (1981): 15–44.

———. "The Neubacher Plan and Practical Schemes for the Establishment of a Greater Serbian Federation, 1943–1944." In *The Third Reich and Yugoslavia, 1933–1945,* edited by Pero Moraca. Belgrade: Institute for Contemporary History, 1977.

Martin, David. *Ally Betrayed: The Uncensored Story of Tito and Mihailovich.* New York: Prentice-Hall, 1946.

———. *Patriot or Traitor: The Case of General Mihailovich.* Stanford, Calif.: Hoover Institution Press, 1978.

———. *The Web of Disinformation: Churchill's Yugoslav Blunder.* New York: Harcourt, Brace, Jovanovich, 1990.

Middle East Headquarters. *The National Liberation Movement of Yugoslavia: A Survey of the Partisan Movement, April 1941–March 1944.* Cairo [?], 1944.

"Mihailovich Eclipsed." *Time,* December, 1942, 48–50.

Moraca, Pero, ed. *The Third Reich and Yugoslavia, 1933–1945.* Belgrade: Institute for Contemporary History, 1977.

National Committee of American Airmen to Aid General Mihailovich and the Serbian People. *Press Clippings.* 3 Vols. Chicago: Privately printed, 1946.

Nuremberg Military Tribunals. *Proceedings of the International Military Tribunals at Nuremberg.* 42 vols. Nuremberg, 1946–47.

Padev, Michael. *Marshal Tito.* London: Frederick Mueller, 1944.

Pavlowitch, Stevan K. "Neither Heroes nor Traitors: Suggestions for a Reappraisal of the Yugoslav Resistance." In *War and Society: A Yearbook of Military History,* edited by Brian Bond and Ian Roy. New York: Holmes and Meier Publishers, 1975.

Pijade, Mosha. *About the Legend That the Yugoslav Uprising Owed Its Existence to Soviet Assistance.* London, 1950.

Raditdsa, Bodgan. "Tito's Partisans." *The Nation* 157 (October 2, 1943): 381.

Rendel, George. *The Sword and the Olive: Recollections of Diplomacy and the Foreign Service, 1913–1954.* London: John Murray, 1954.

Research Institute of Ljubljana. *Allied Airmen and Prisoners of War Rescued by the Slovene Partisans.* Ljubljana, Yugoslavia, 1946.

Roberts, Walter. *Tito, Mihailović, and the Allies, 1941–1945.* New Brunswick, N.J.: Rutgers University Press, 1973.

Roosevelt, Elliot, ed. *F.D.R.: His Personal Letters, 1928–1945,* Vol. 2. New York: Duell, Sloan and Pearce, 1950.

Rootham, Jasper. *Miss Fire: The Chronicle of a British Mission to Mihailovich, 1943–1944.* London: Chatto and Windus, 1946.

Schramm, Ernst, ed., *Kriegstagebuch des Oberkommandos der Wehrmacht.* 7 vols. Frankfurt am Main: Bernard & Graefer, 1961–1965.

Smith, Bradley. *The Shadow Warriors: O.S.S. and the Origins of the C.I.A.* New York: Basic Books, 1983.

Smith, R. Harris, *OSS: The Secret History of America's First Central Intelligence Agency.* Los Angeles: University of California Press, 1972.

Stafford, David. *Britain and European Resistance, 1940–1945: A Survey of the Special Operations Executive with Documents.* Toronto: University of Toronto Press, 1980.

St. John, Robert. *Foreign Correspondent.* Garden City, N.Y.: Doubleday and Company, 1957.

———. *From the Land of Silent People.* Garden City, N.Y.: Halcyon House, 1943.

Sulzberger, Cyrus L. *A Long Row of Candles: Memoirs and Diaries, 1945–1954.* New York: Macmillan Company, 1969.

Sweet-Escott, Bickham. *Baker Street Irregular.* London: Methuen & Co., 1965.

"Swing to Tito." *Newsweek,* November 22, 1943, 33.

Thayer, Charles W. *Hands Across the Caviar.* New York: J. B. Lippincott Company, 1952.

Todorovich, Boris. *Last Words: A Memoir of World War II and the Yugoslav Tragedy.* Edited by J. Stryder and Andrew Karp. New York: Walker and Company, 1989.

Tomasevich, Jozo. *War and Revolution in Yugoslavia, 1941–1945: The Chetniks.* Stanford, Calif.: Stanford University Press, 1975.

Trial of Dragoljub-Draža Mihailović, The. Belgrade: The Union of the Journalists Association of the Federative Peoples Republic of Yugoslavia, 1946.

United States. *Statutes at Large.* Vol. 56.

U.S. Air Force. *History of the Fifteenth Air Force, Operational History, March 1–May 31, 1944* (Copy in Archives, Fifteenth Air Force Records, Albert F. Simpson Historical Research Center, Montgomery, Alabama).

————. *The History of M.A.A.F., September 1, 1944 to May 9, 1945* (Copy in Archives, Fifteenth Air Force Records, Albert F. Simpson Historical Research Center, Montgomery, Alabama).

U.S. Department of the Army. *German Antiguerrilla Operations in the Balkans, 1941–1944.* No. 20-243 (1954).

————. *The German Campaigns in the Balkans, Spring 1941.* No. 20-260 (1953).

————. *Supplementary to the Balkan Campaign.* No. MS-B 525 (n.d.).

U.S. Department of State. *Documents on German Foreign Policy, 1918–1945.* Washington, D.C.: U.S. Government Printing Office, 1949.

————. *Foreign Relations of the United States: The Cairo and Teheran Conferences, 1943.* Washington, D.C.: U.S. Government Printing Office, 1961.

————. *Foreign Relations of the United States: The Malta and Yalta Conference, 1945.* Washington, D.C.: U.S. Government Printing Office, 1955.

————. *Foreign Relations of the United States, 1941,* 2. Washington, D.C.: U.S. Government Printing Office, 1962.

————. *Foreign Relations of the United States, 1943,* 2. Washington, D.C.: U.S. Government Printing Office, 1964.

————. *Foreign Relations of the United States, 1944,* 4. Washington, D.C.: U.S. Government Printing Office, 1966.

————. *Nazi Conspiracy and Aggression.* 8 vols. Washington, D.C.: U.S. Government Printing Office, 1946.

————. *Register of the Department of State.* Washington, D.C.: U.S. Government Printing Office, 1947.

U.S.S.R. Ministry of Foreign Affairs. *Correspondence Between the Chairman of the Council of Ministers of the U.S.S.R. and the Presidents of the U.S.A. and the Prime Ministers of Great Britain During the Great Patriotic War of 1941–1945.* Moscow: Foreign Languages Publishing House, 1957.

Warlimont, Walter. *Inside Hitler's Headquarters, 1939–1945.* Translated by R. H. Barry. New York: Frederick A. Praeger, 1964.

Warren, Harris G. *Special Operations: AAF Aid to European Resistance Movements, 1943–1945."* Washington, D.C.: USAAF Historical Office, 1947.

"War within a War." *Time,* February 8, 1943, 29.

West, Nigel. *MI6: British Secret Intelligence Service Operations, 1909–1945.* New York: Random House, 1983.

Wheeler, Mark C. *Britain and the War for Yugoslavia, 1940–1943.* Boulder, Colo.: East European Monographs, 1980.

Wilson, Henry Maitland. *Eight Years Overseas, 1939–1947.* London: Hutchinson, 1948.

Winks, Robin W. *Cloak and Gown: Scholars in the Secret War, 1939–1961.* New York: Morrow, 1987.

Wolff, Robert Lee. *The Balkans in Our Time.* Cambridge, Mass.: Harvard University Press, 1956.

Woodward, Ernest Llewellyn. *British Foreign Policy in the Second World War*. Vols. 1 and 3. London: H.M.S.O., 1970–71.

Zalar, Charles, *Yugoslav Communism: A Critical Study*. 87th Cong., 1st sess., 1961. Washington, D.C.: U.S. Government Printing Office, 1961.

Index

Yarrow, Bernard, 165
Yugoslav Army in the Fatherland, 6
Yugoslav Army of National Liberation, 151, 155
Yugoslav Communist Party, 7
Yugoslavia, x–xi, 3, 8, 10, 22, 28–29, 33; beginning of resistance in, 6–7; British policy in, 33–36; civil war in, 31, 56–57, 69–71,

76–81, 106–107, 119–20, 138–39, 151; defeat of, 5; joint OSS-SOE operations in, 15; surrender of Italian forces in, 17–19; Teheran decisions and, 34–36; Tripartite Pact and, 4–5; U.S. and, 12, 36, 39–41, 106, 119–20, 167–69

Zlatibor, 21

OSS and the Yugoslav Resistance, 1943–1945 was composed into type on a Compugraphic digital phototypesetter in ten point Plantin with two points of spacing between the lines. Plantin was also selected for display. The book was designed by Cameron Poulter, typeset by Metricomp, Inc., printed offset by Thomson-Shore, Inc., and bound by John H. Dekker & Sons, Inc. The paper on which this book is printed carries acid-free characteristics for an effective life of at least three hundred years.

TEXAS A&M UNIVERSITY PRESS : COLLEGE STATION